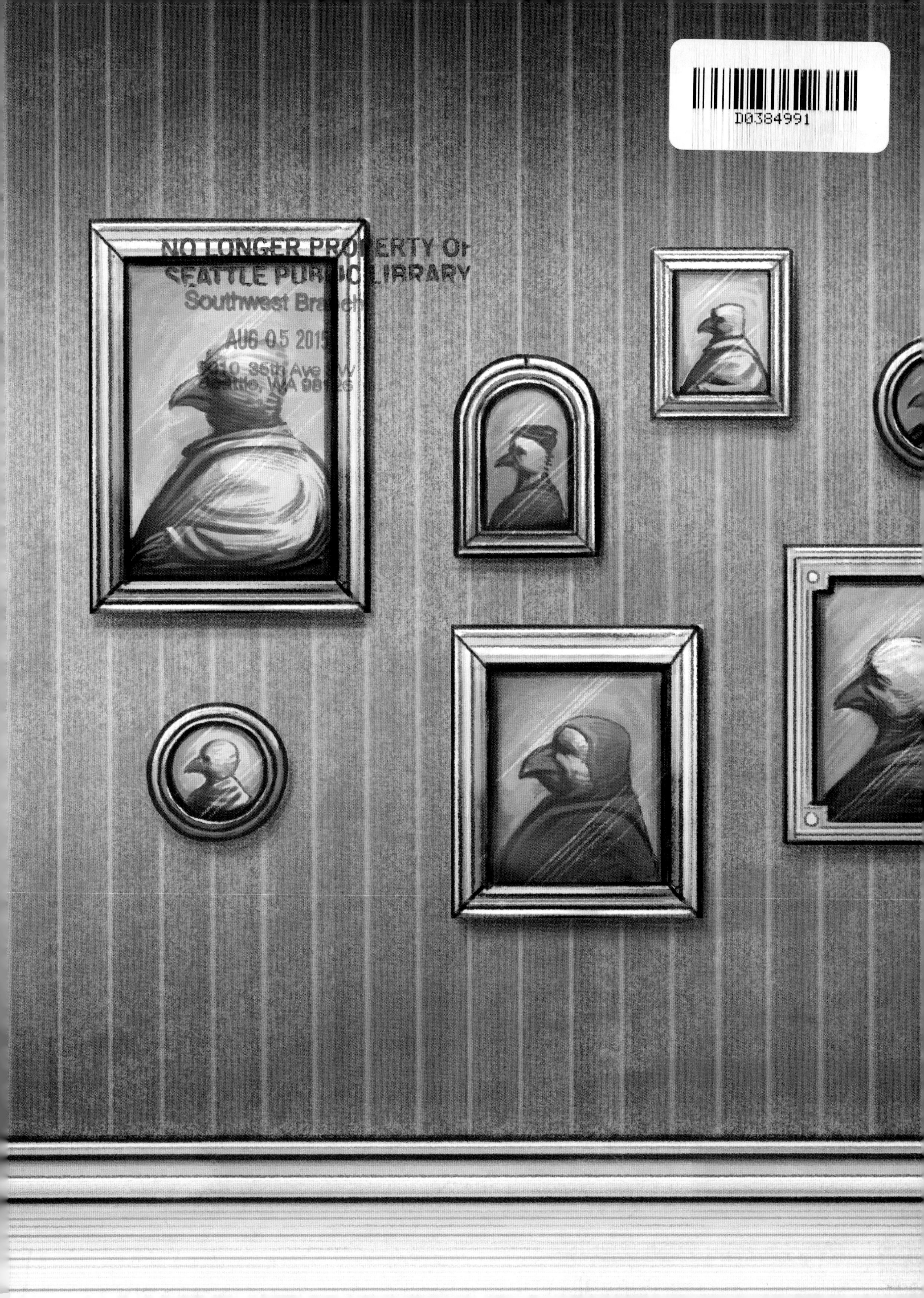

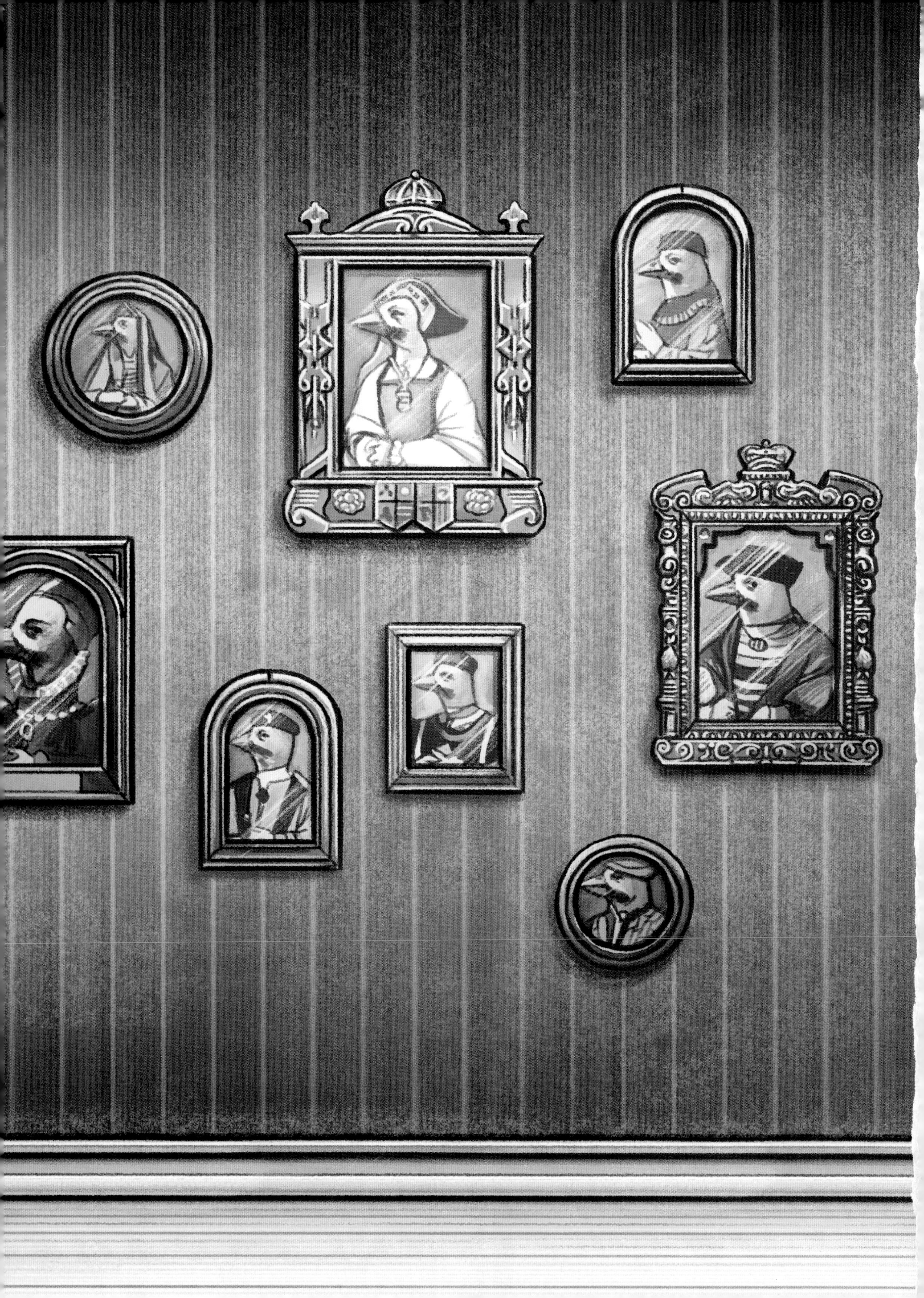

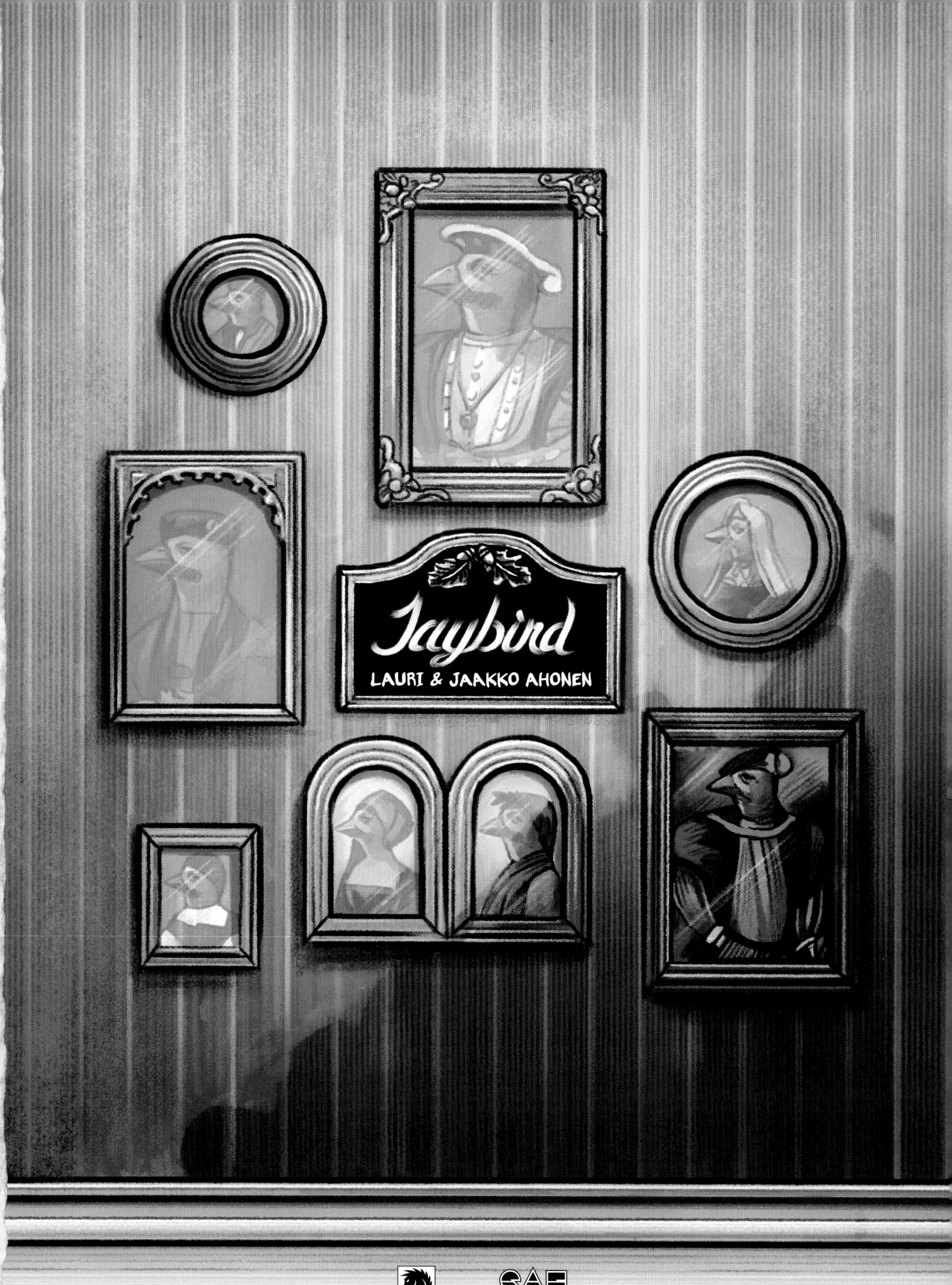
Jaybird
LAURI & JAAKKO AHONEN

DARK HORSE BOOKS
SAF COMICS

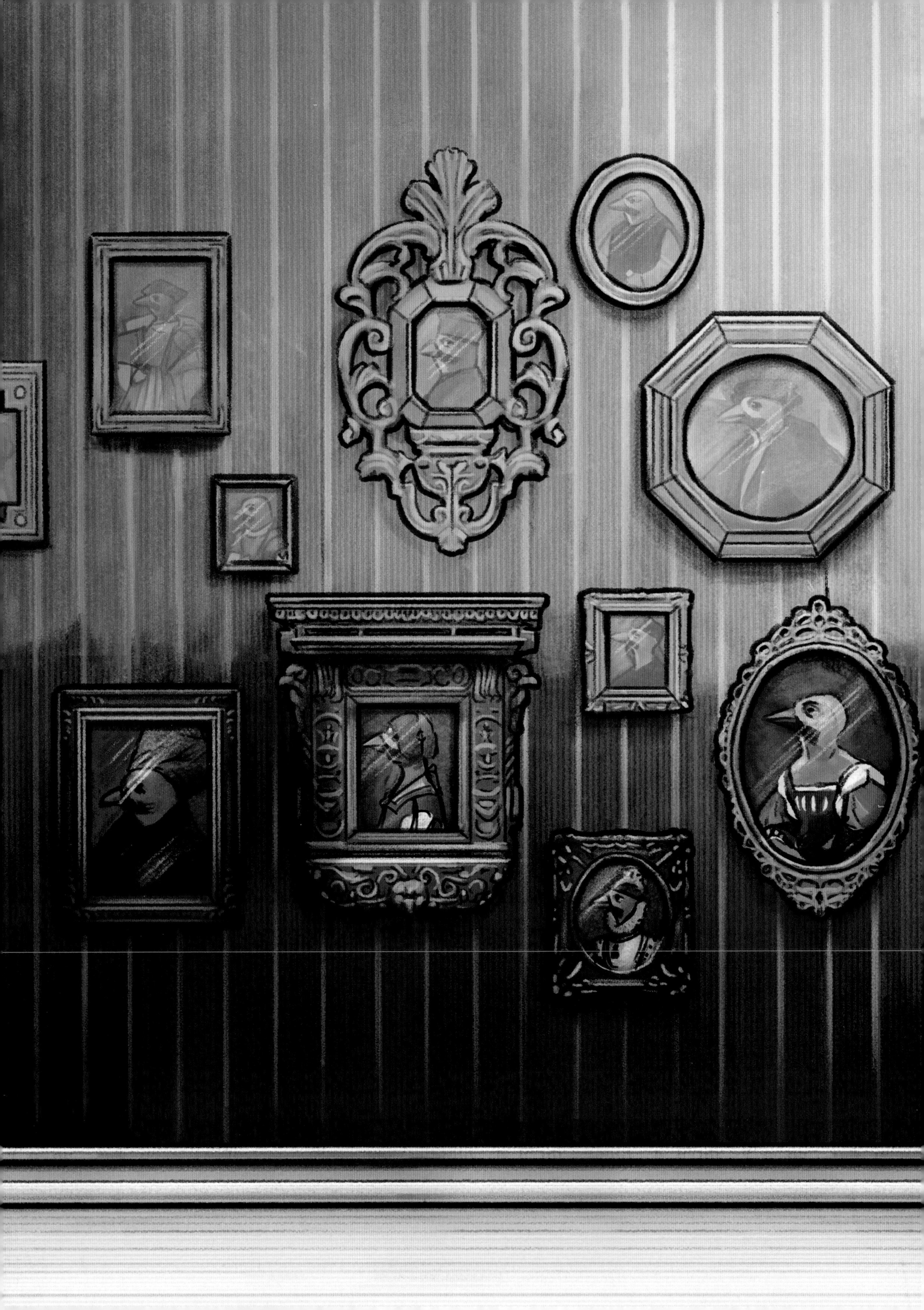

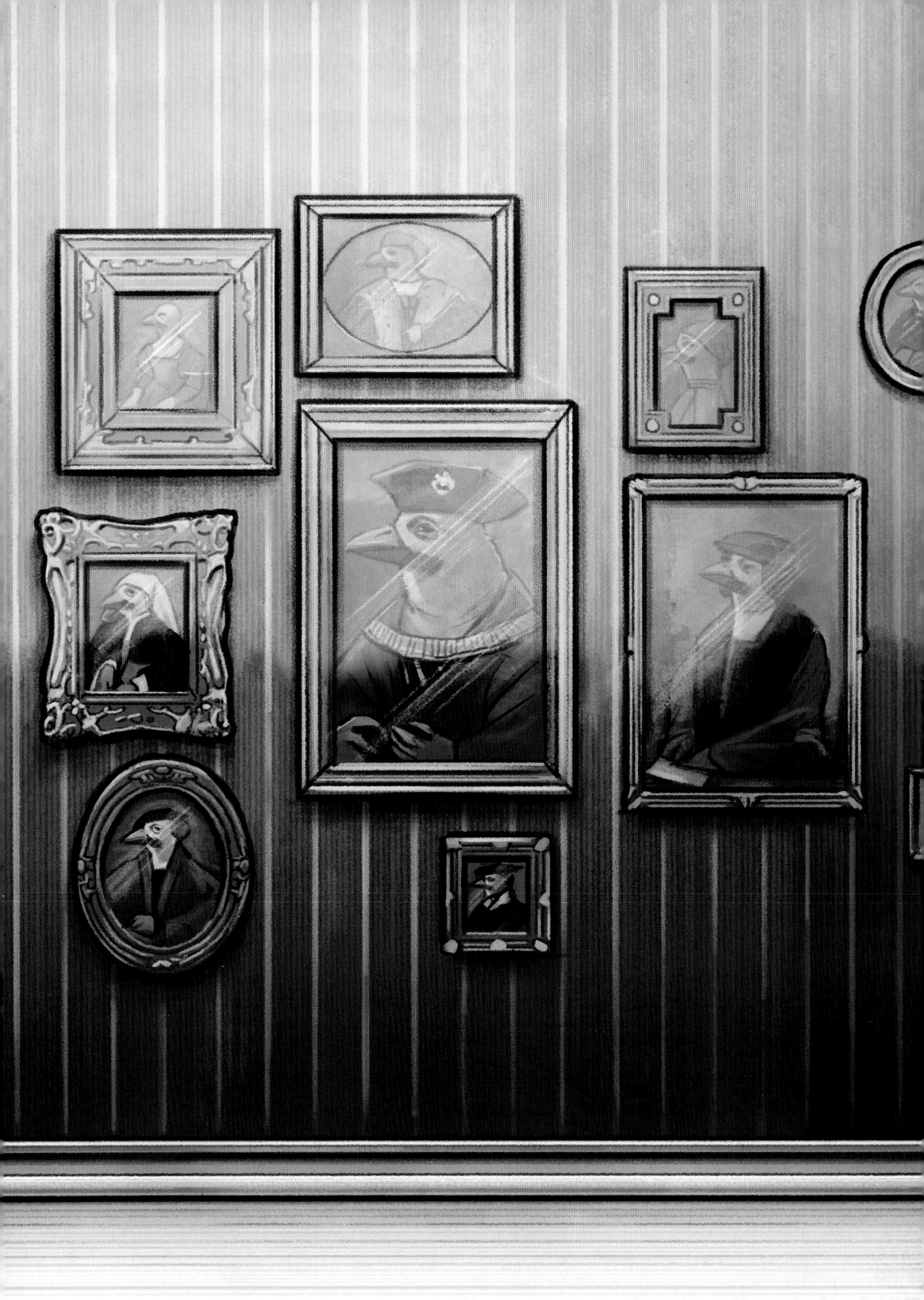

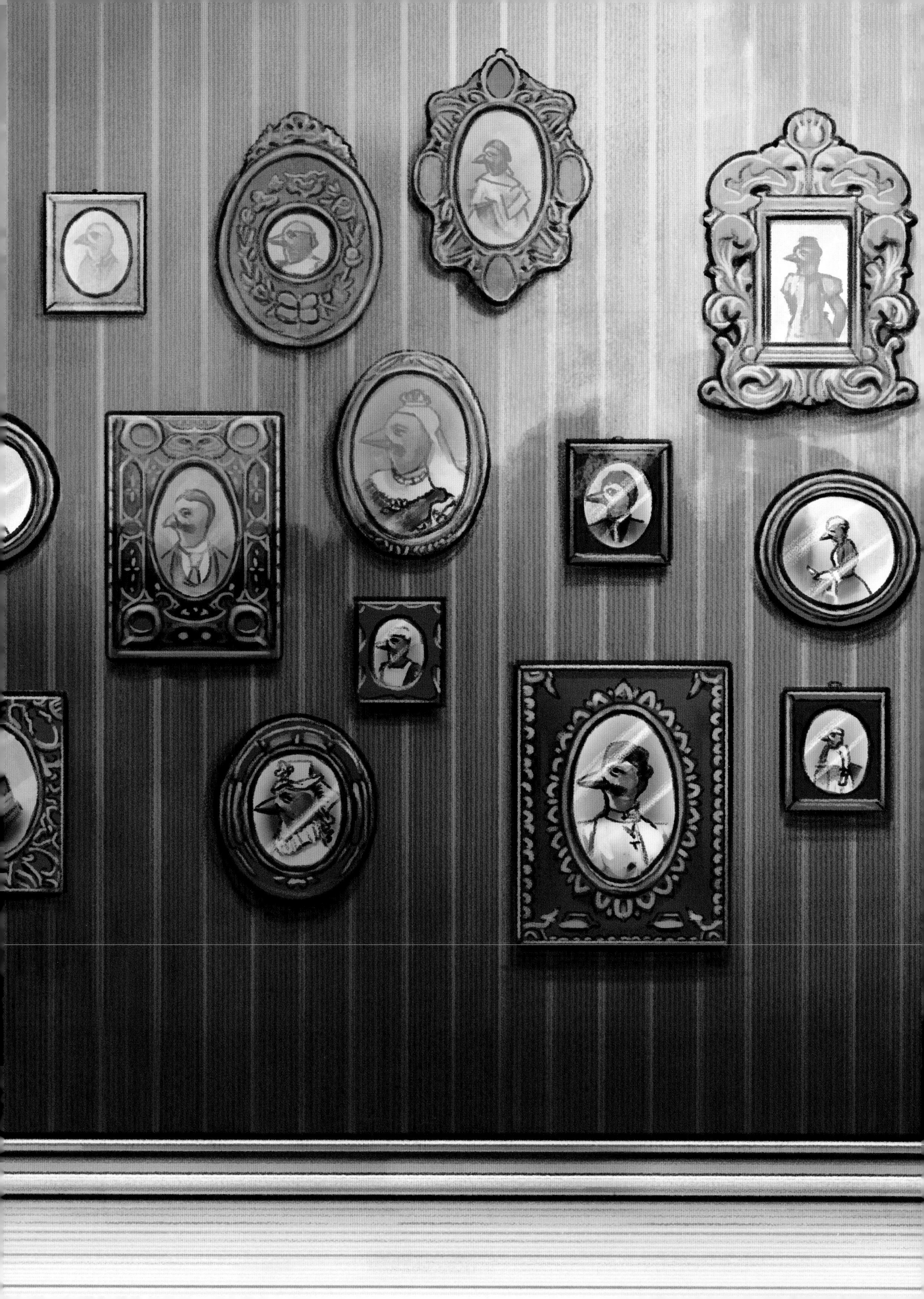

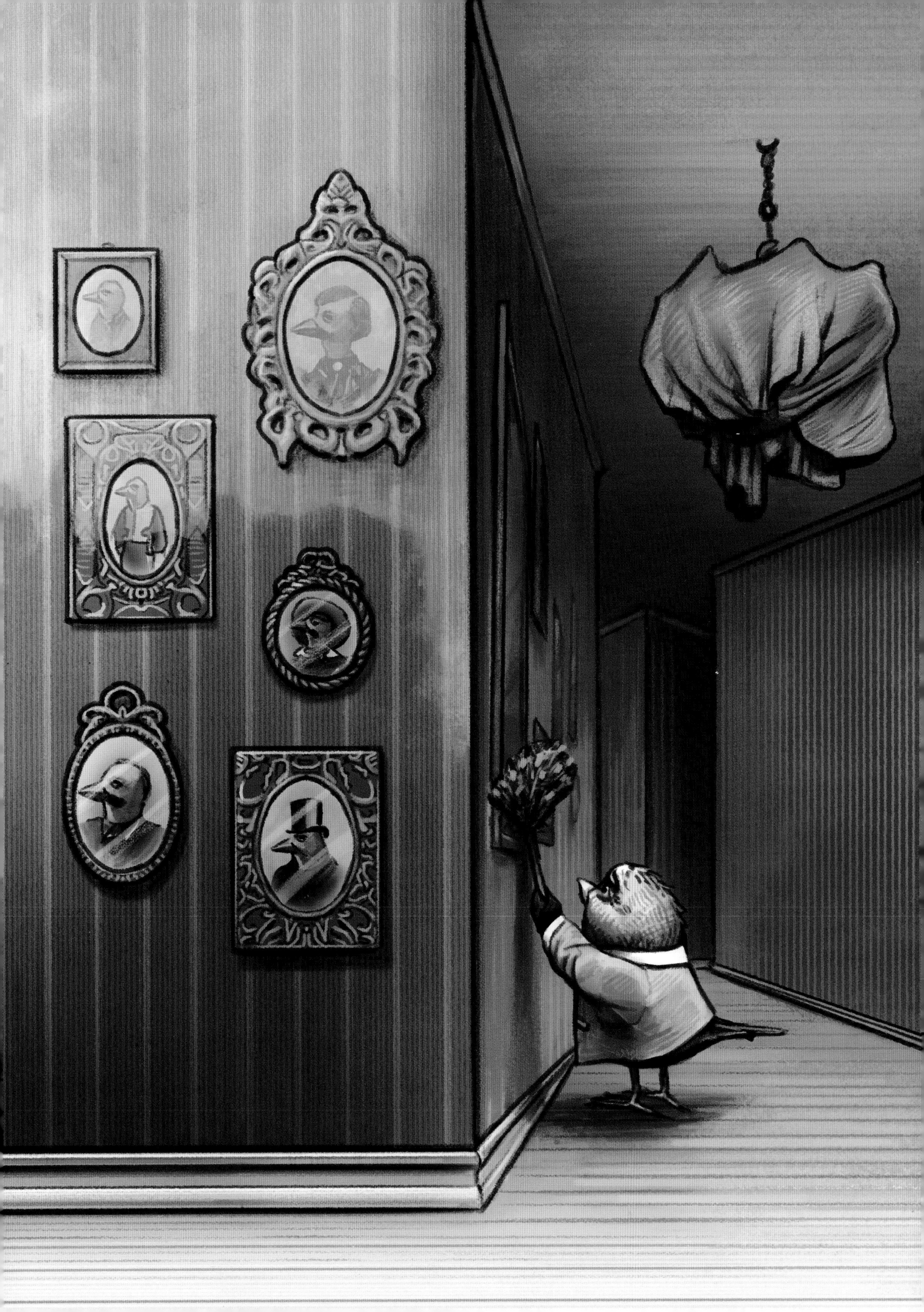

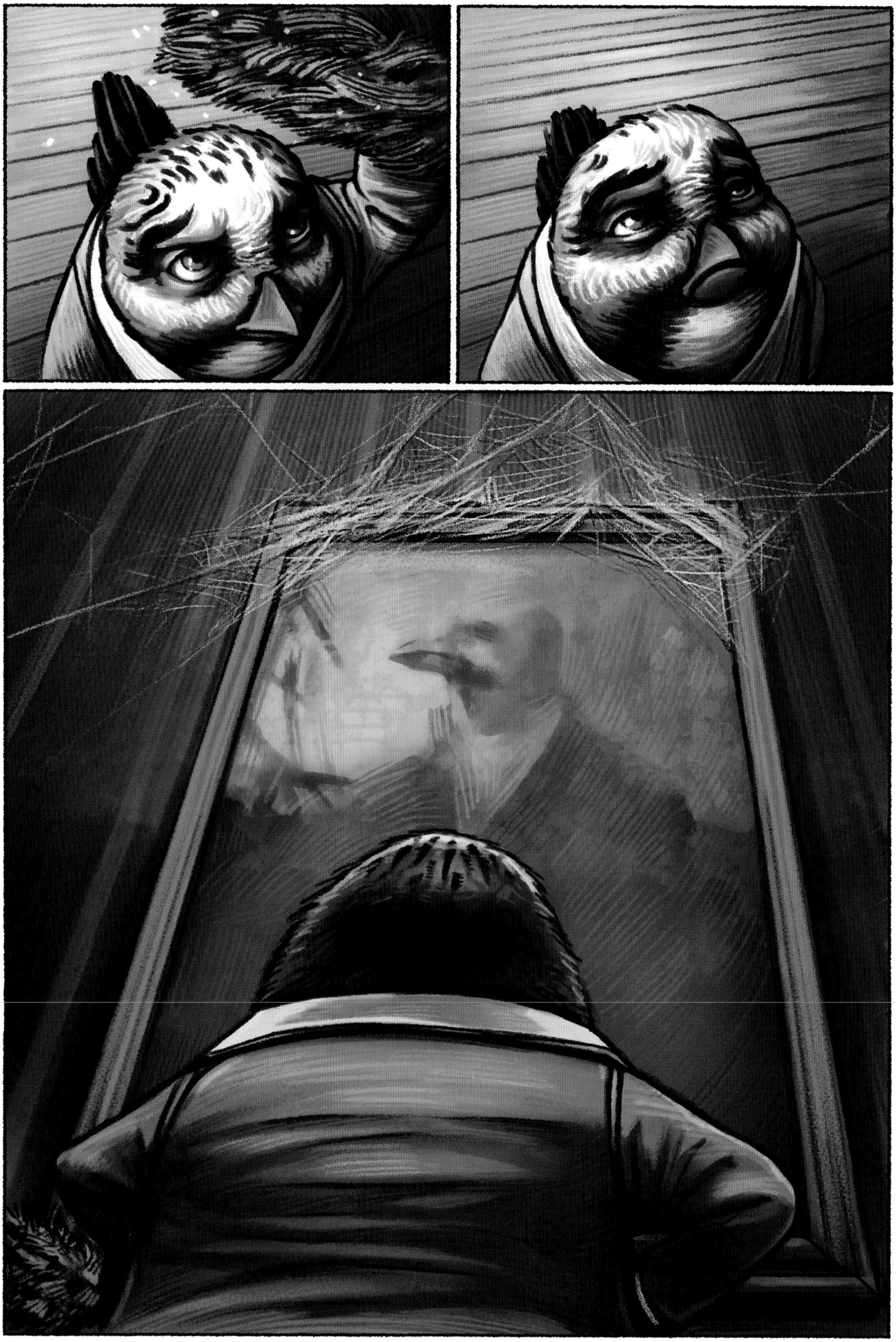

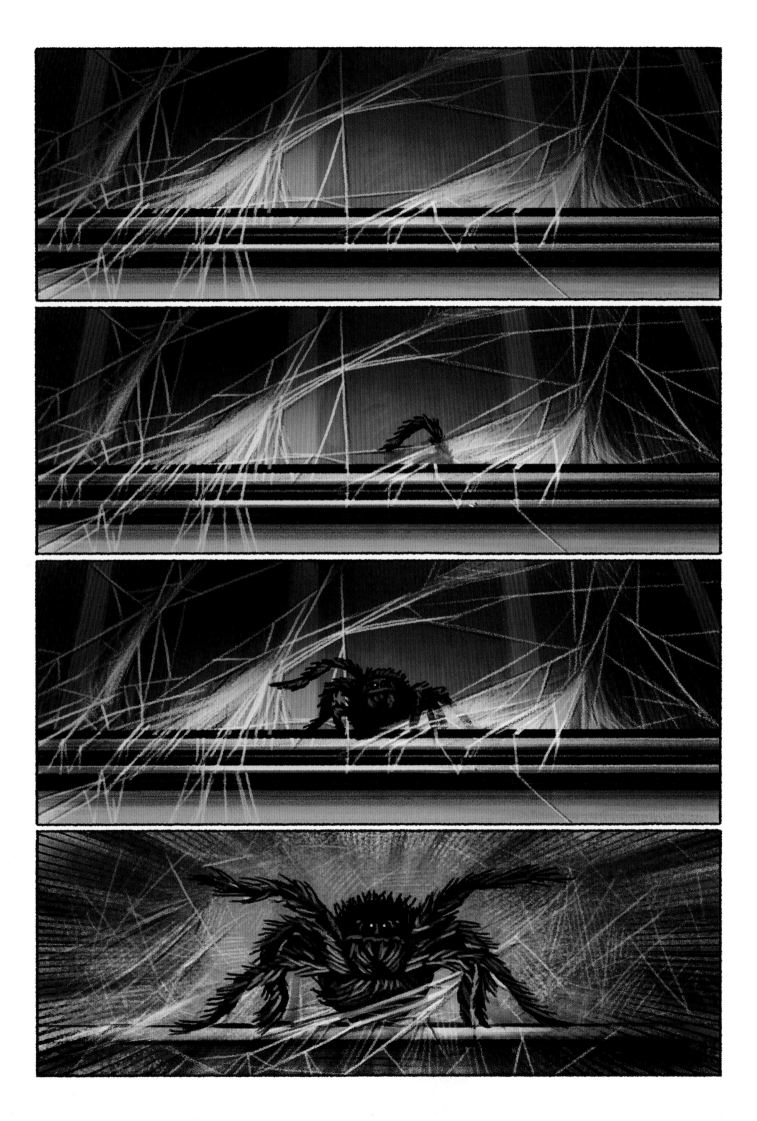

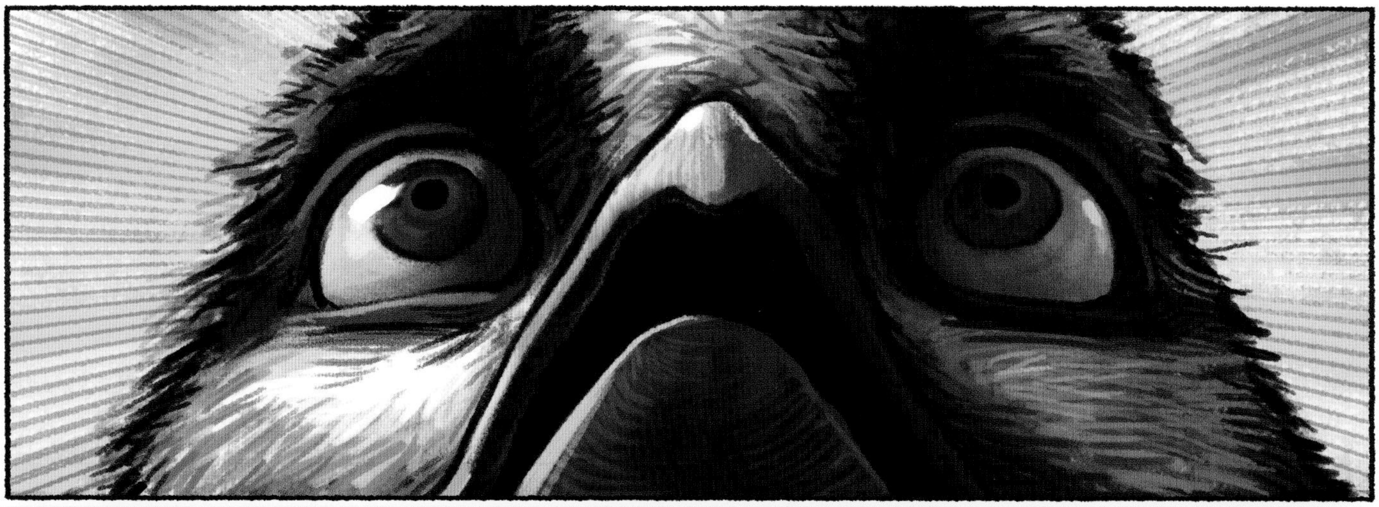

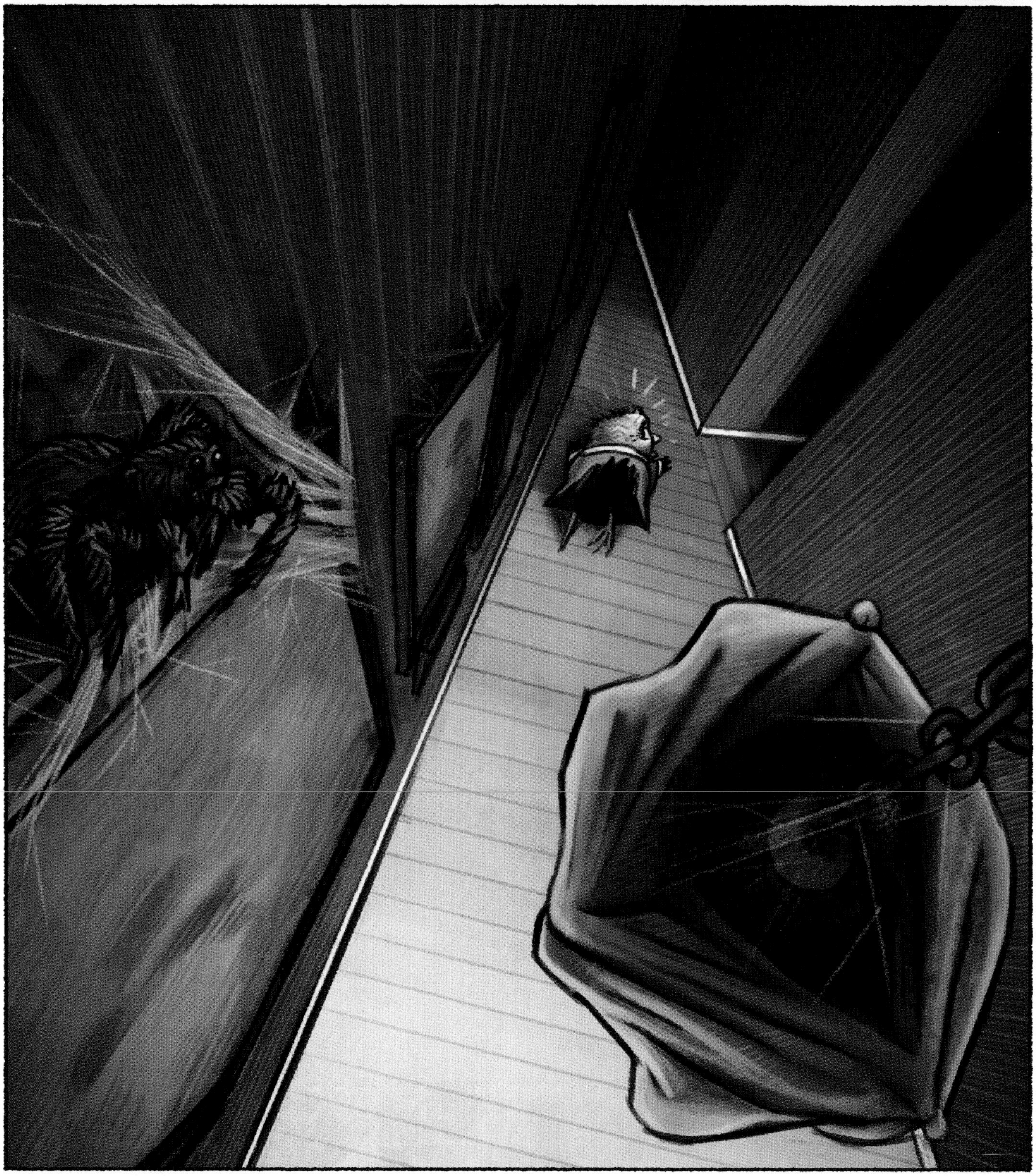

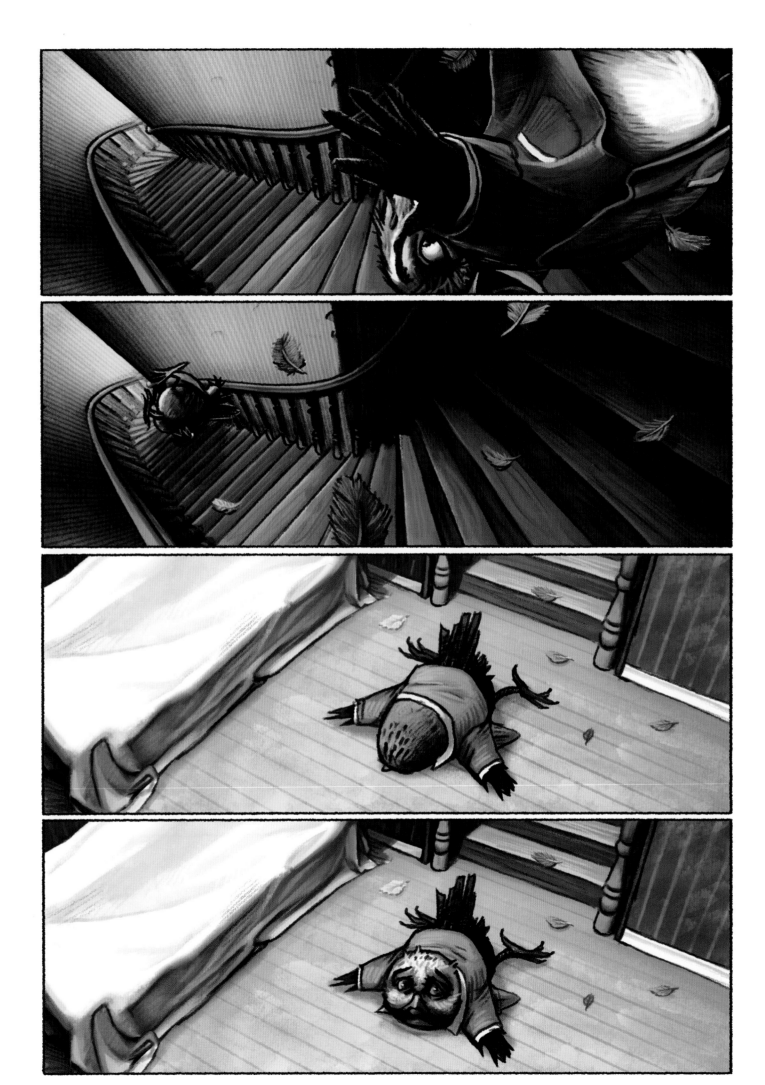

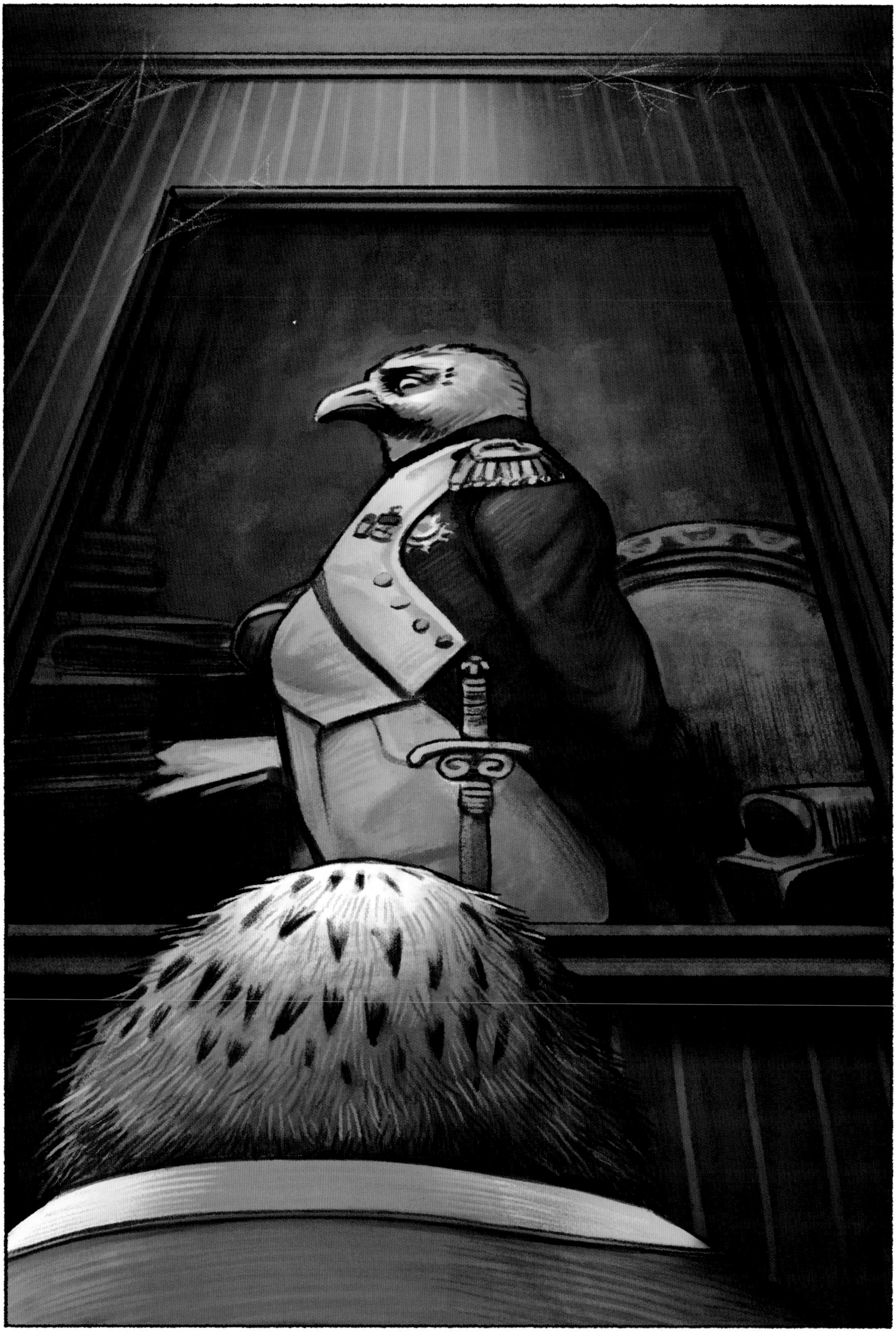

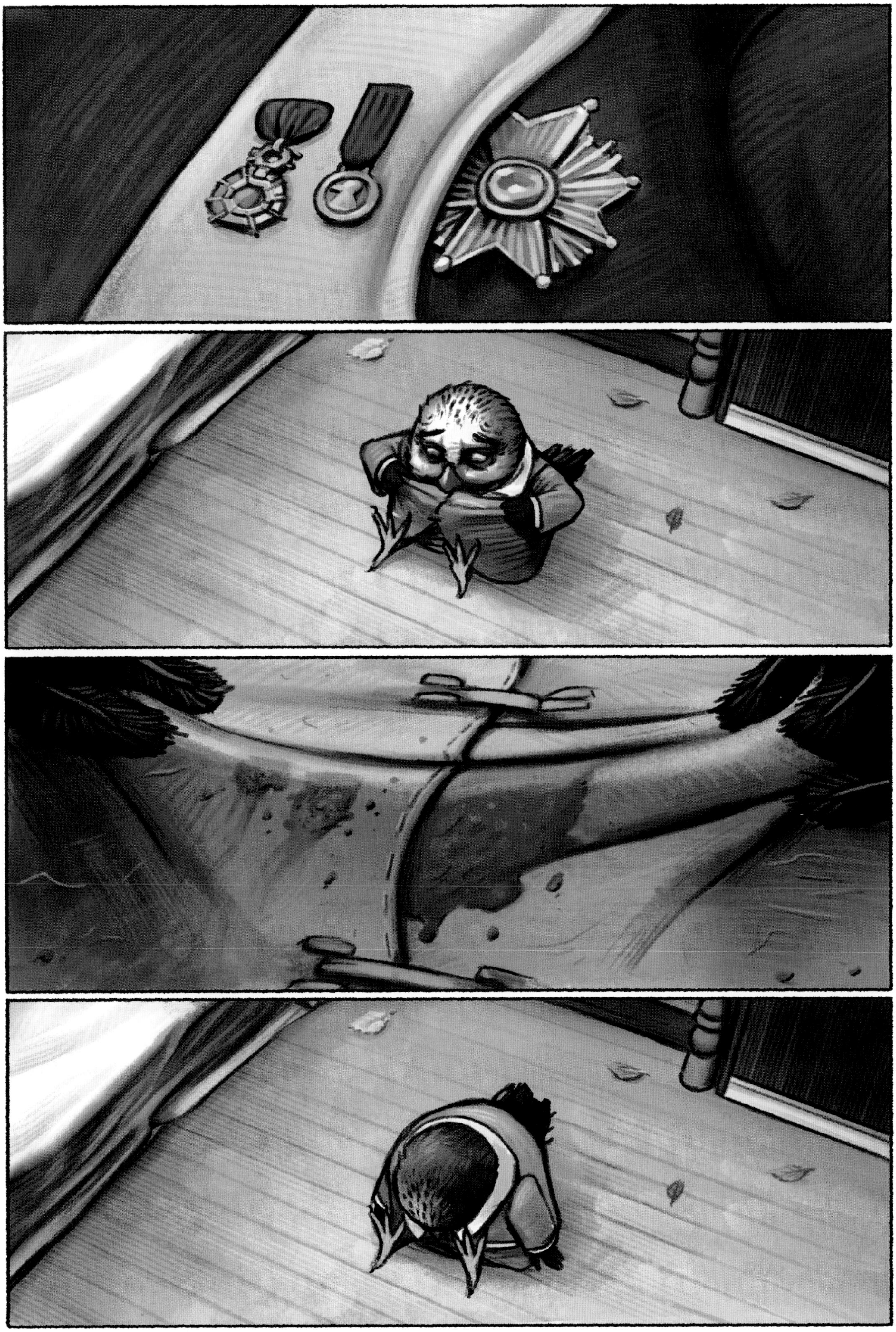

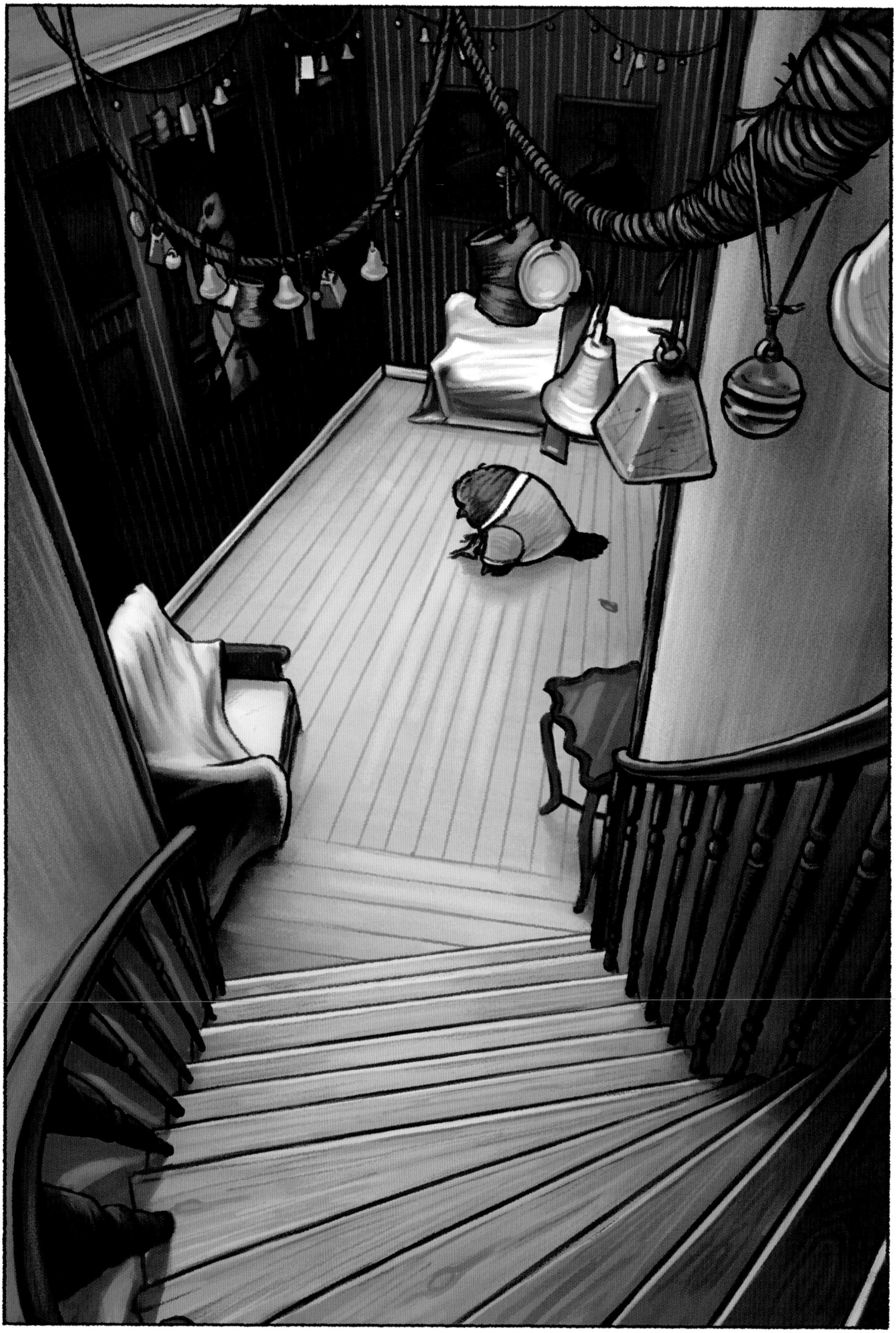

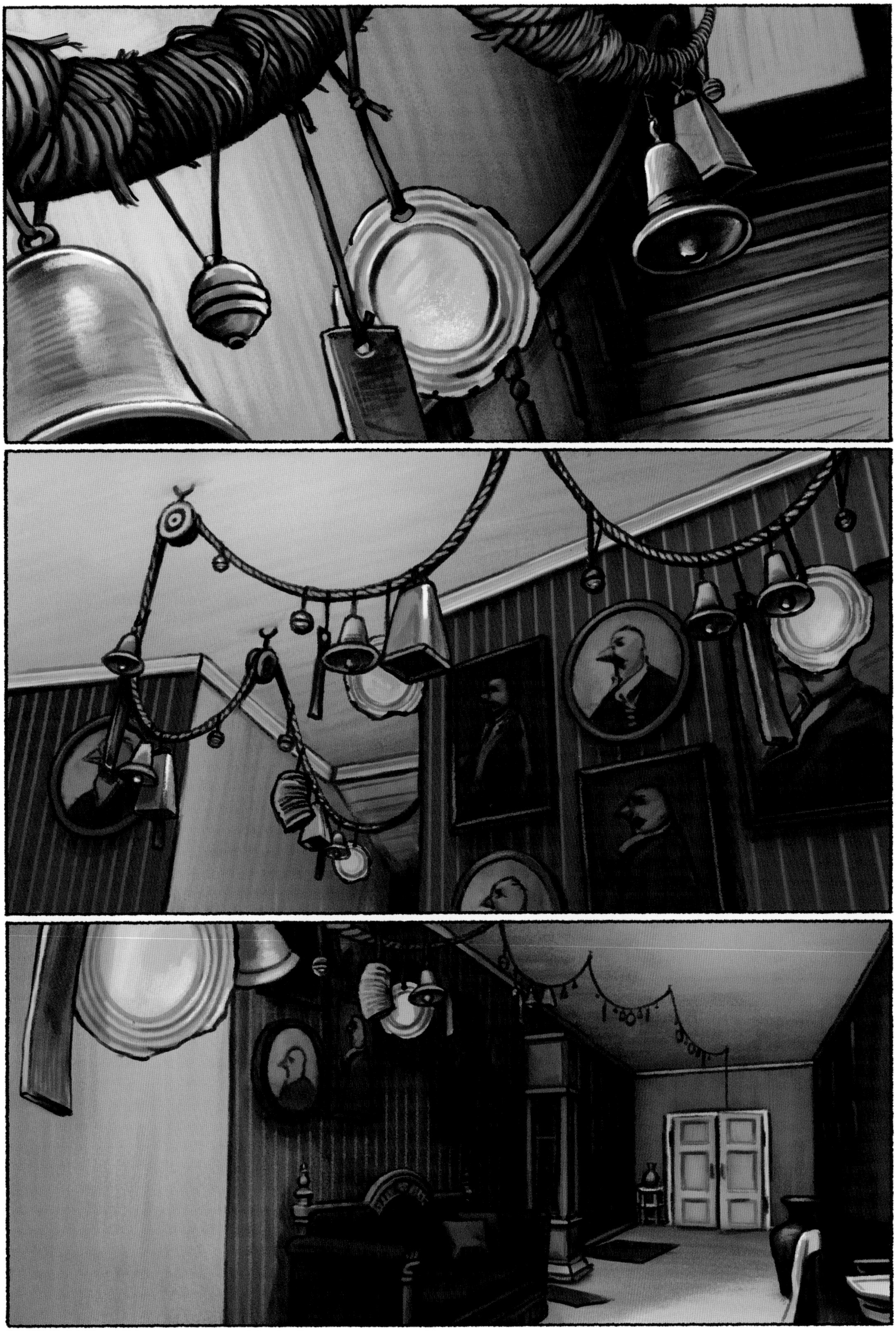

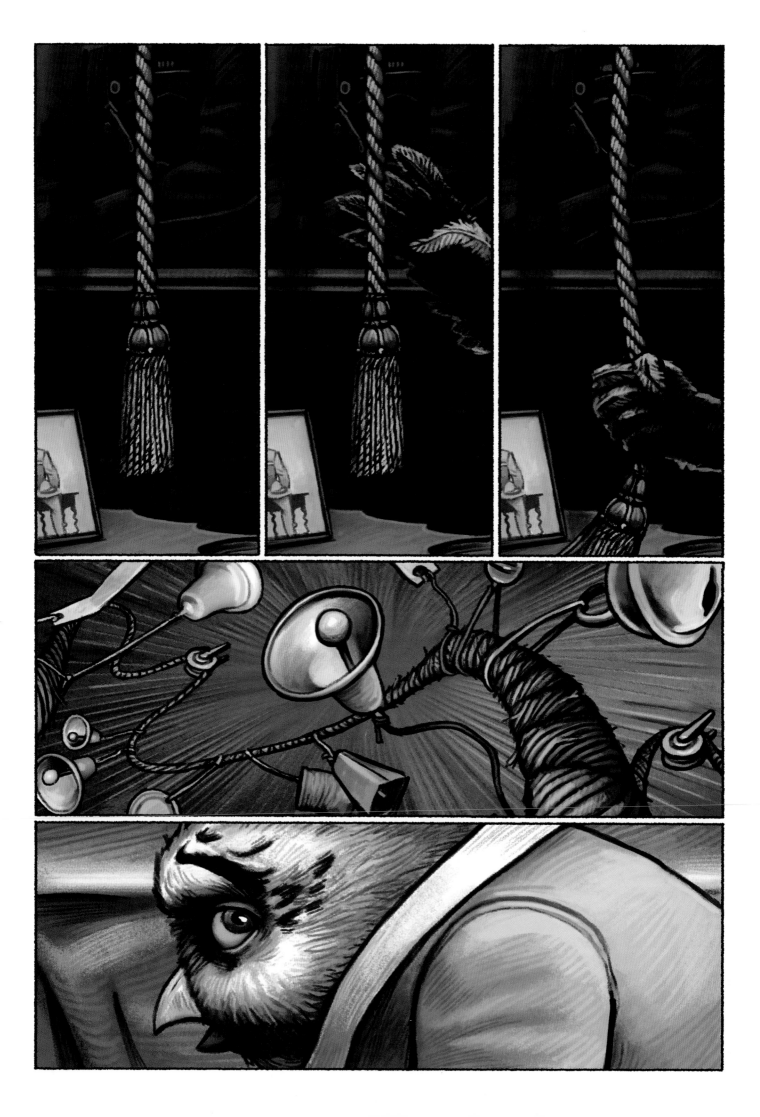

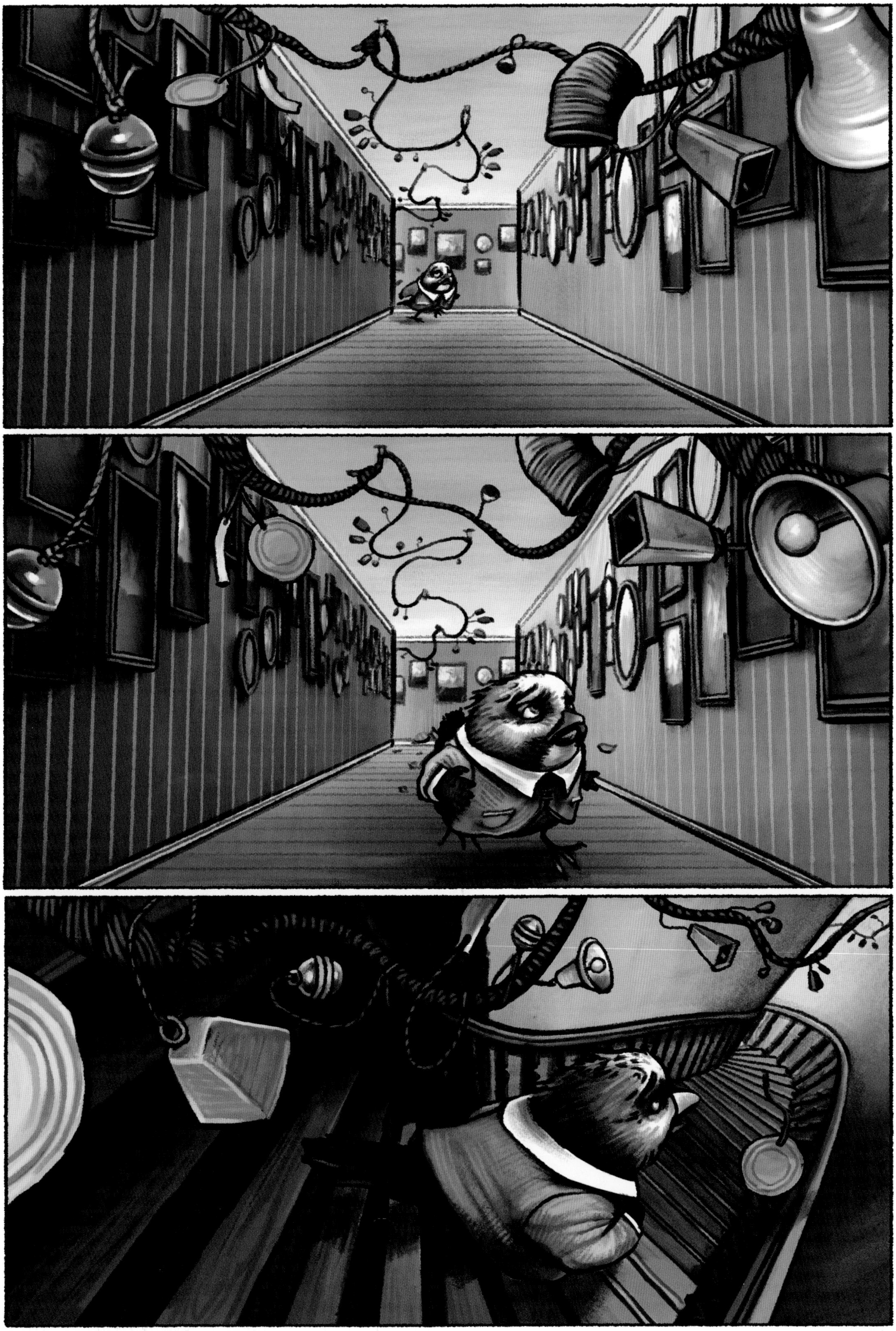

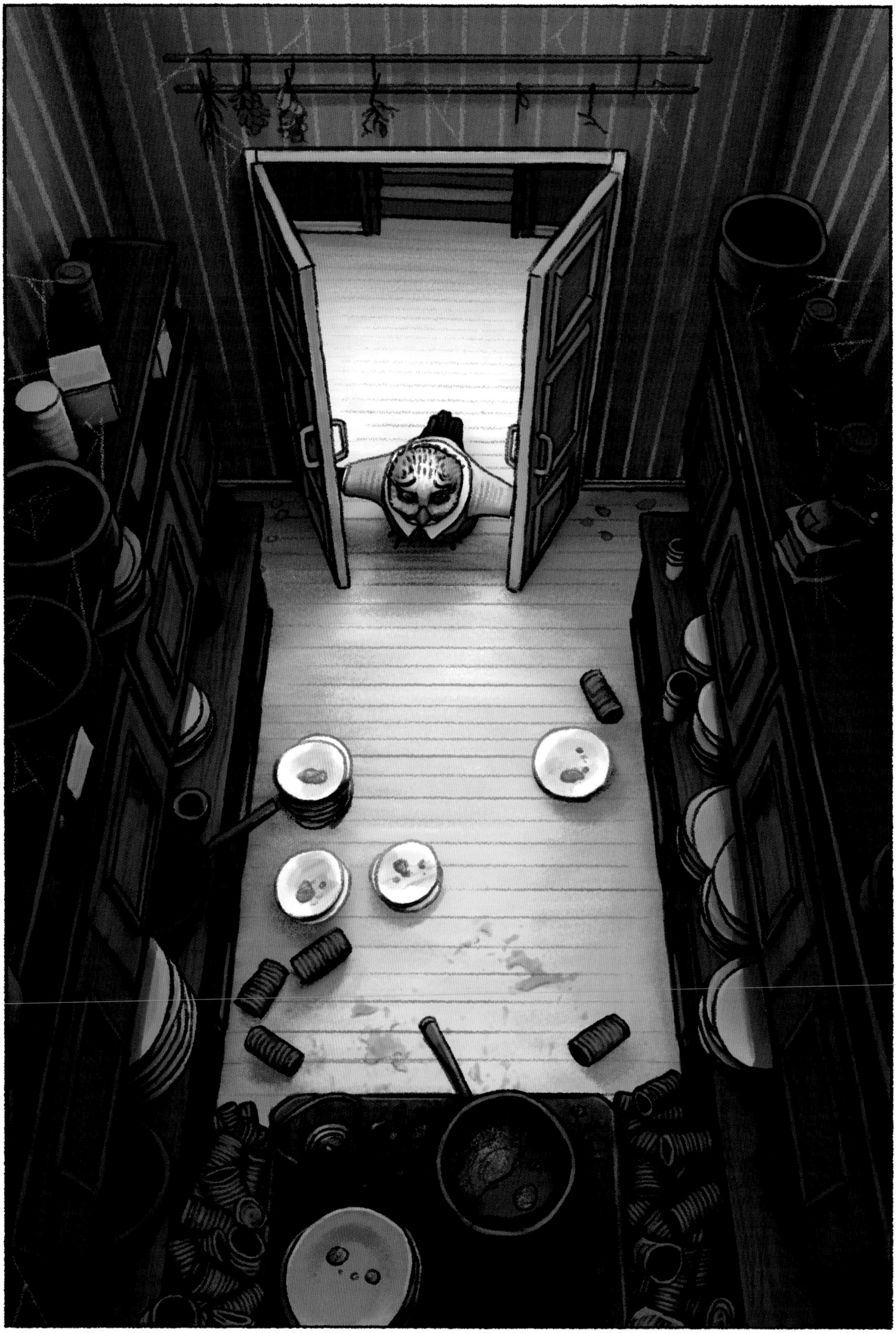

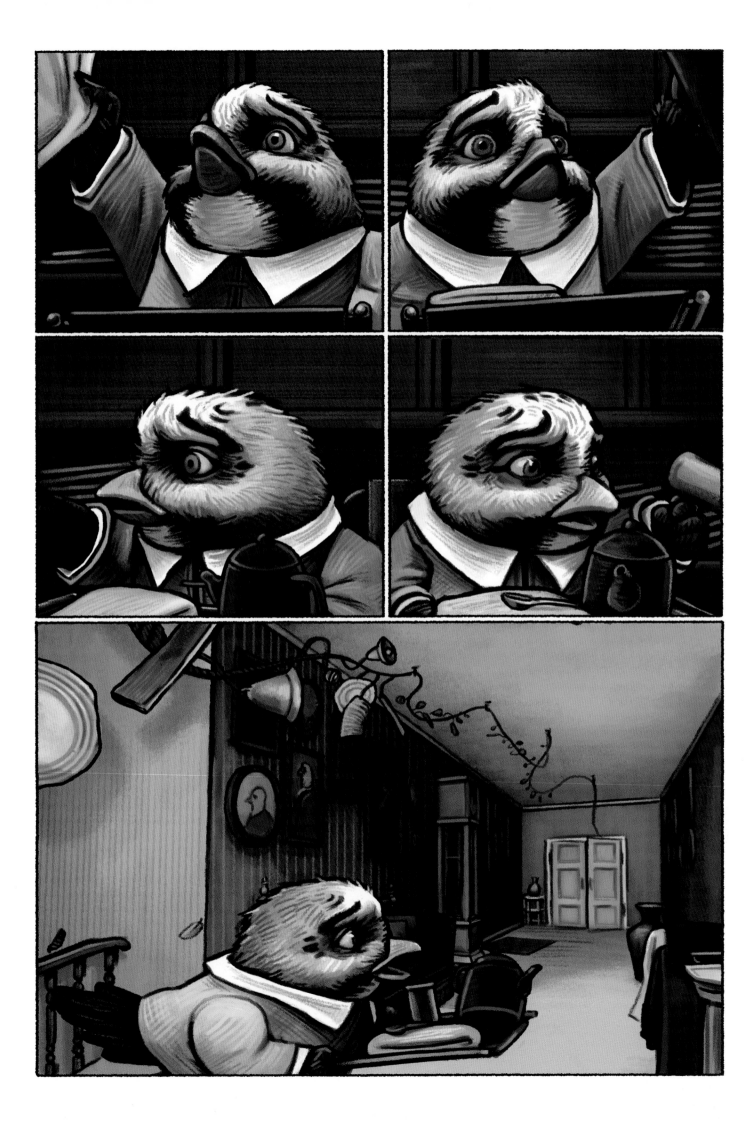

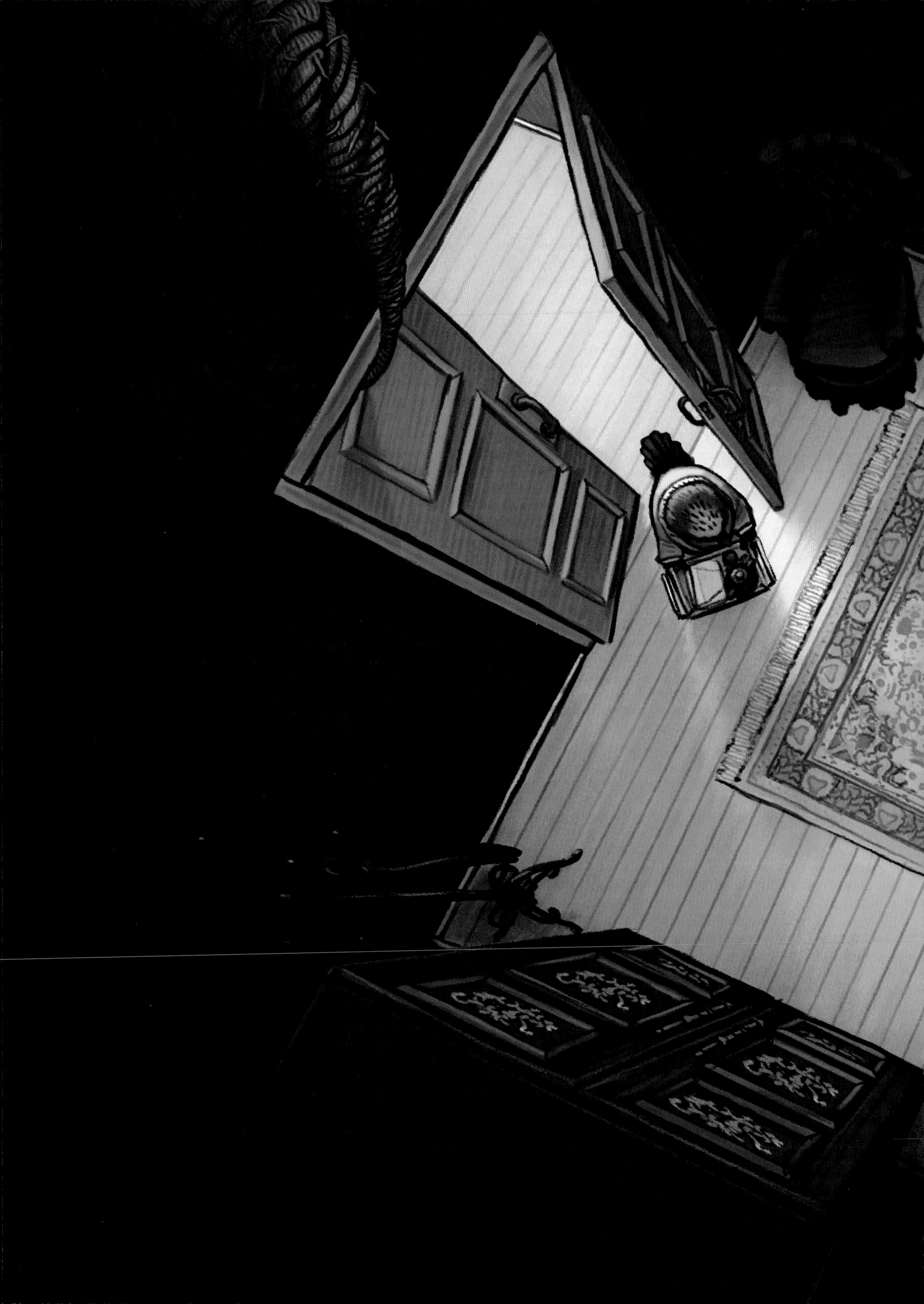

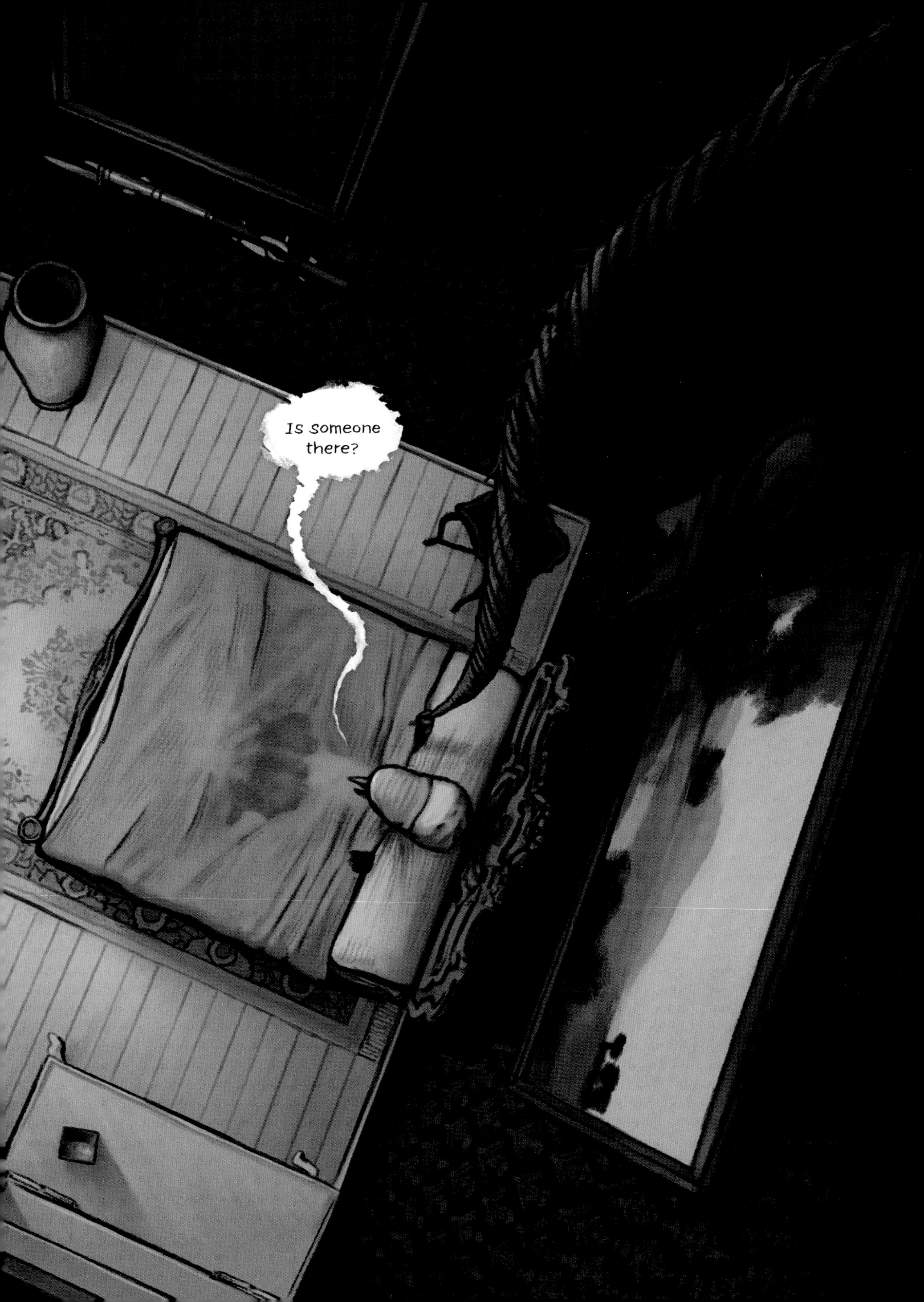
Is someone there?

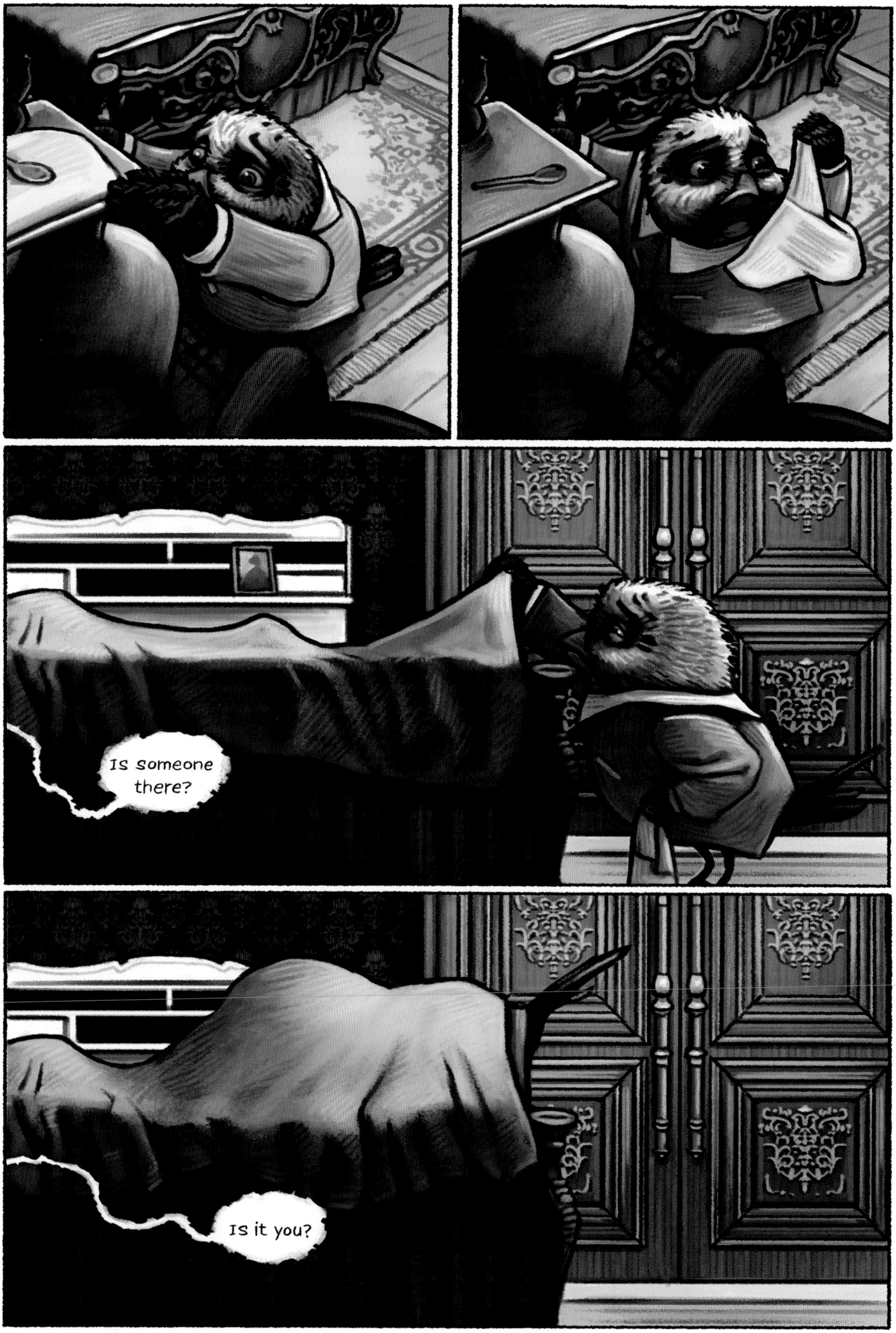
Is someone there?
Is it you?

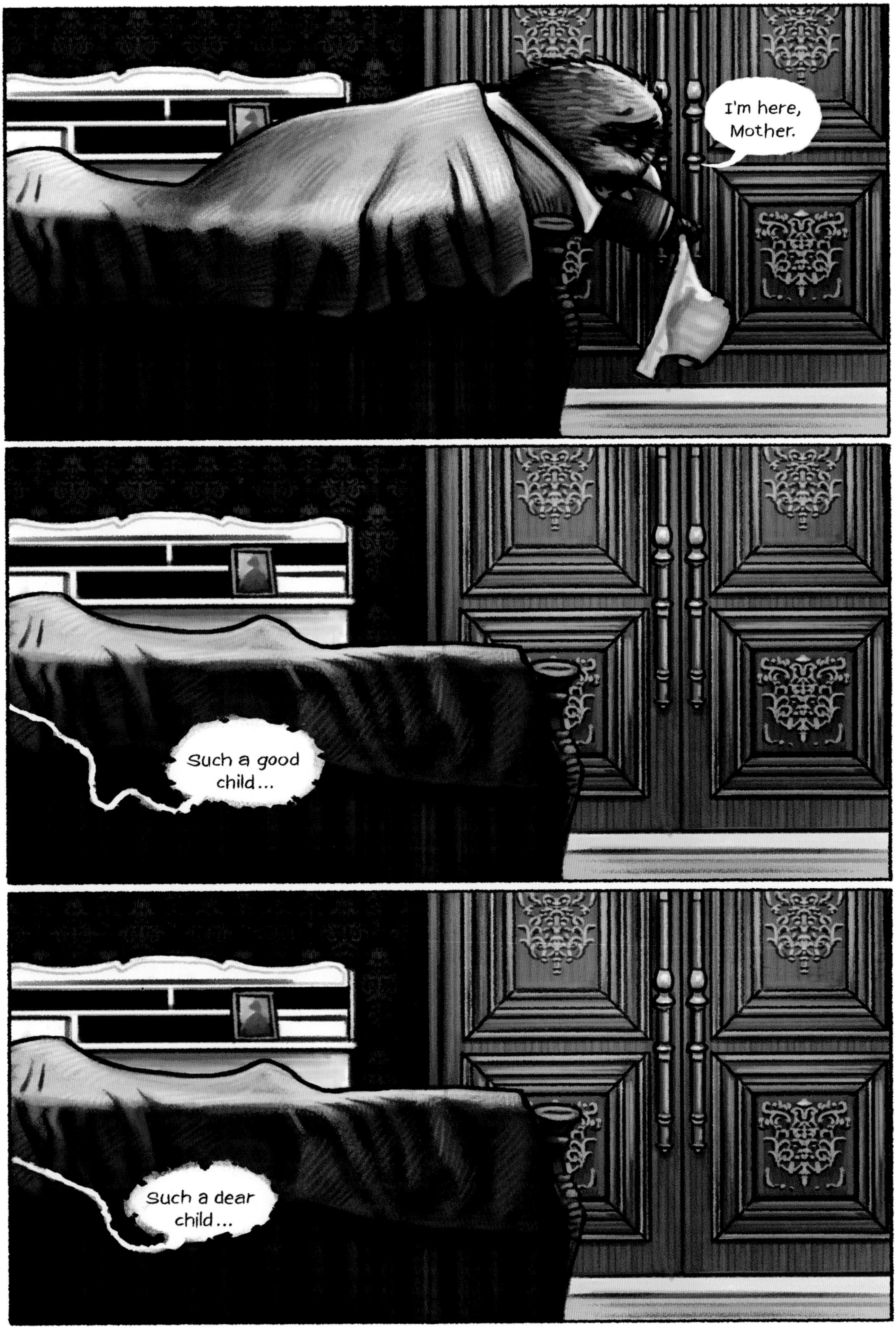
I'm here, Mother.
Such a good child...
Such a dear child...

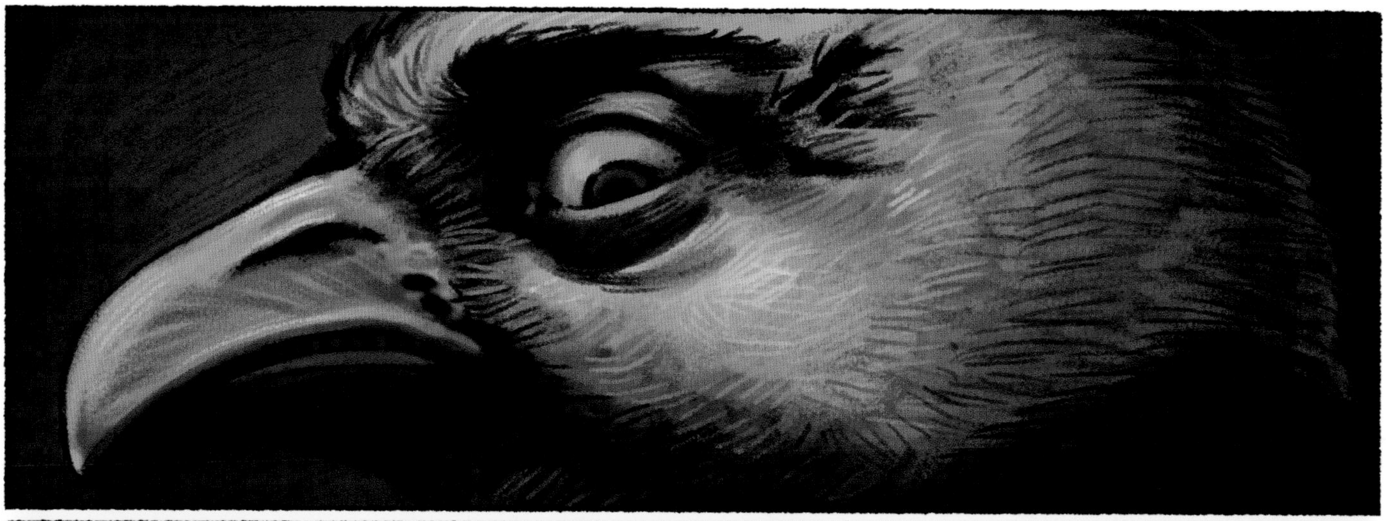
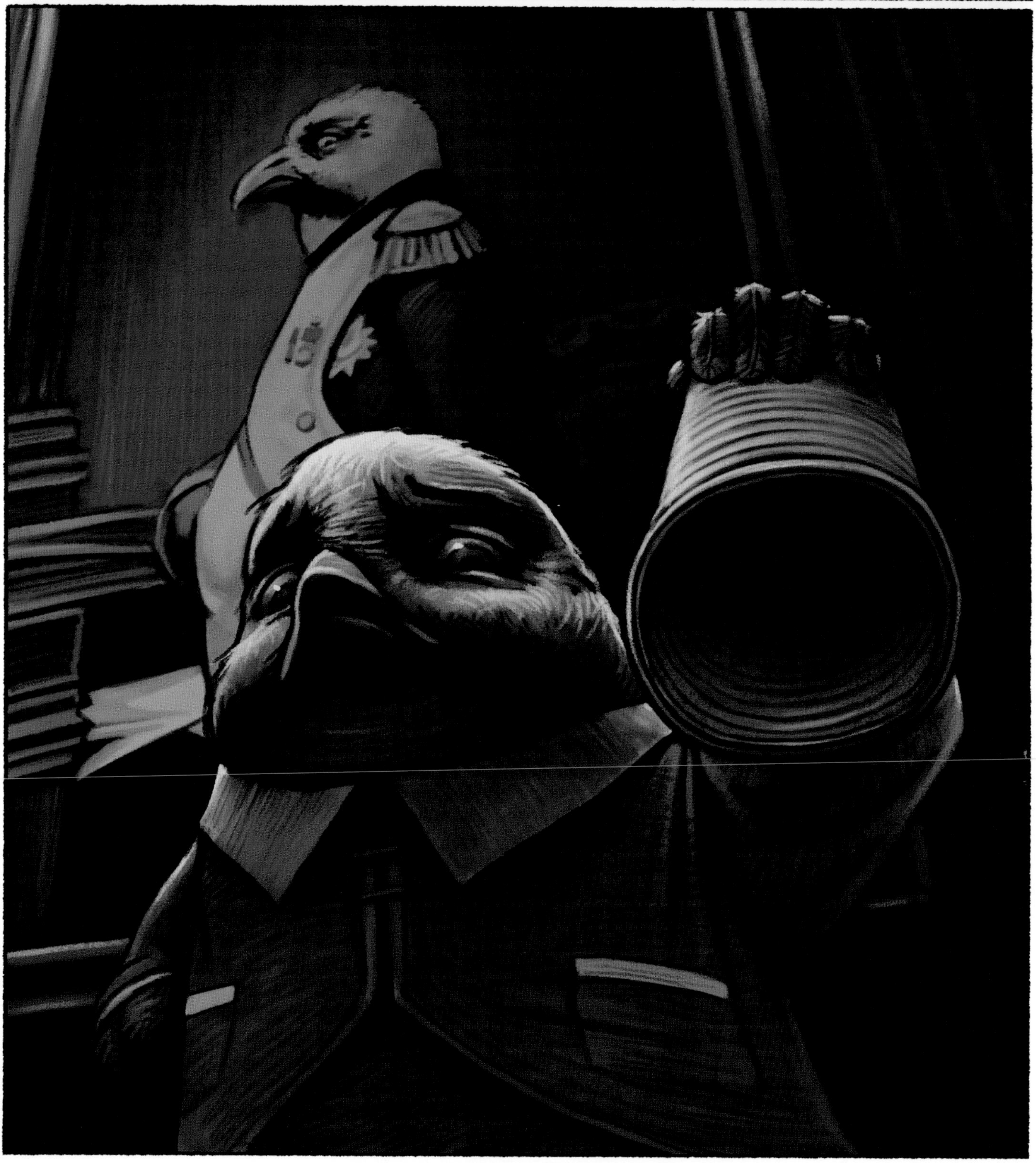

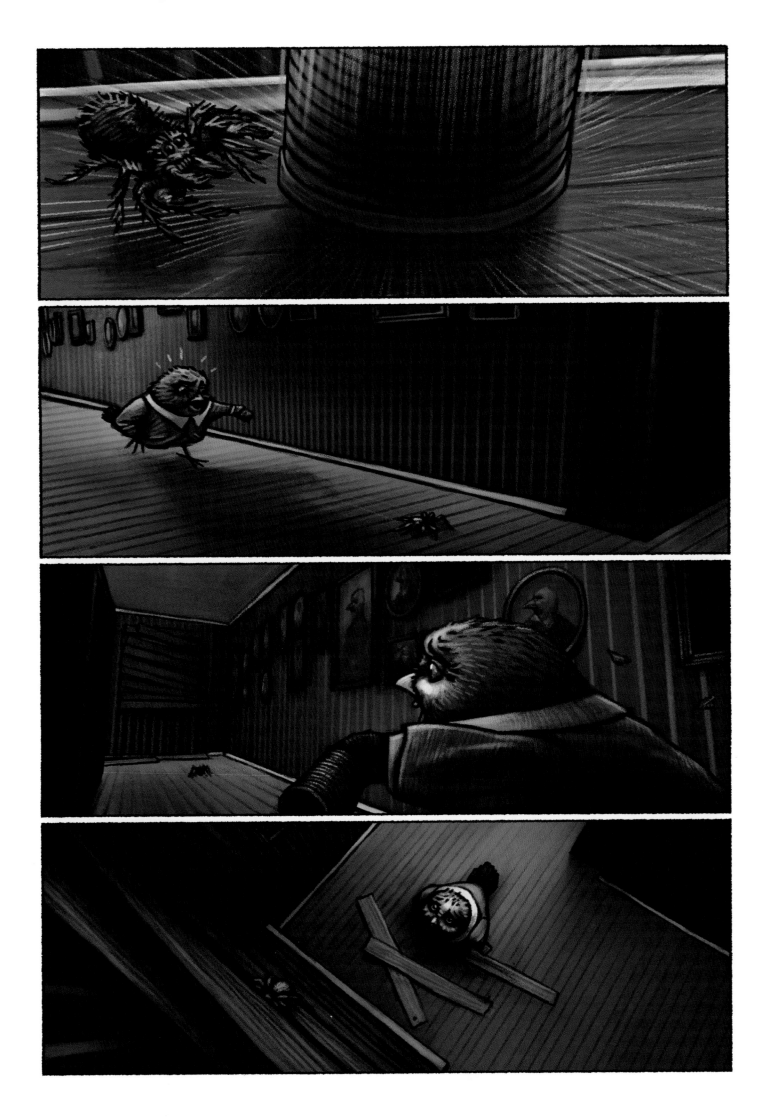

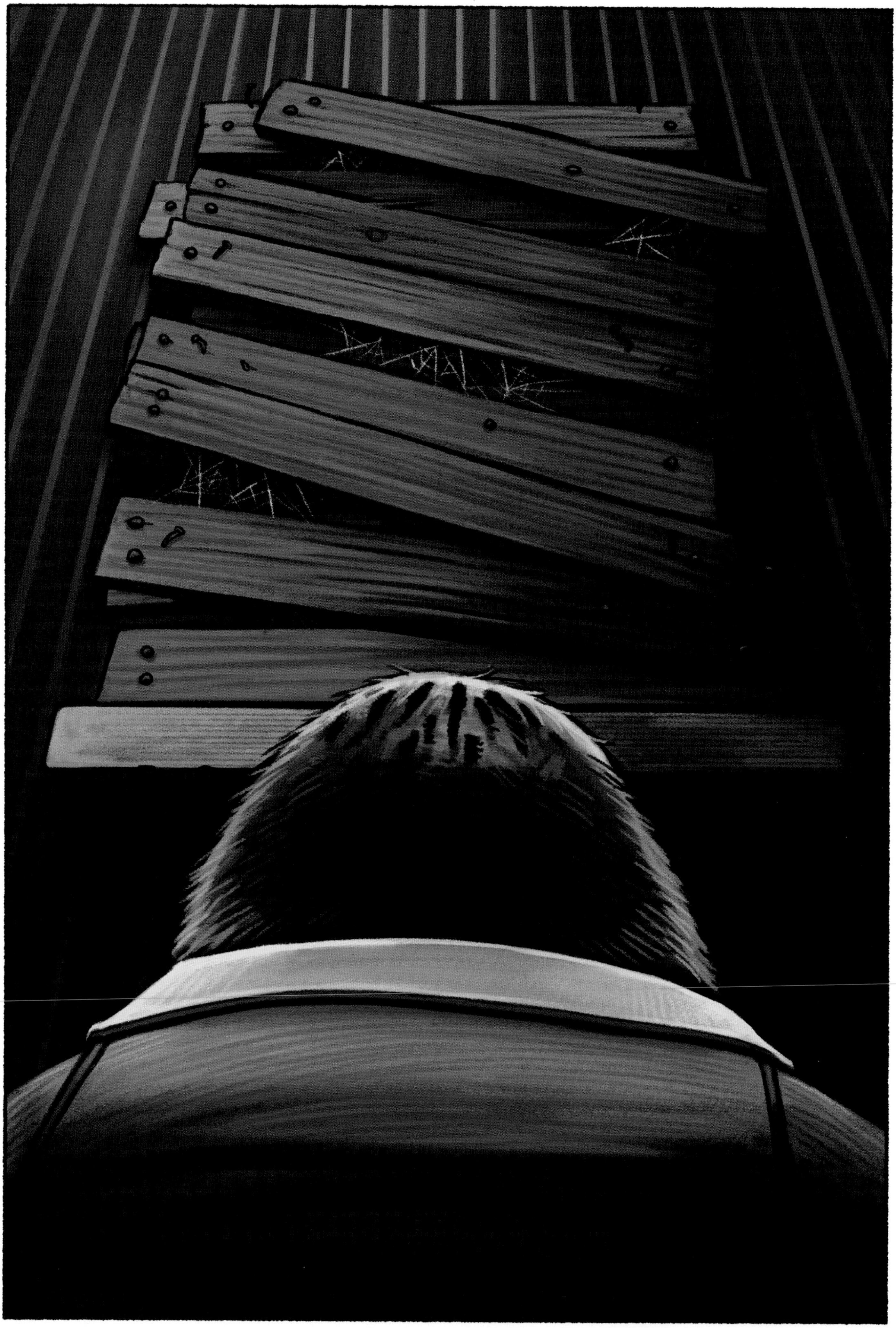

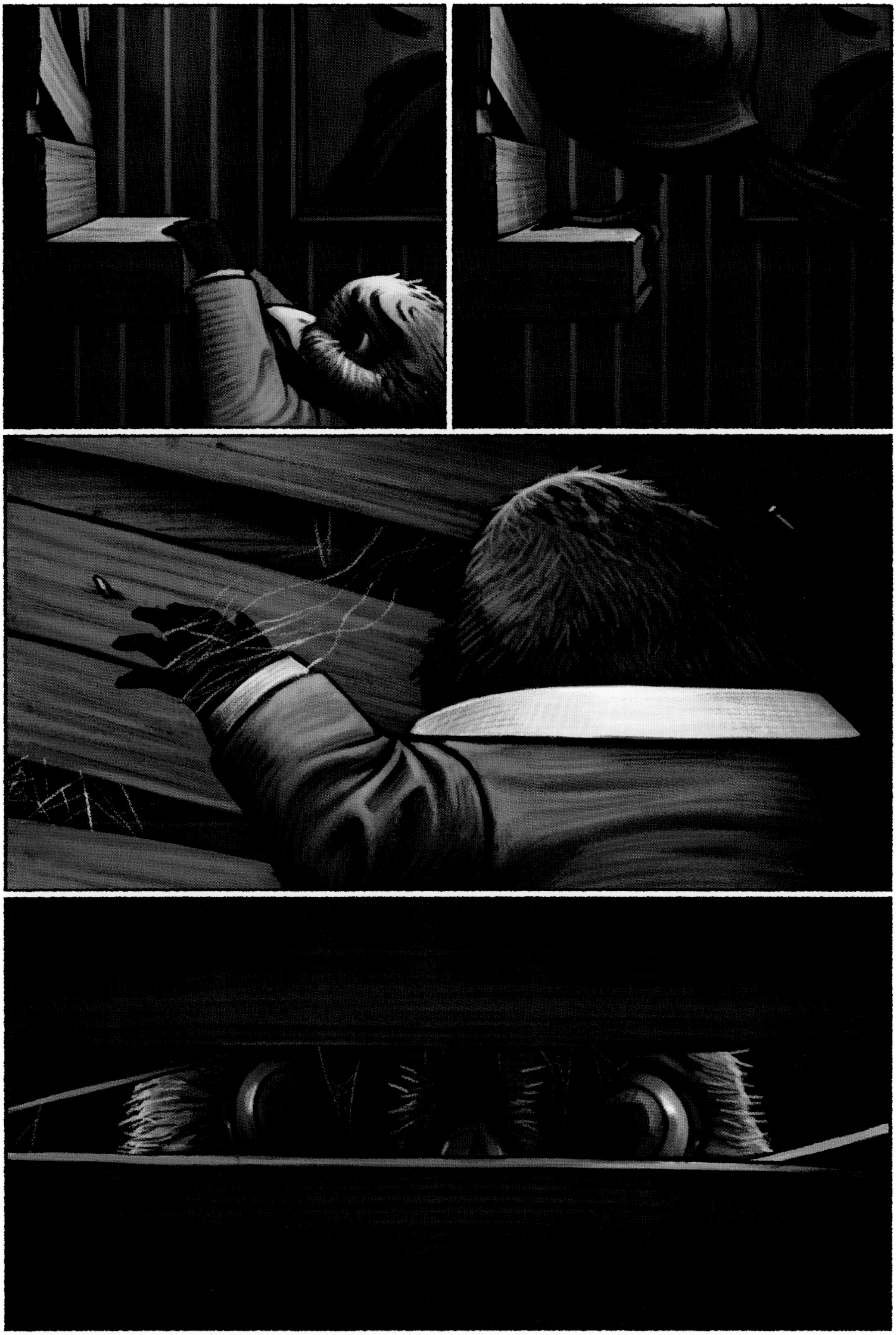

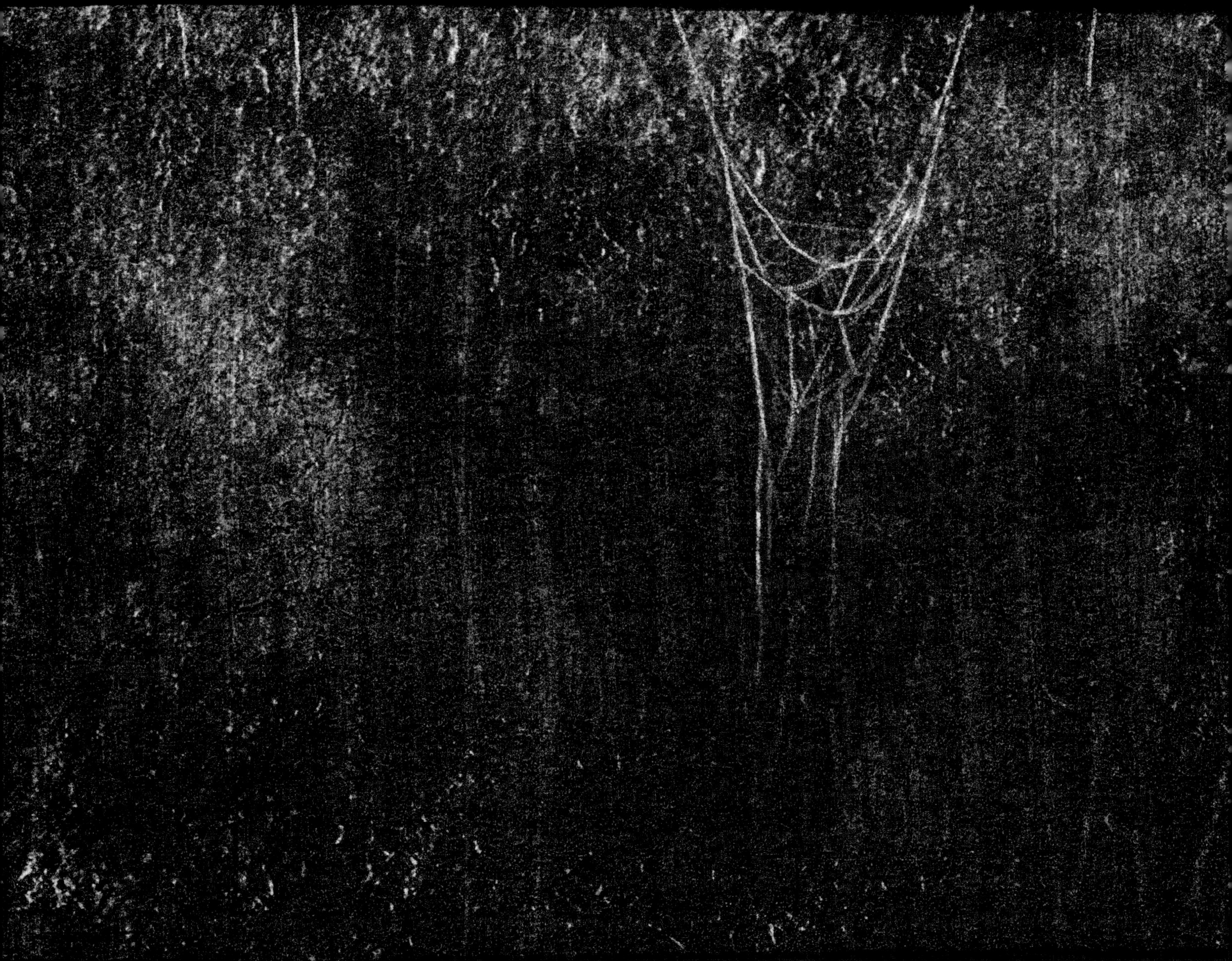

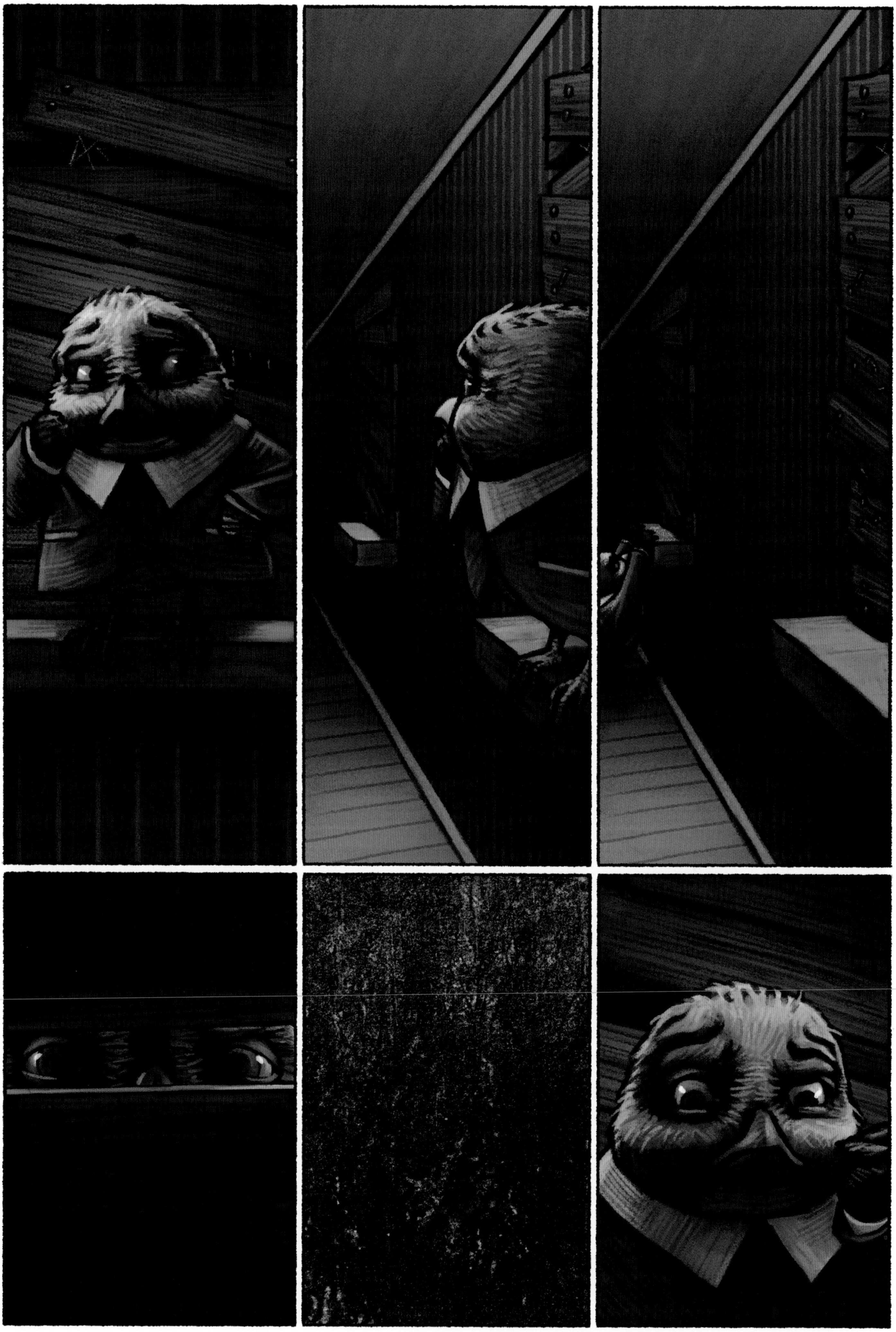

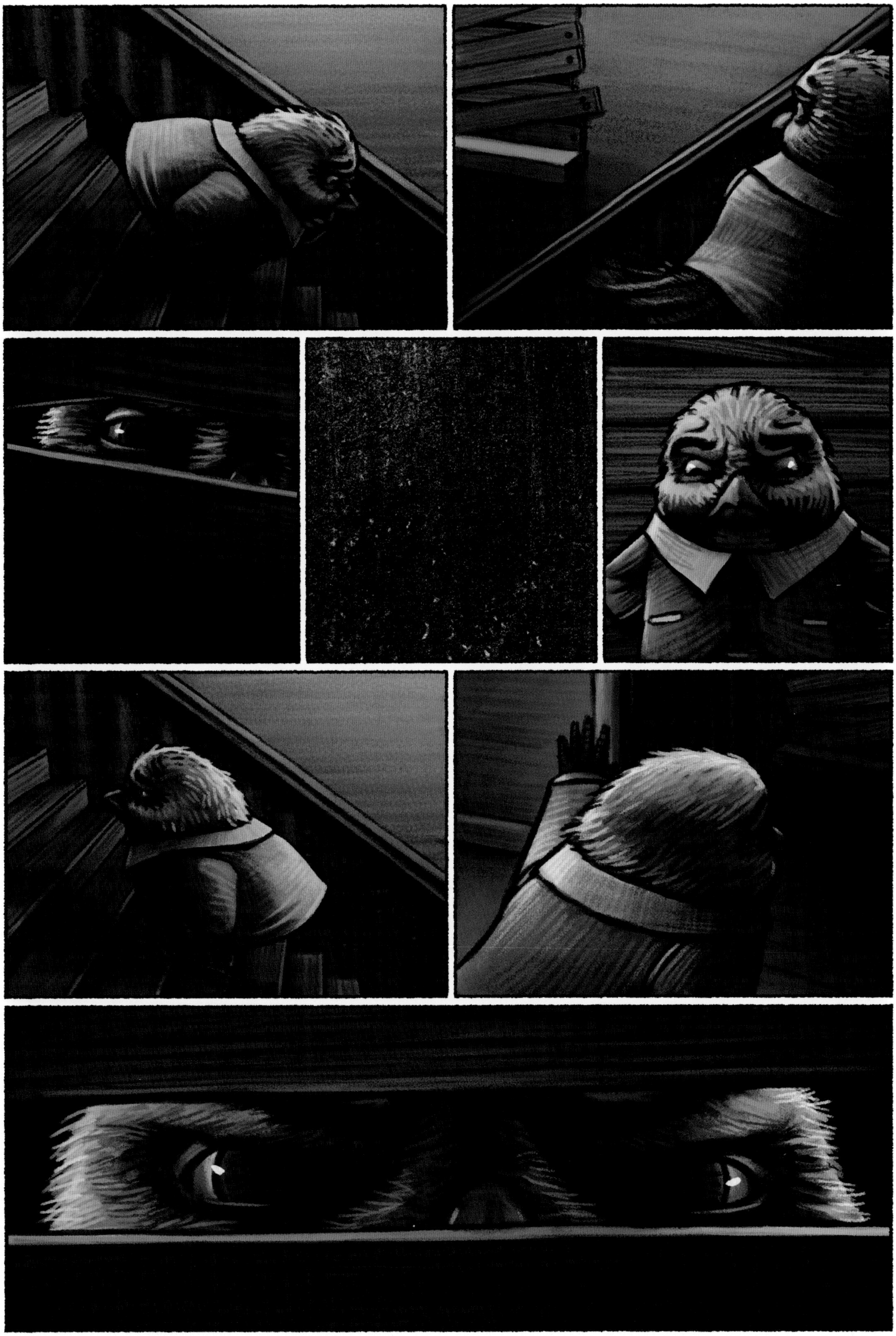

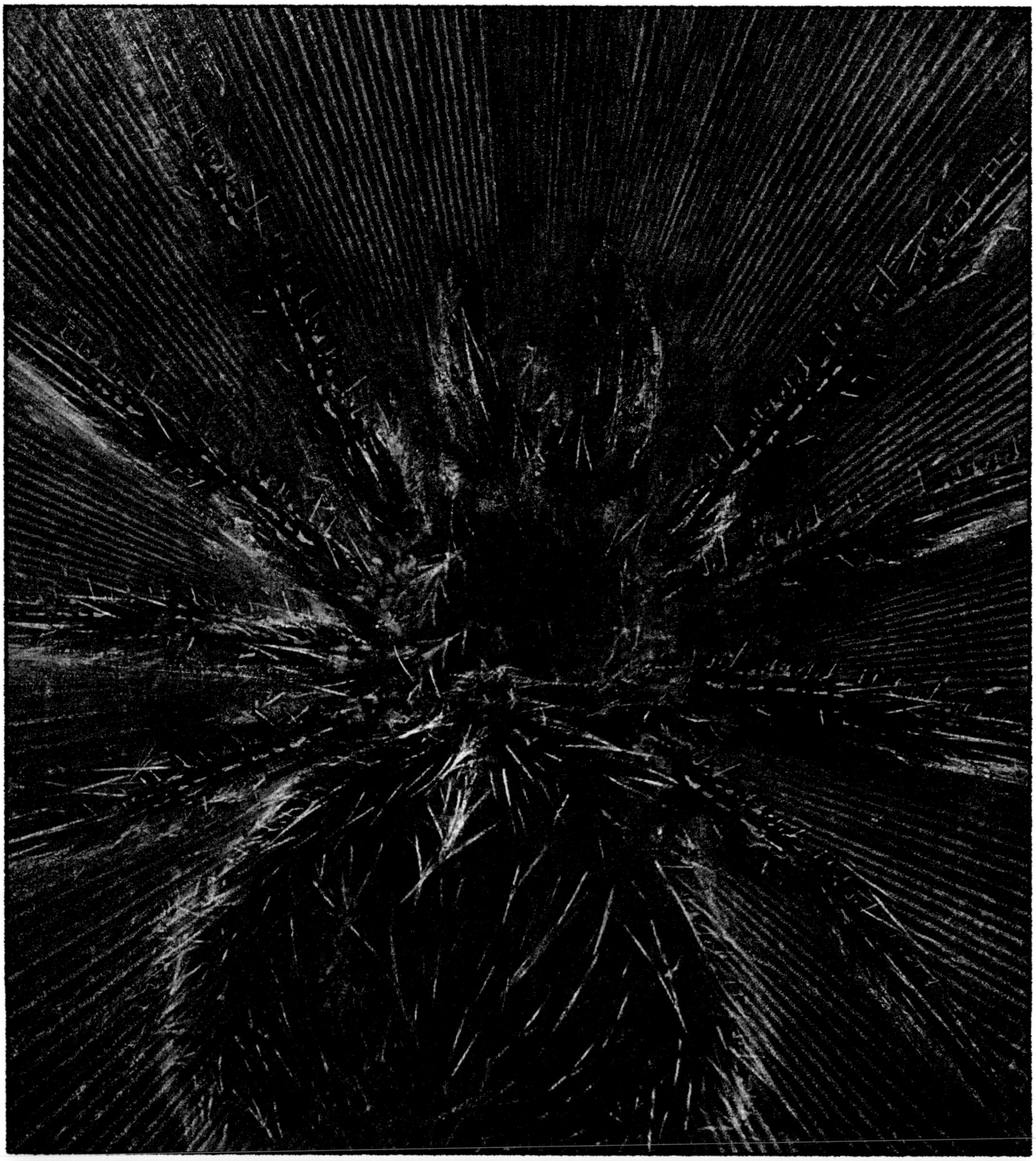

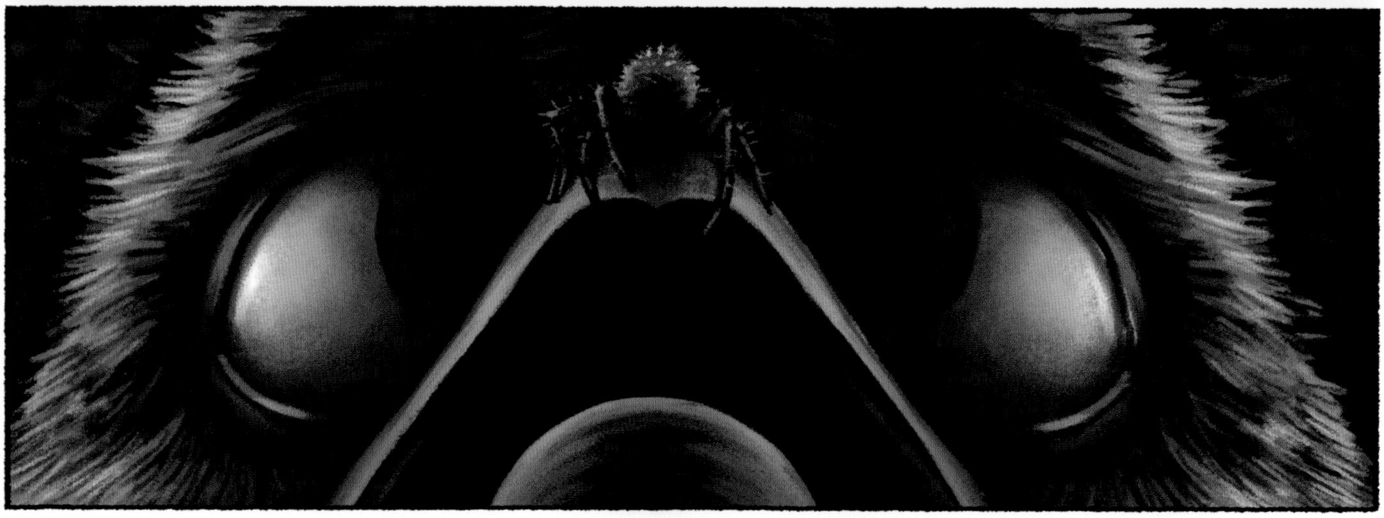

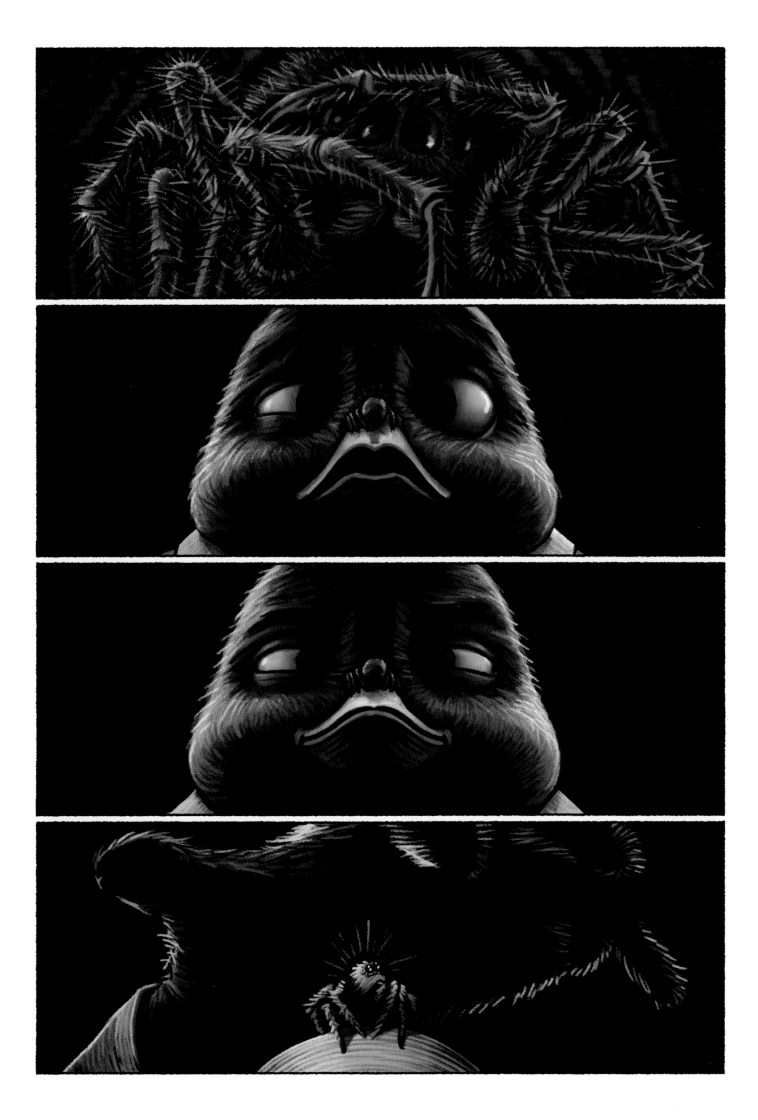

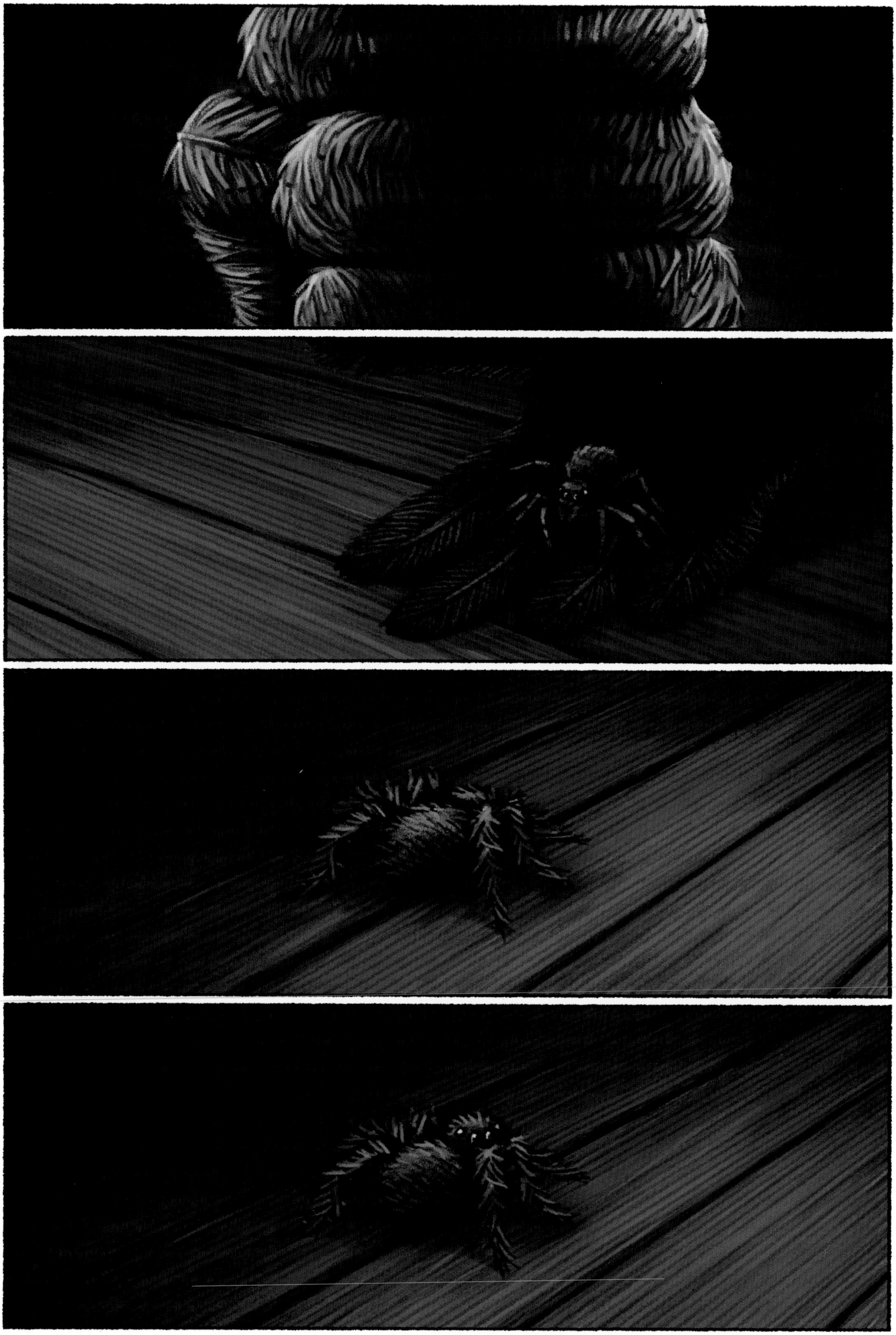

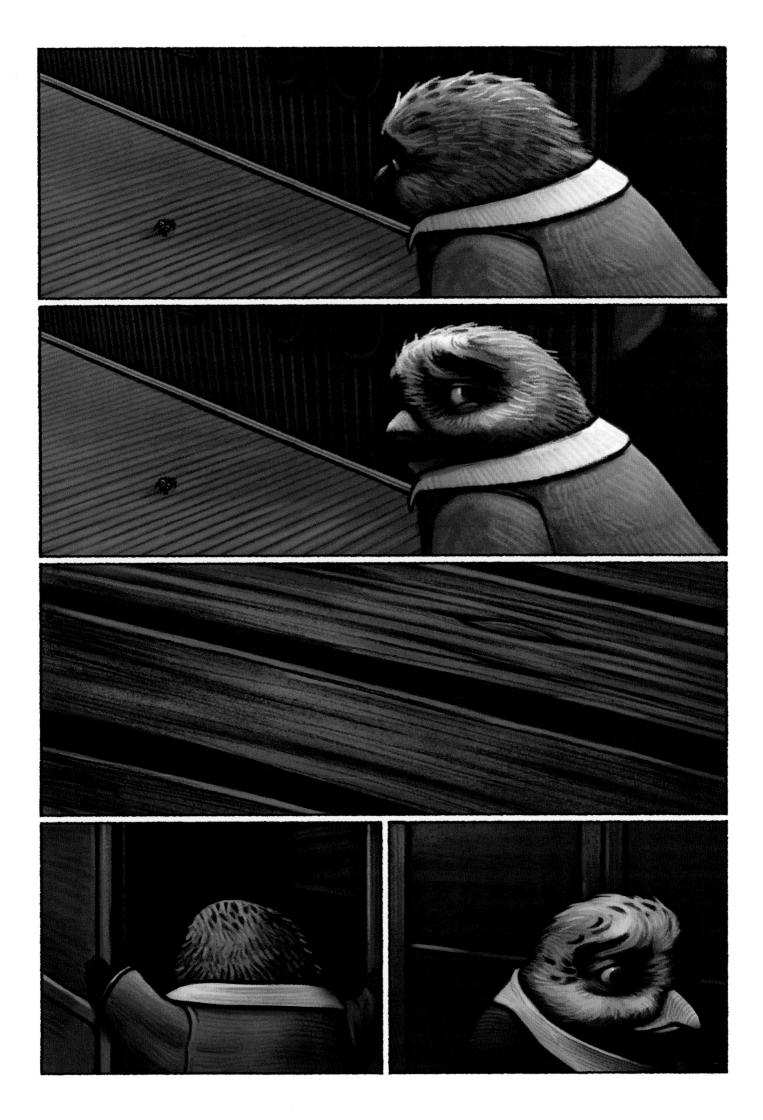

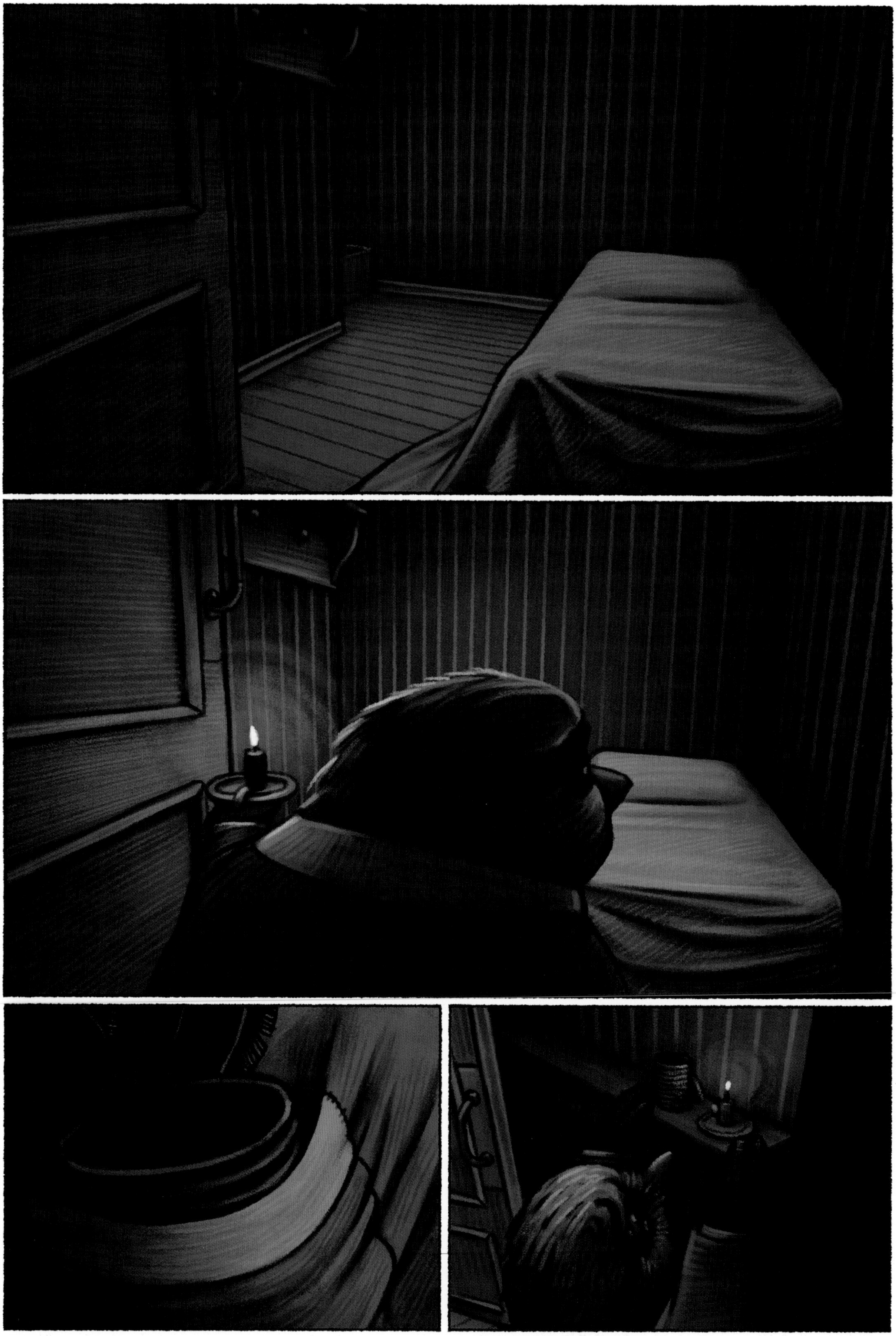

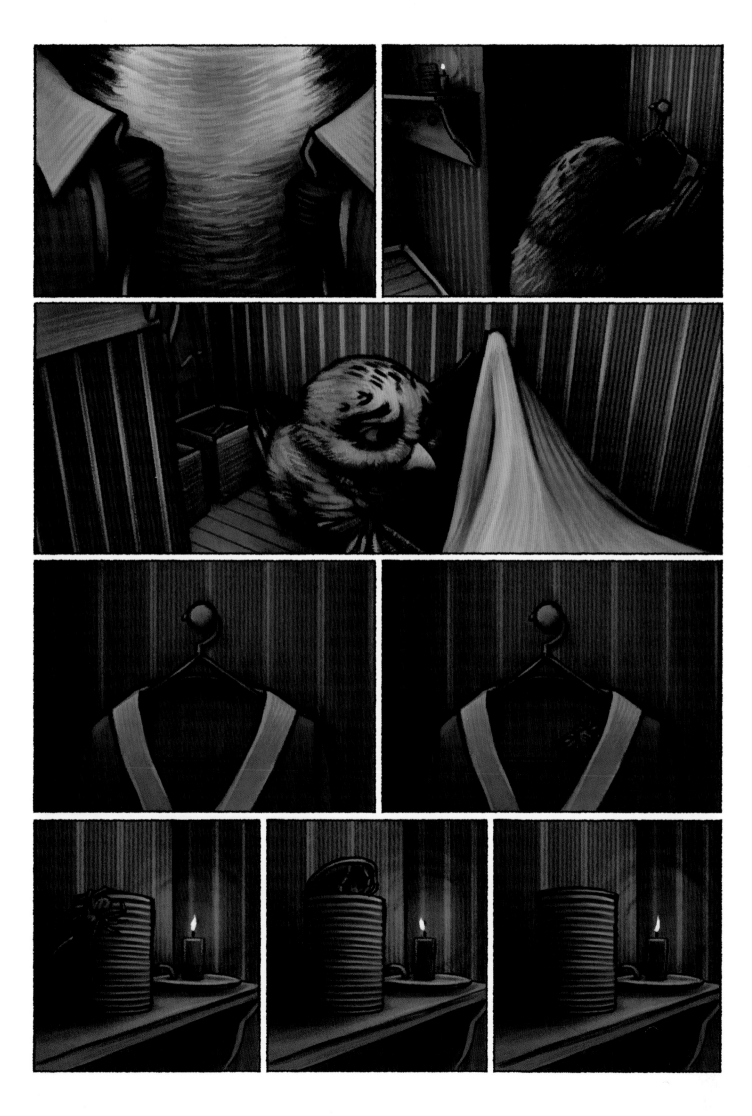

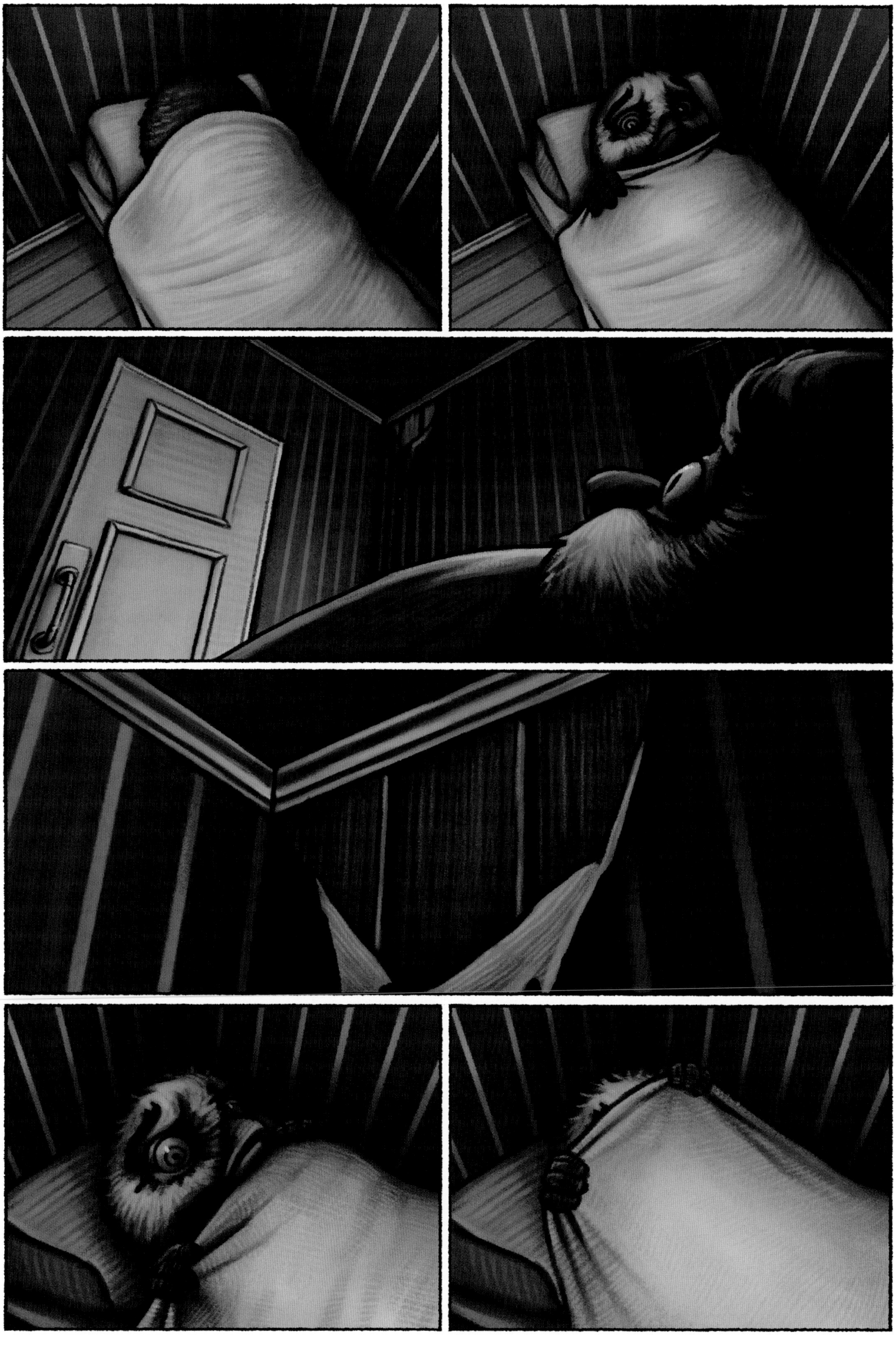

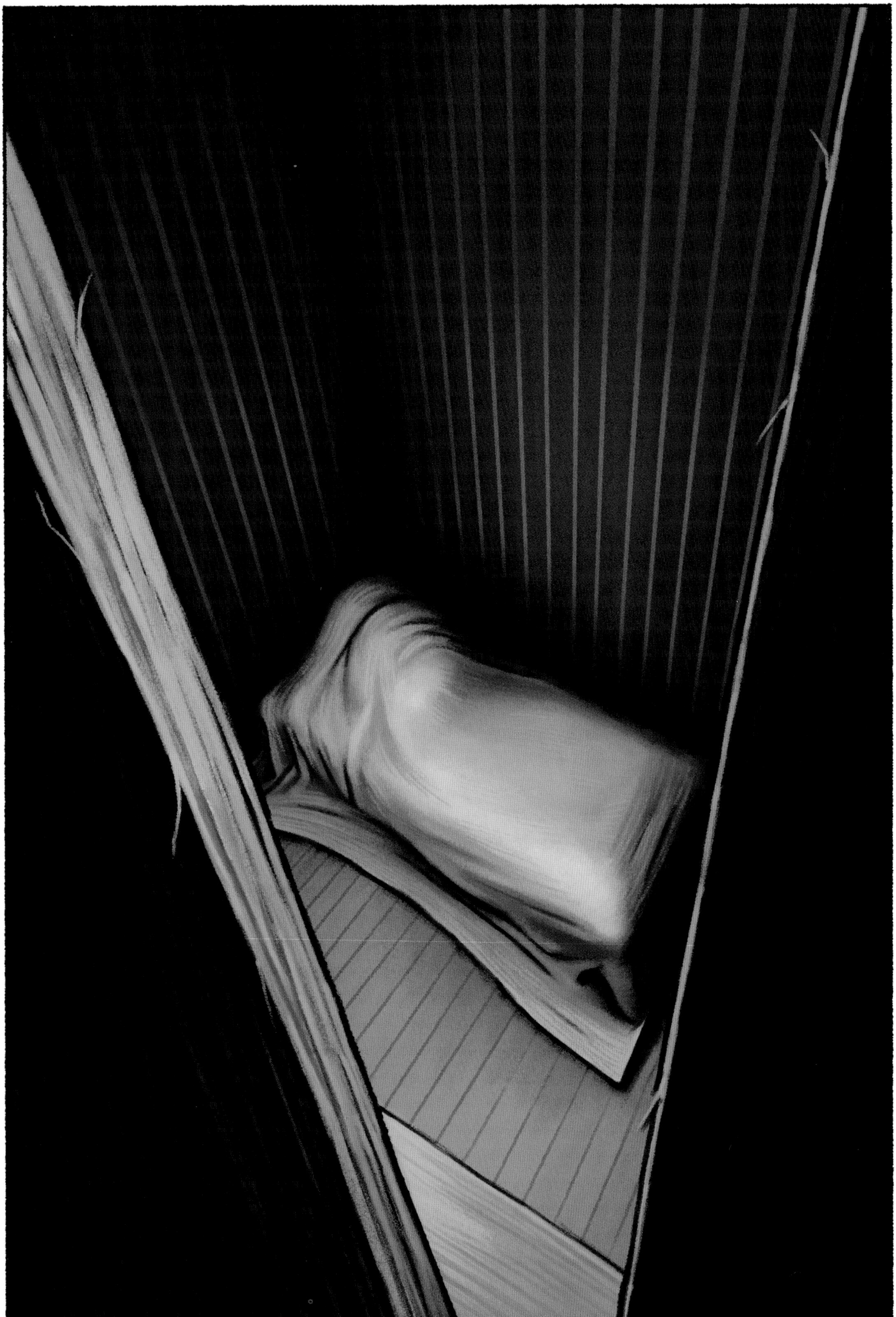

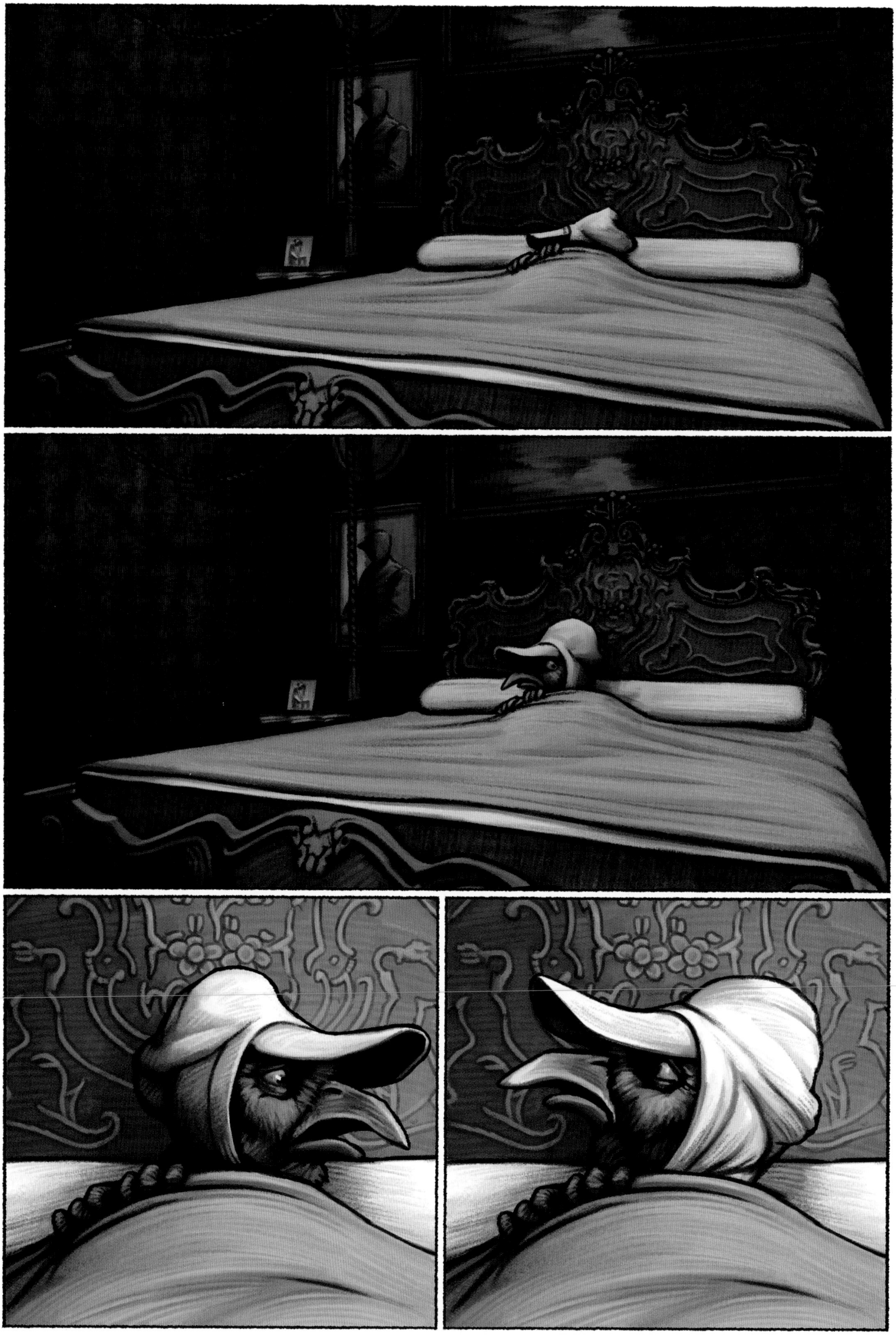

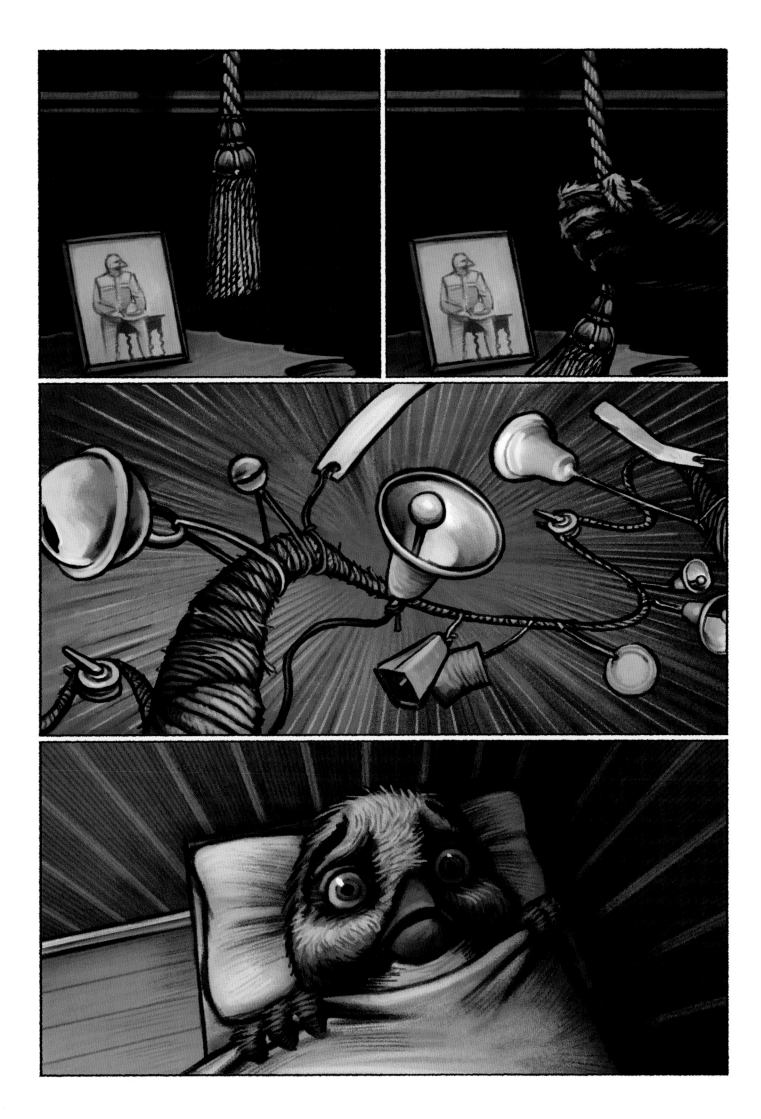

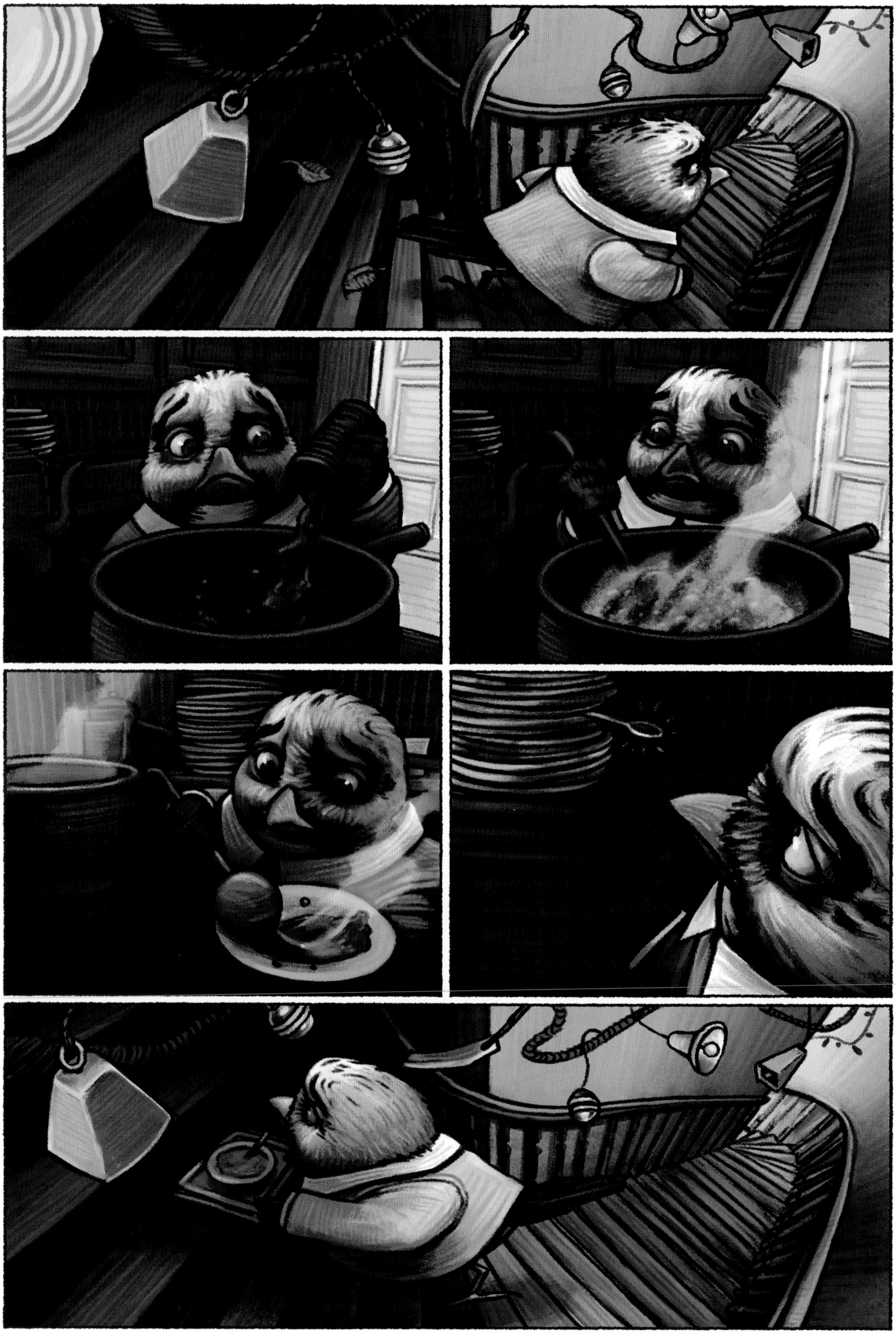

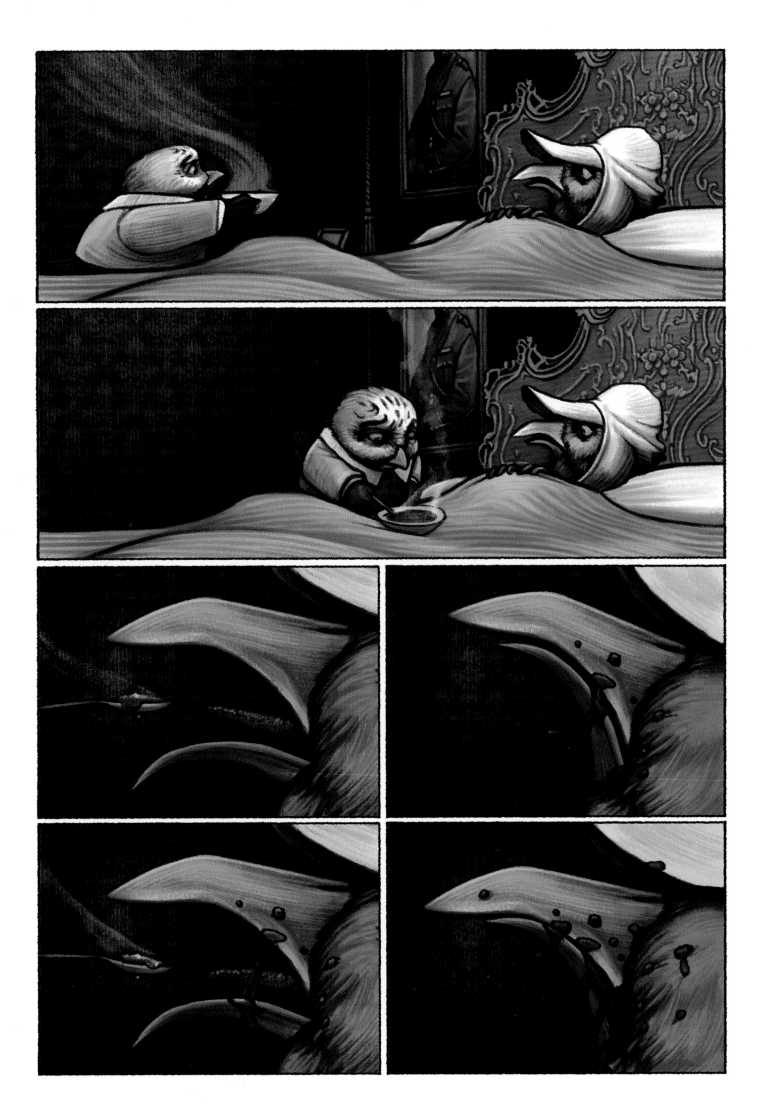

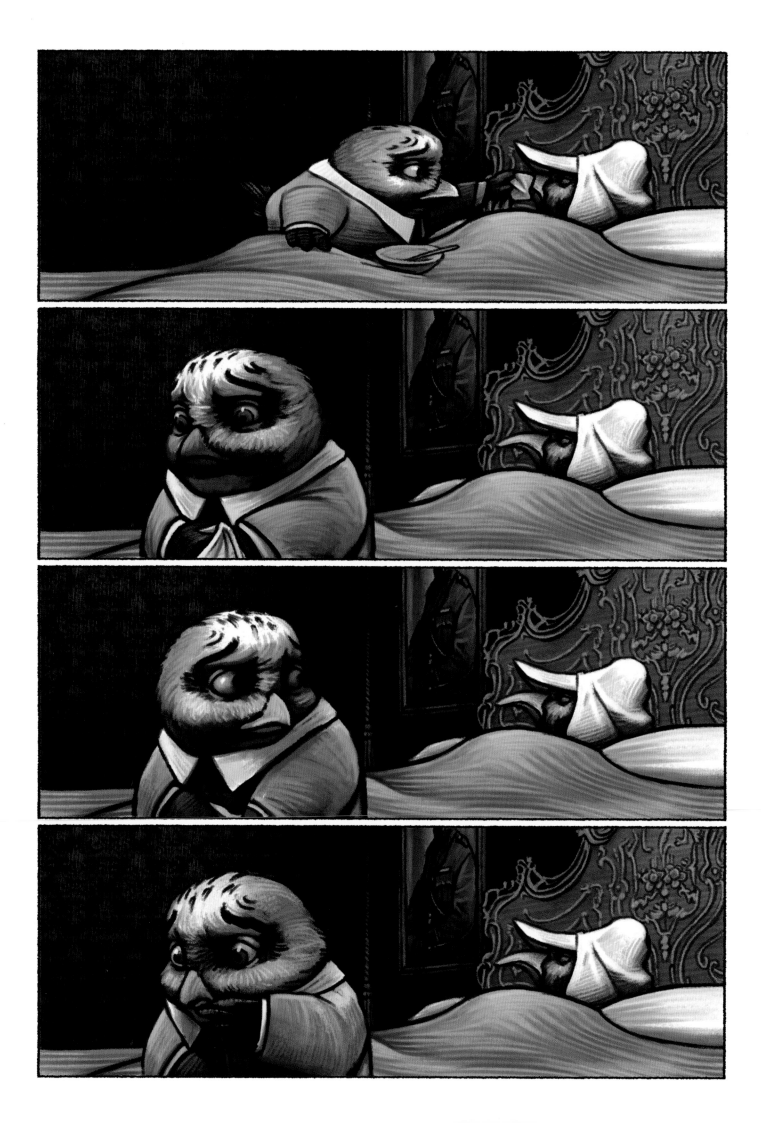

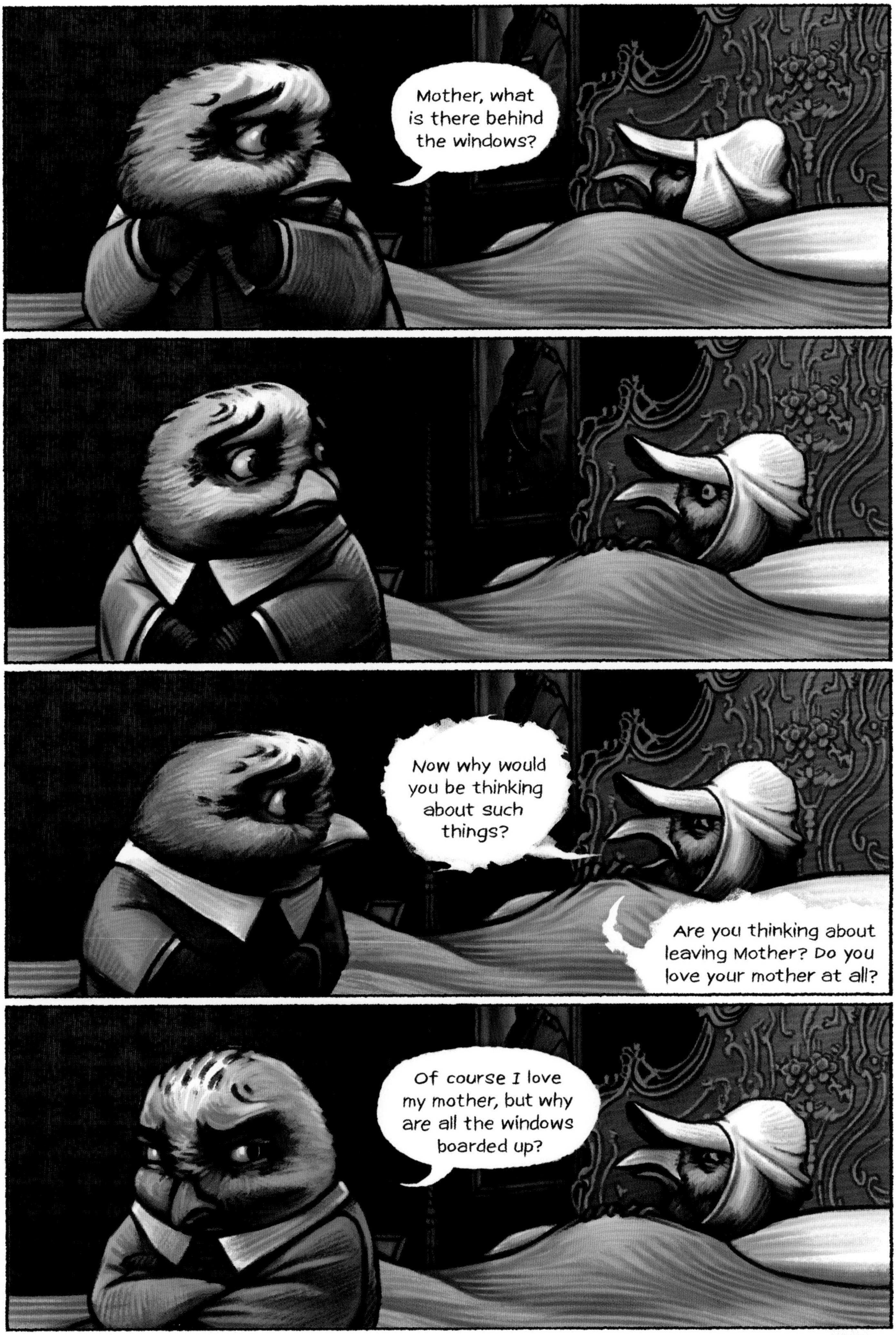
Mother, what is there behind the windows?
Now why would you be thinking about such things?
Are you thinking about leaving Mother? Do you love your mother at all?
Of course I love my mother, but why are all the windows boarded up?

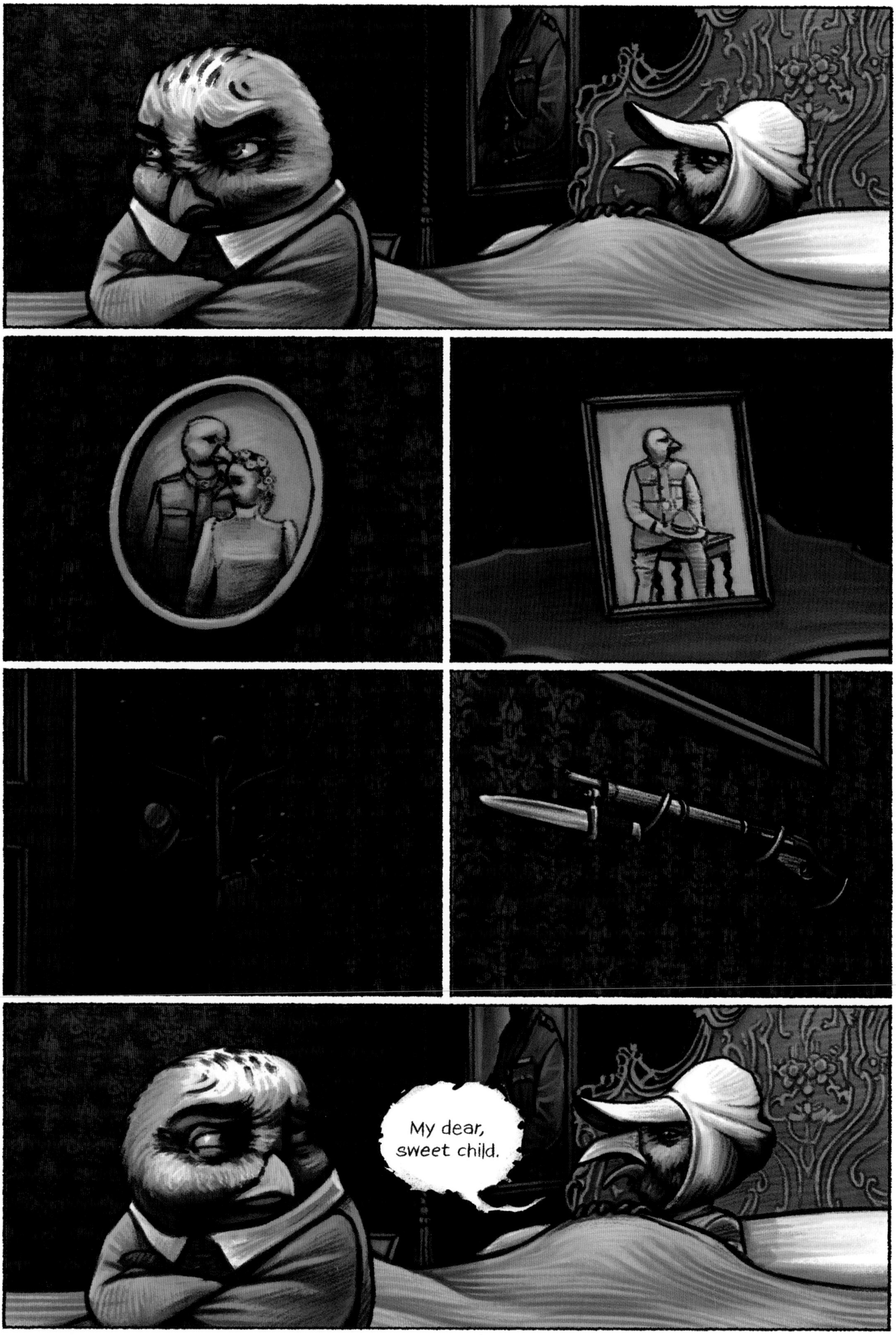
My dear, sweet child.

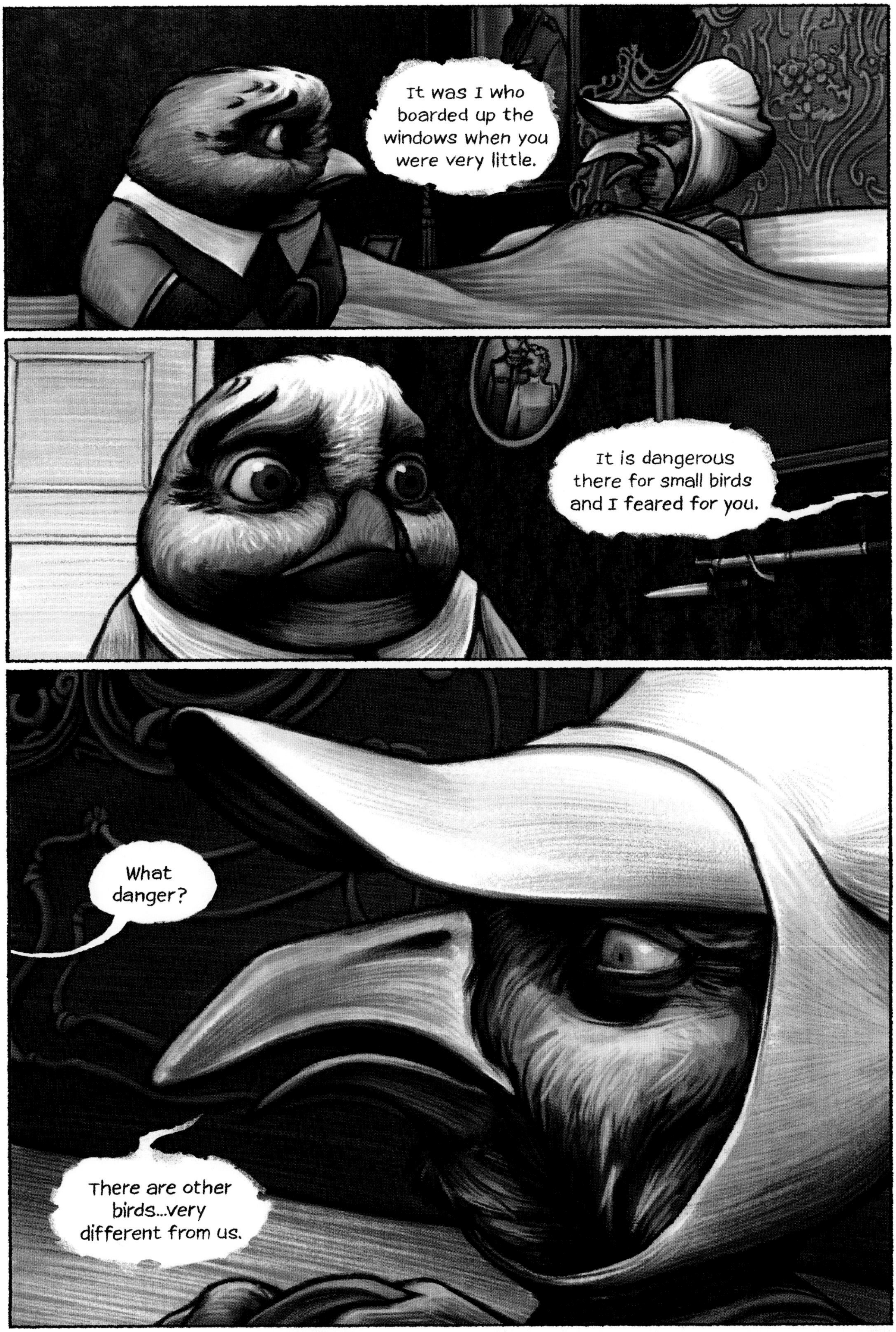

It was I who boarded up the windows when you were very little.
It is dangerous there for small birds and I feared for you.
What danger?
There are other birds...very different from us.

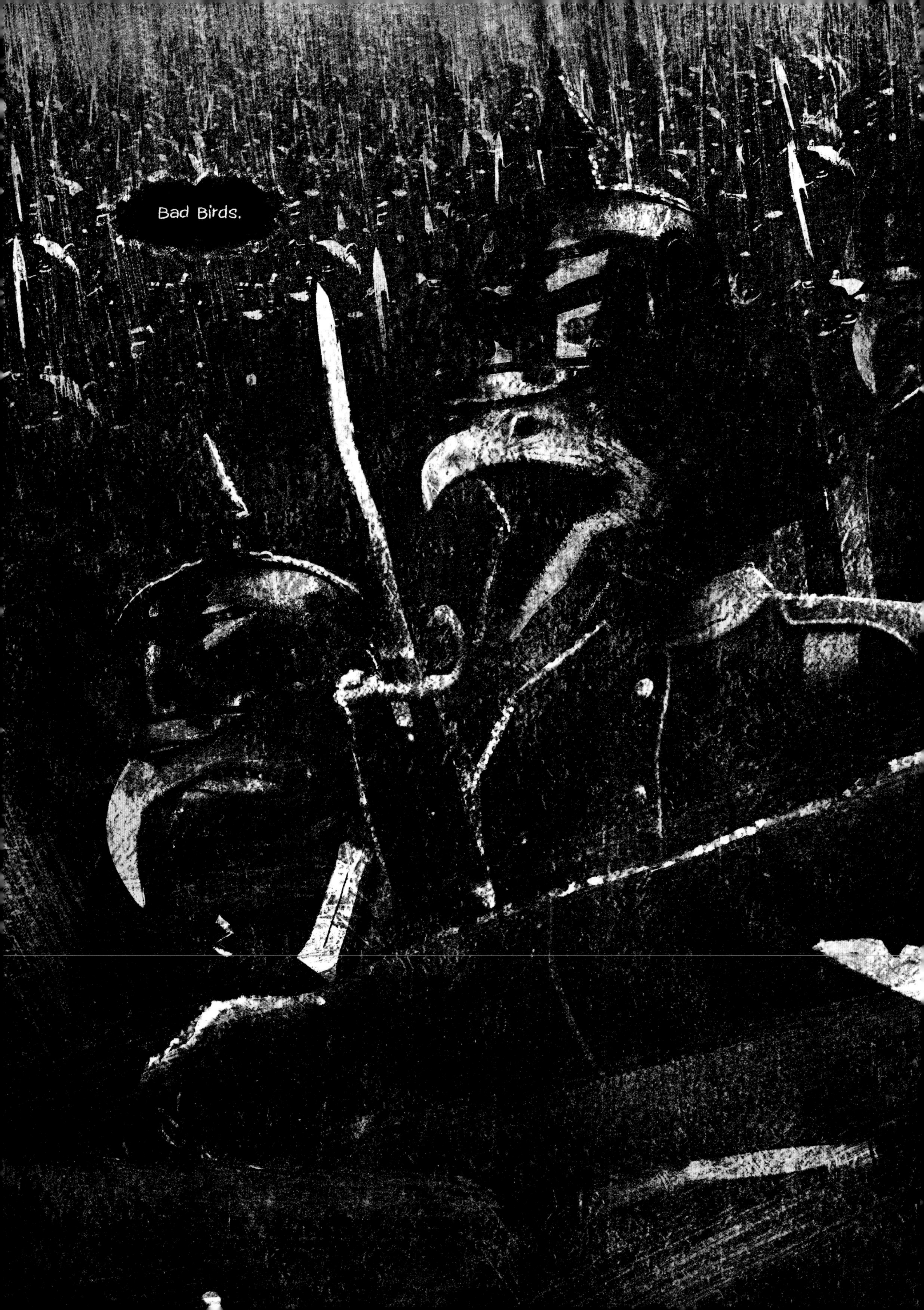
Bad Birds.

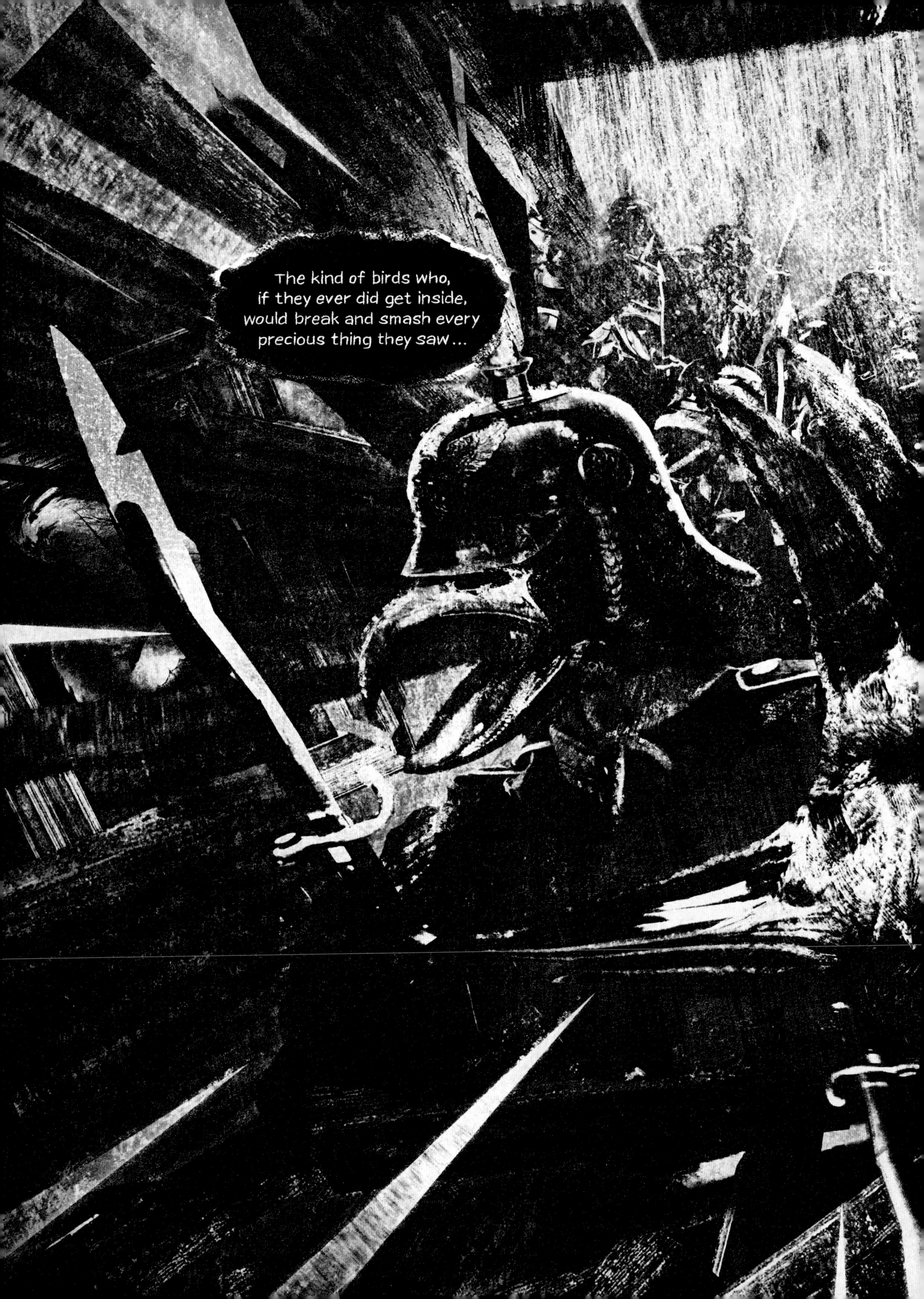
The kind of birds who, if they ever did get inside, would break and smash every precious thing they saw...

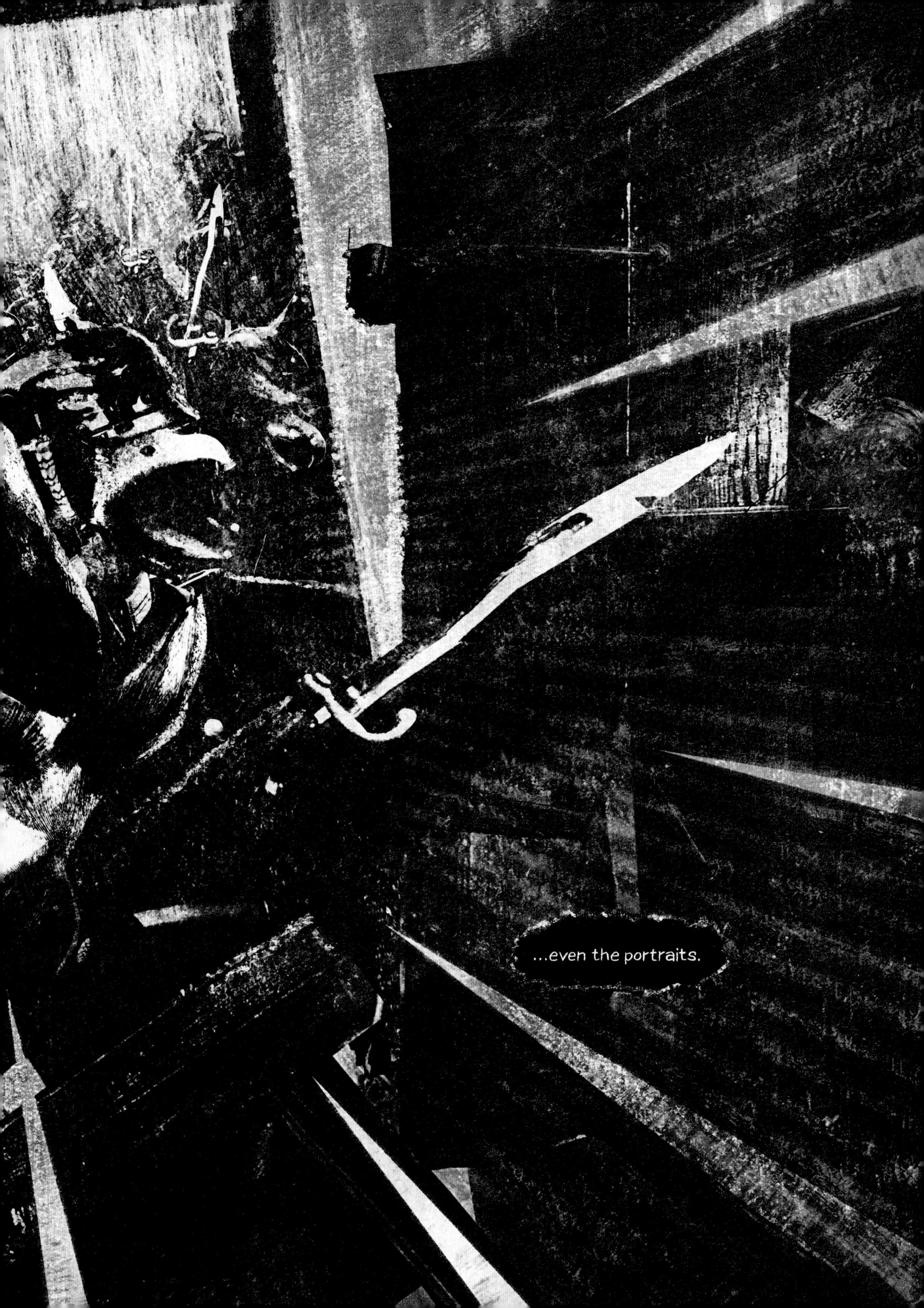
...even the portraits.

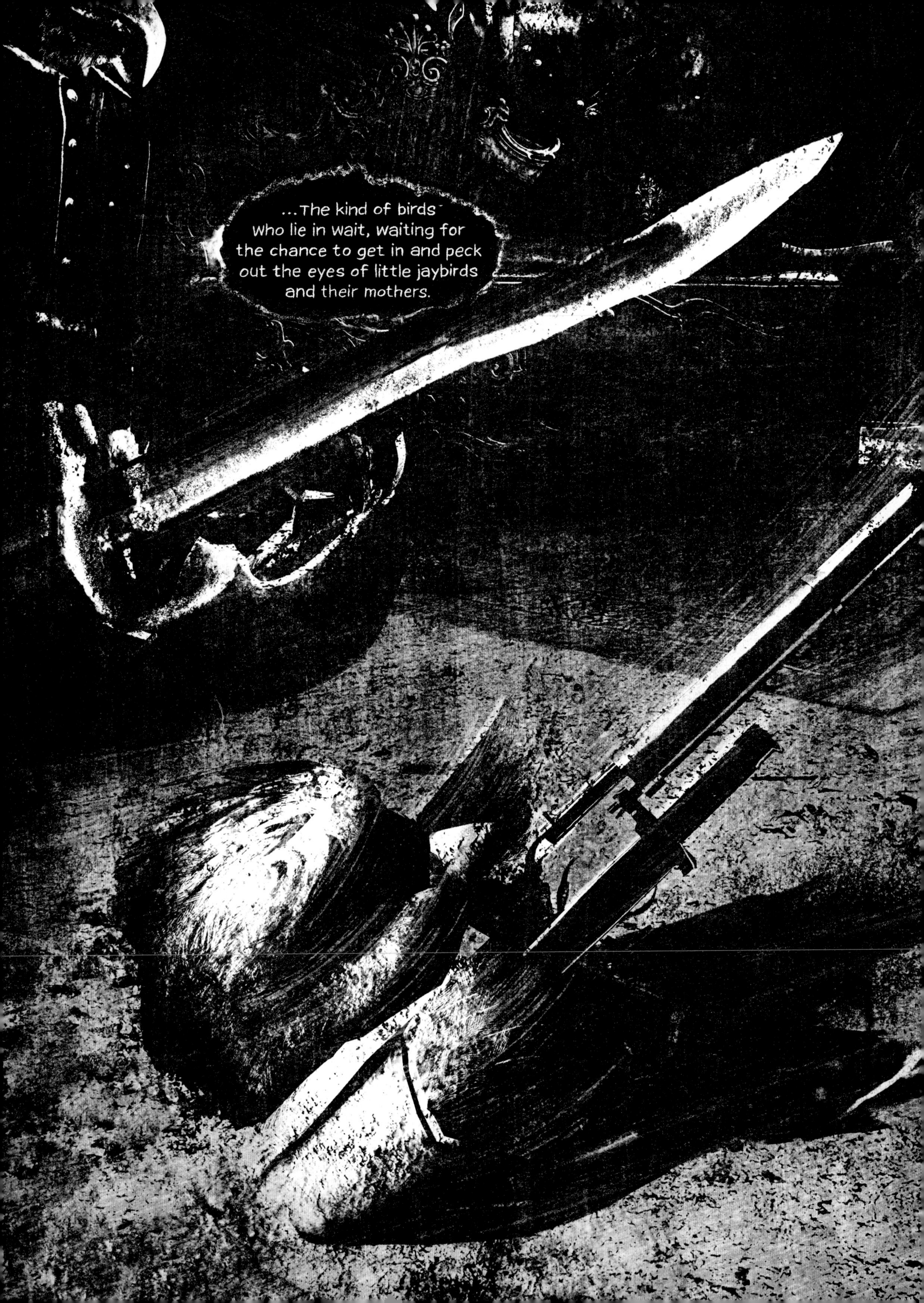
...The kind of birds who lie in wait, waiting for the chance to get in and peck out the eyes of little jaybirds and their mothers.

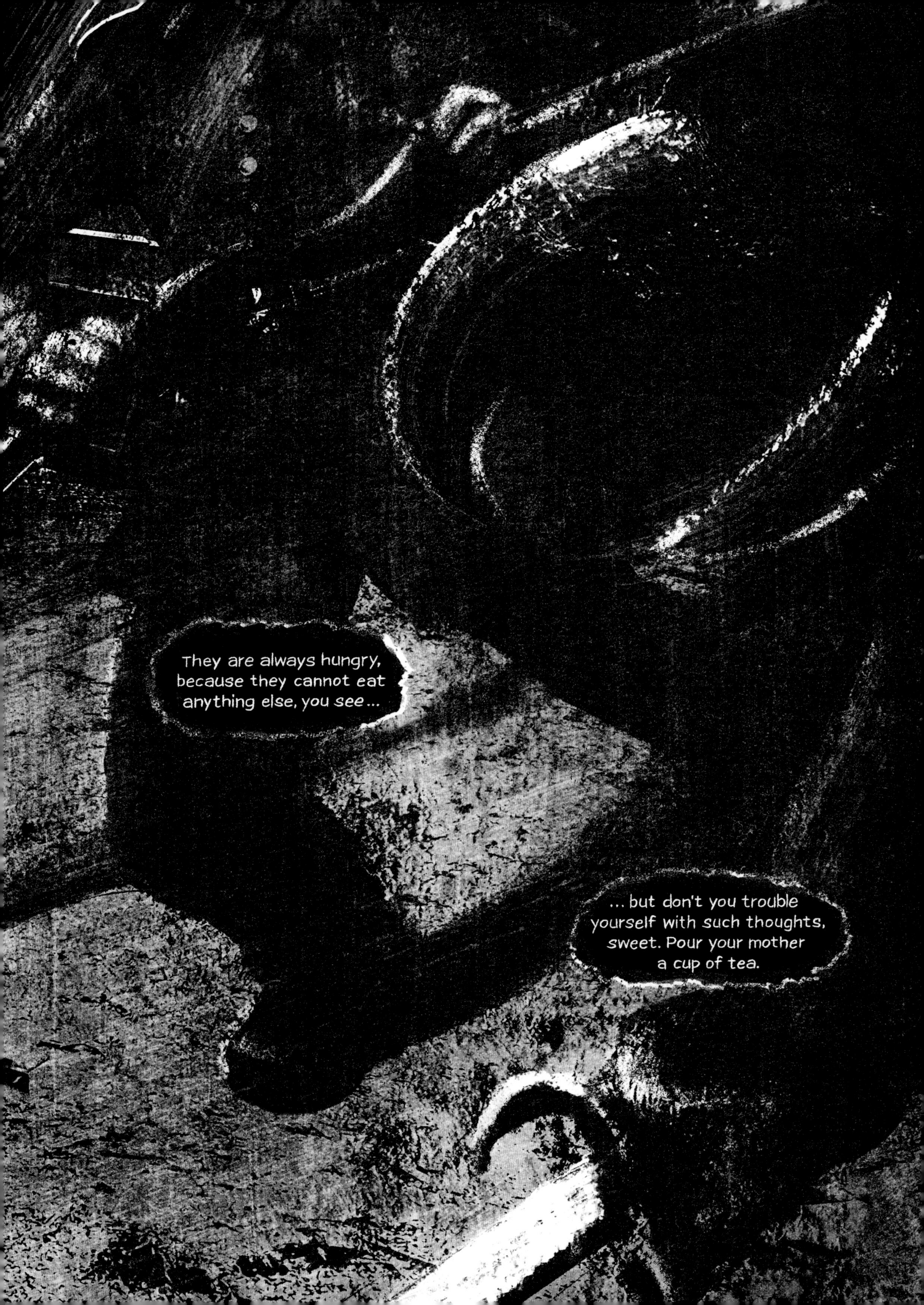
They are always hungry, because they cannot eat anything else, you see...
...but don't you trouble yourself with such thoughts, sweet. Pour your mother a cup of tea.

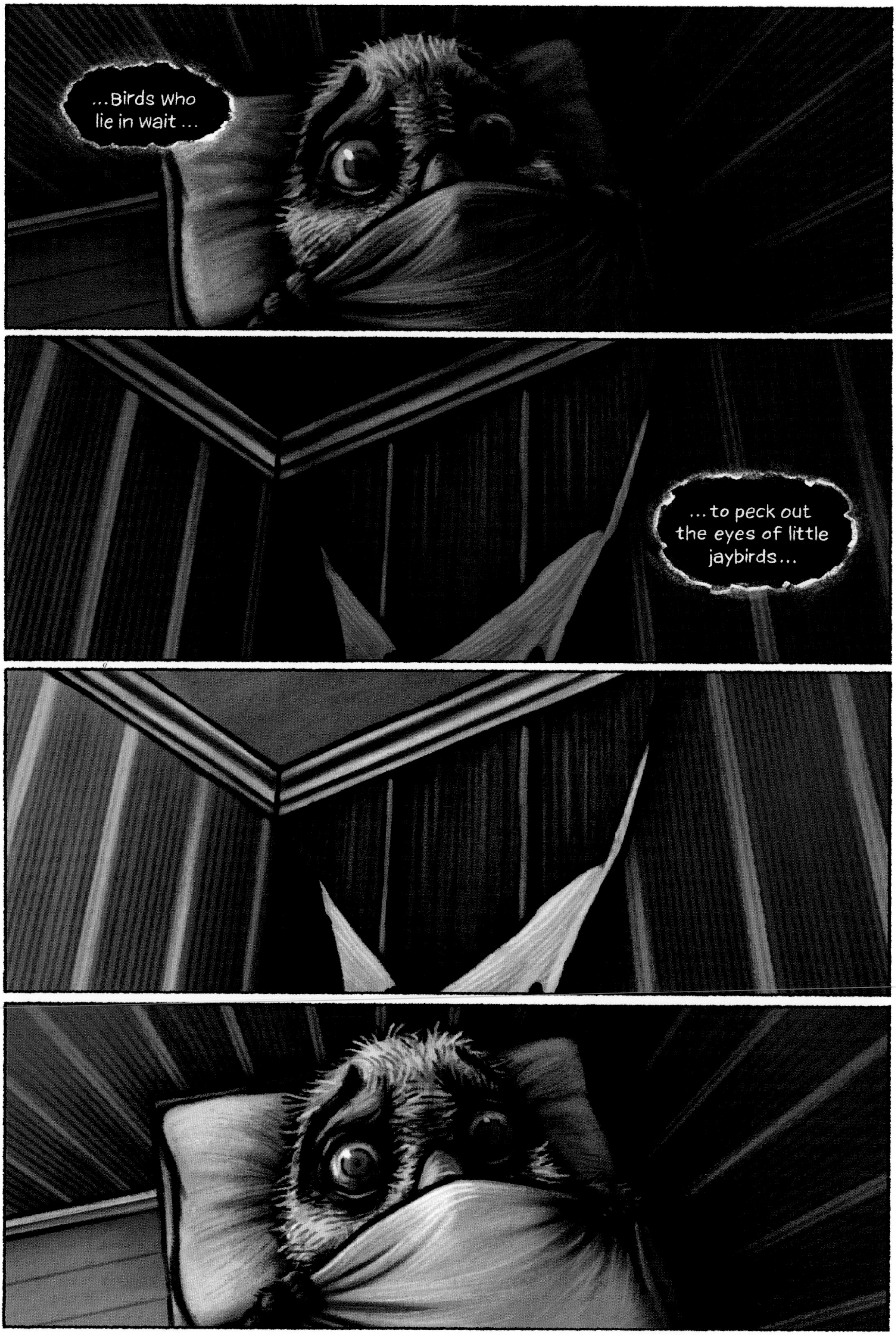
...Birds who lie in wait ...
...to peck out the eyes of little jaybirds...

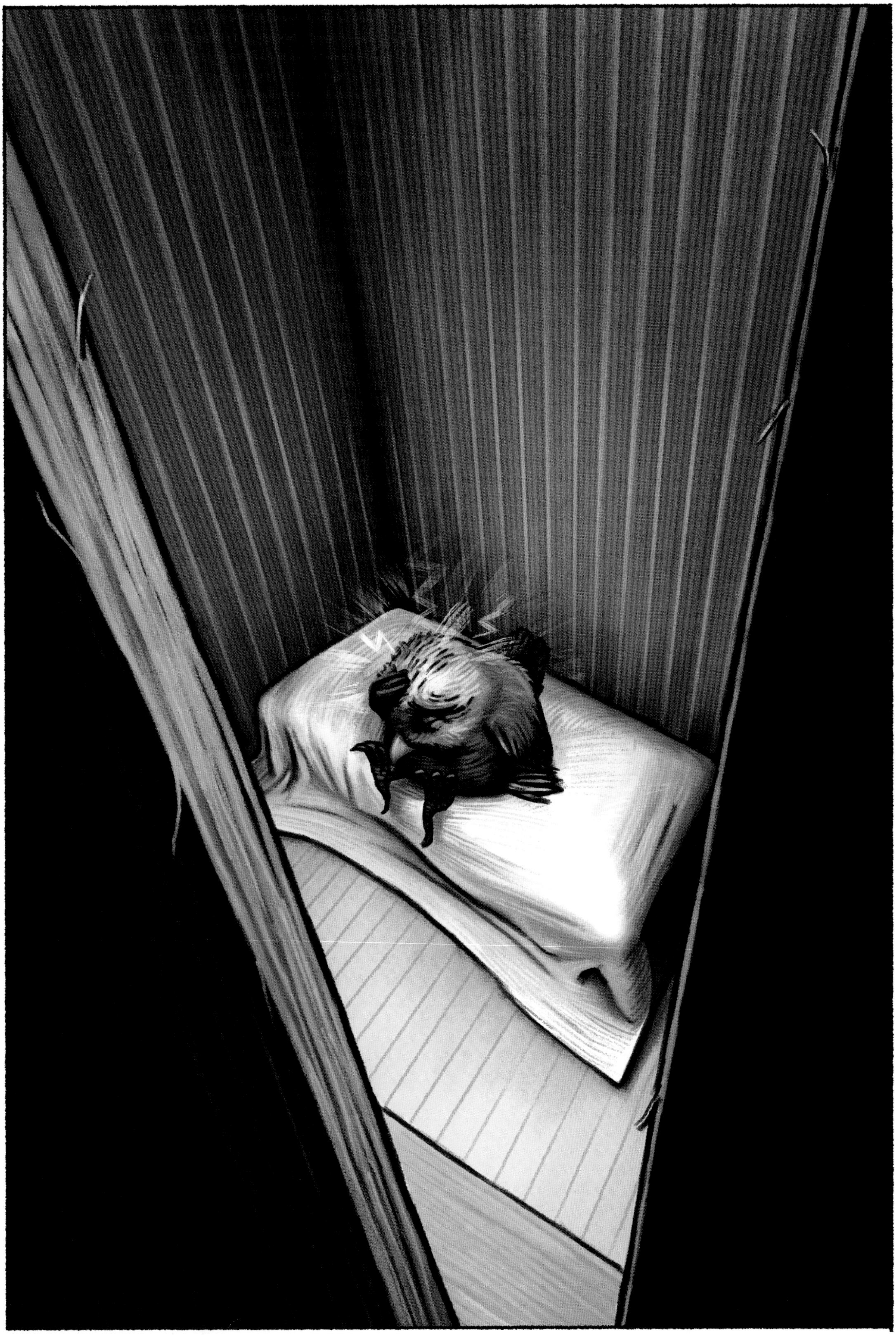

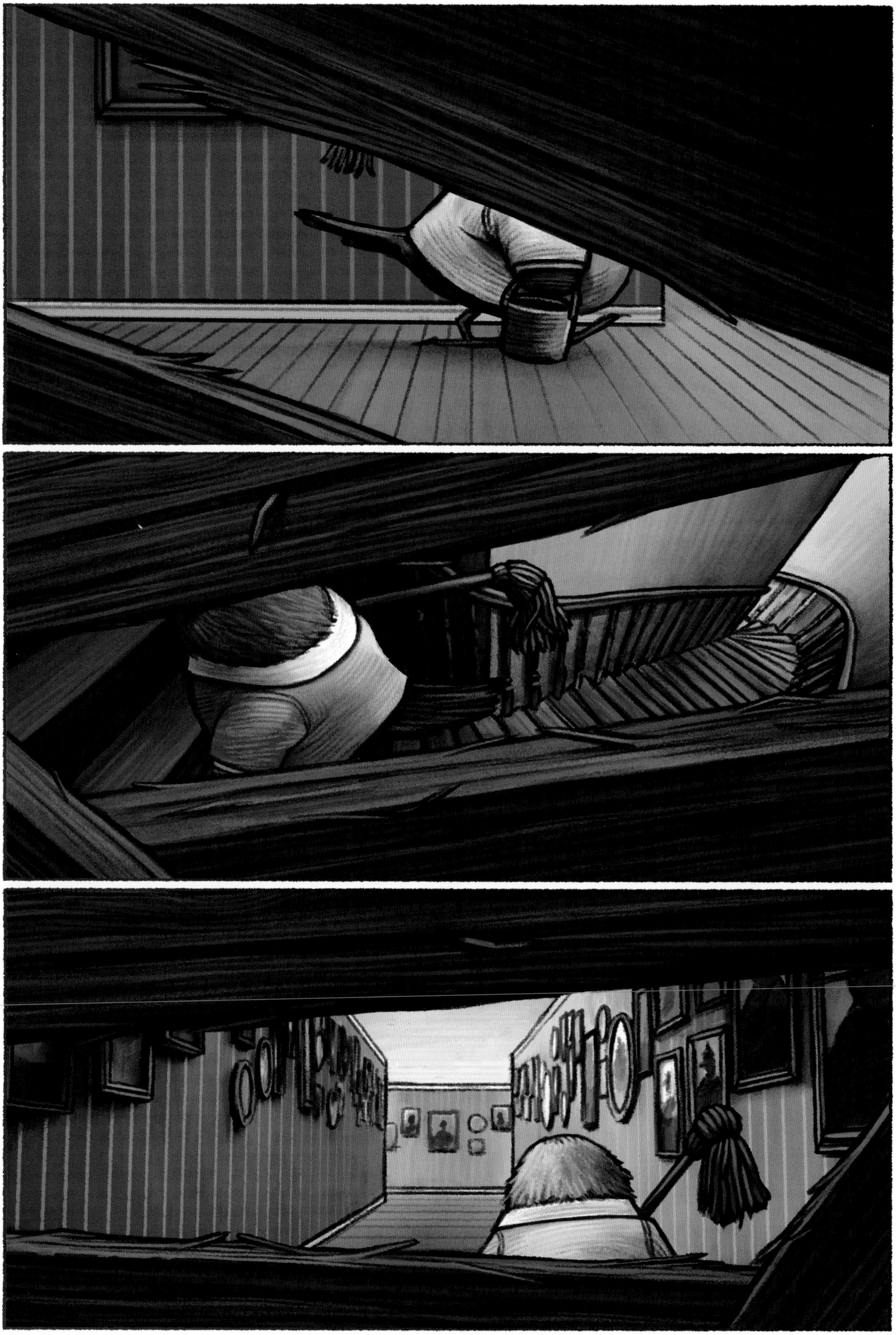

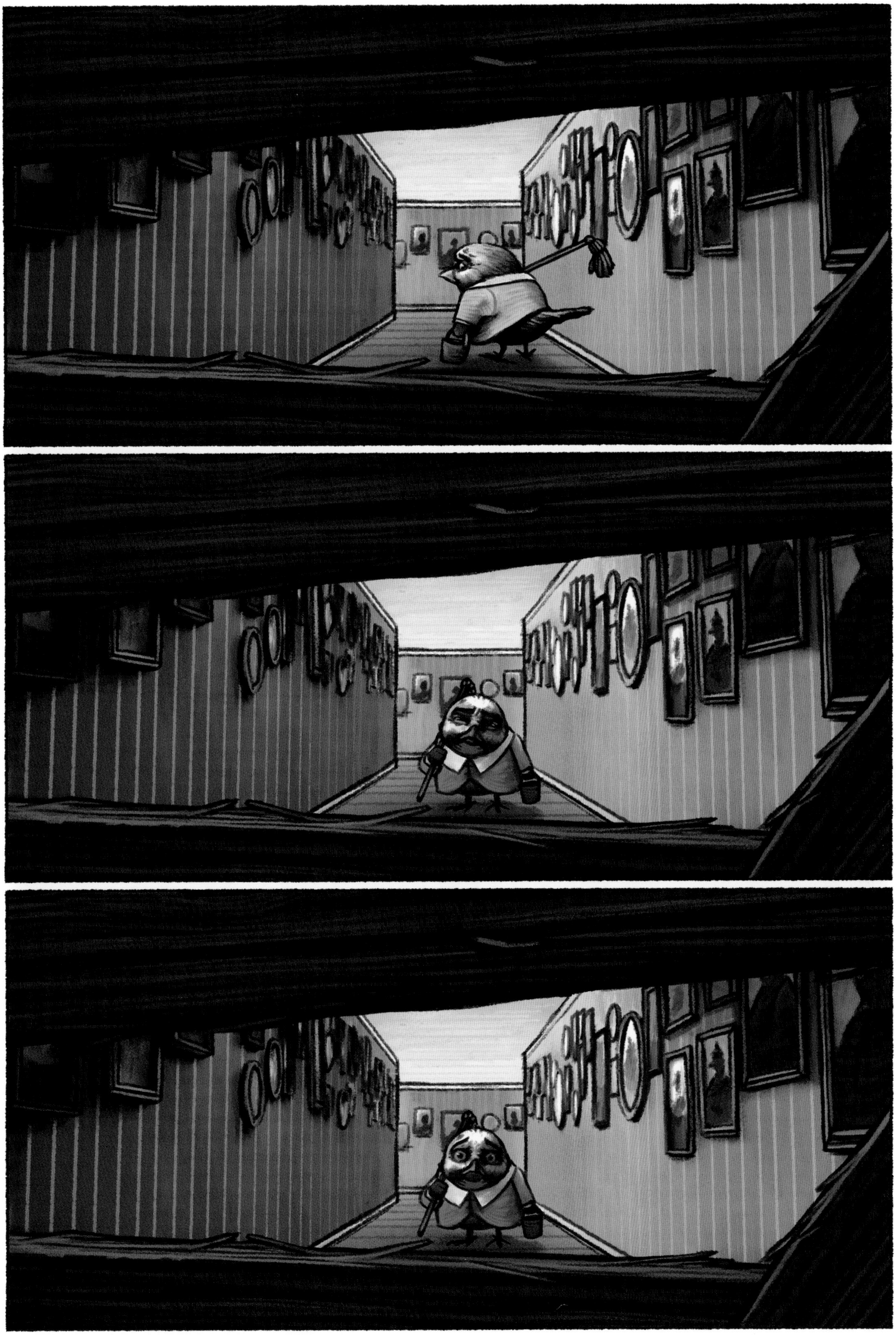

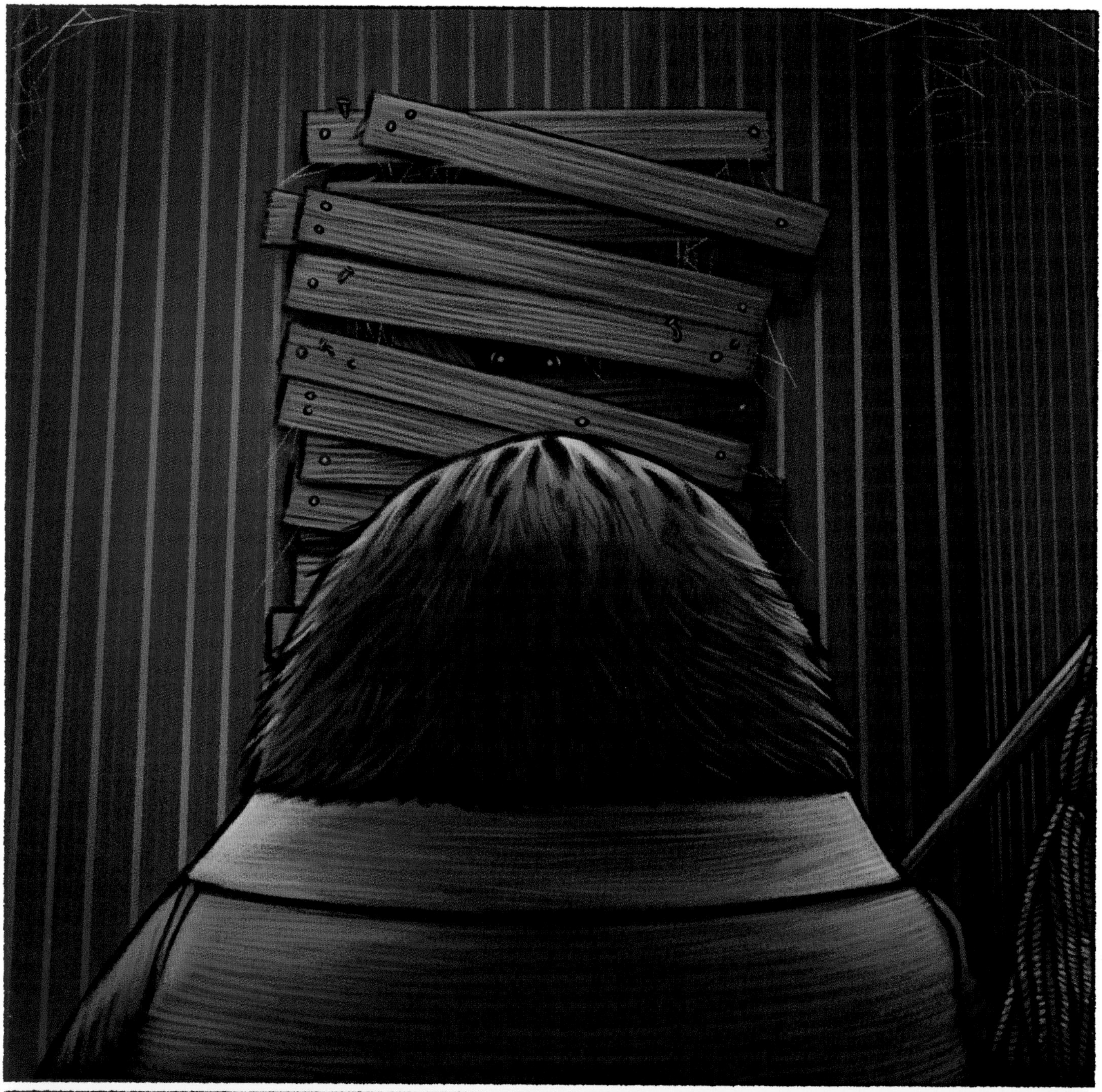

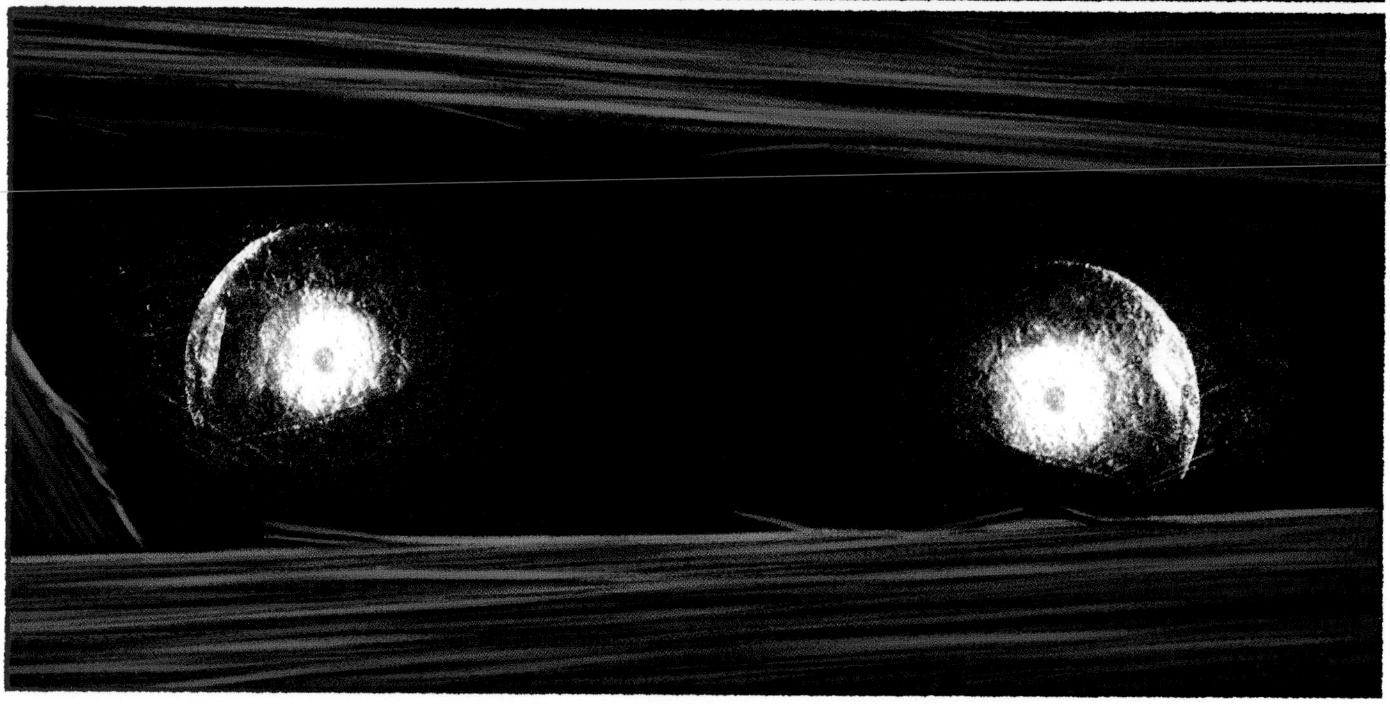

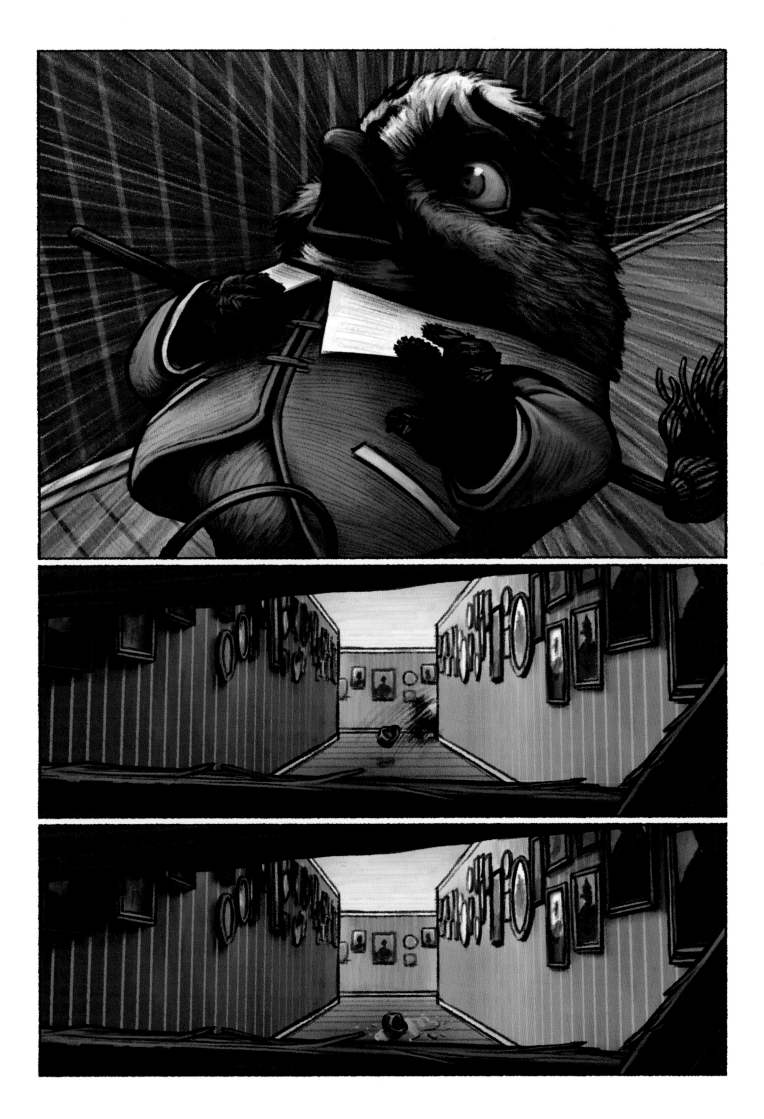

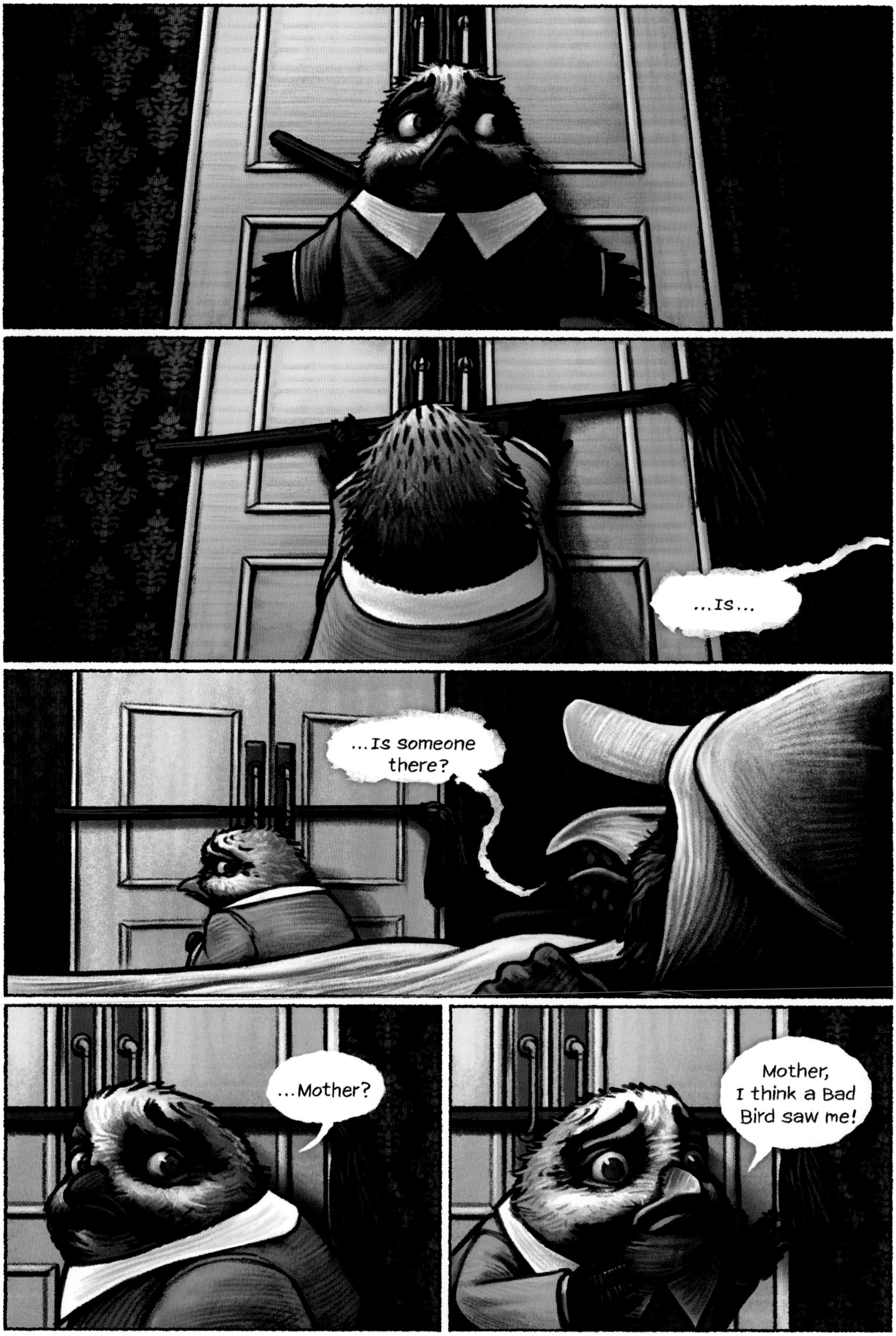
...Is...
...Is someone there?
...Mother?
Mother, I think a Bad Bird saw me!

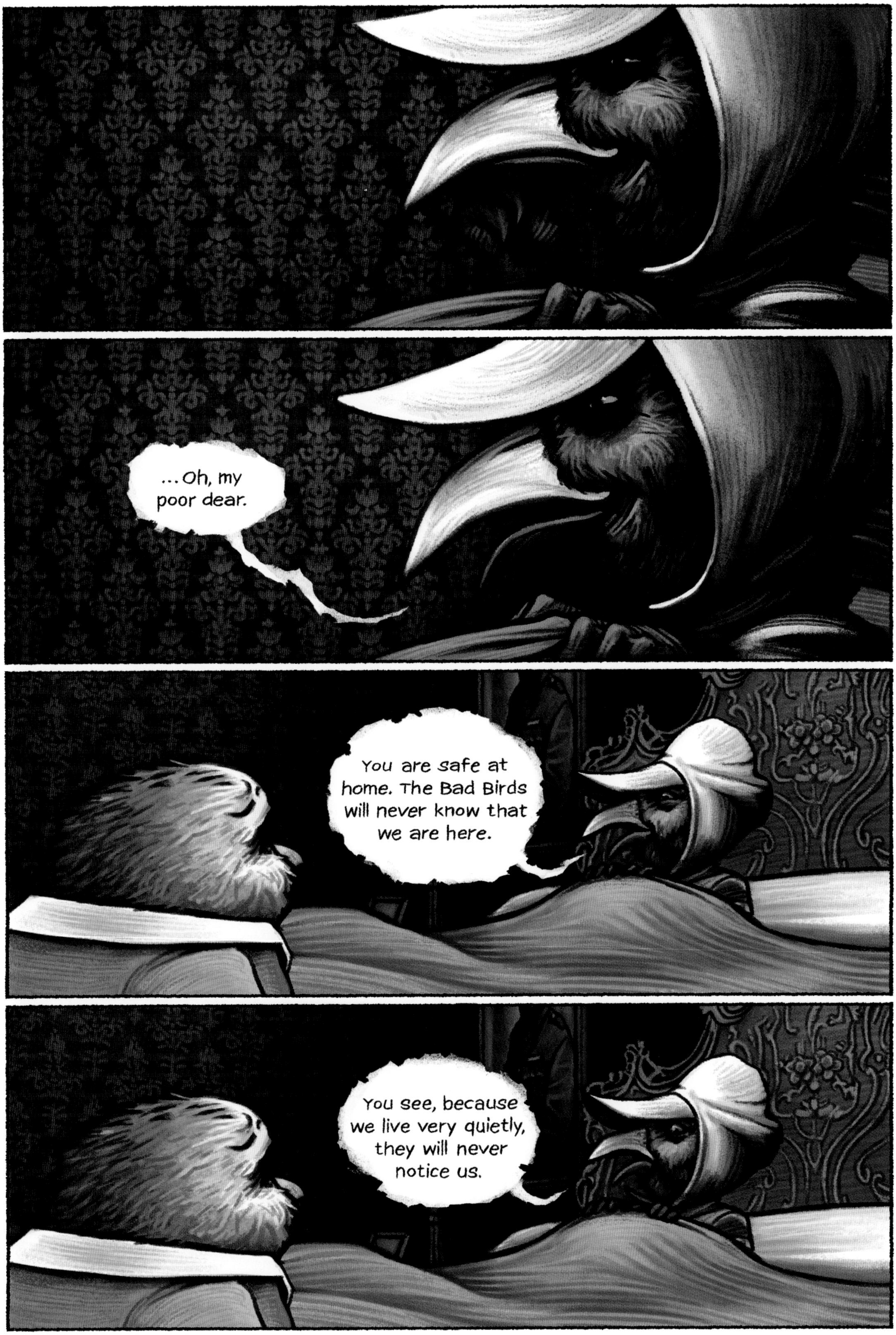
...Oh, my poor dear.
You are safe at home. The Bad Birds will never know that we are here.
You see, because we live very quietly, they will never notice us.

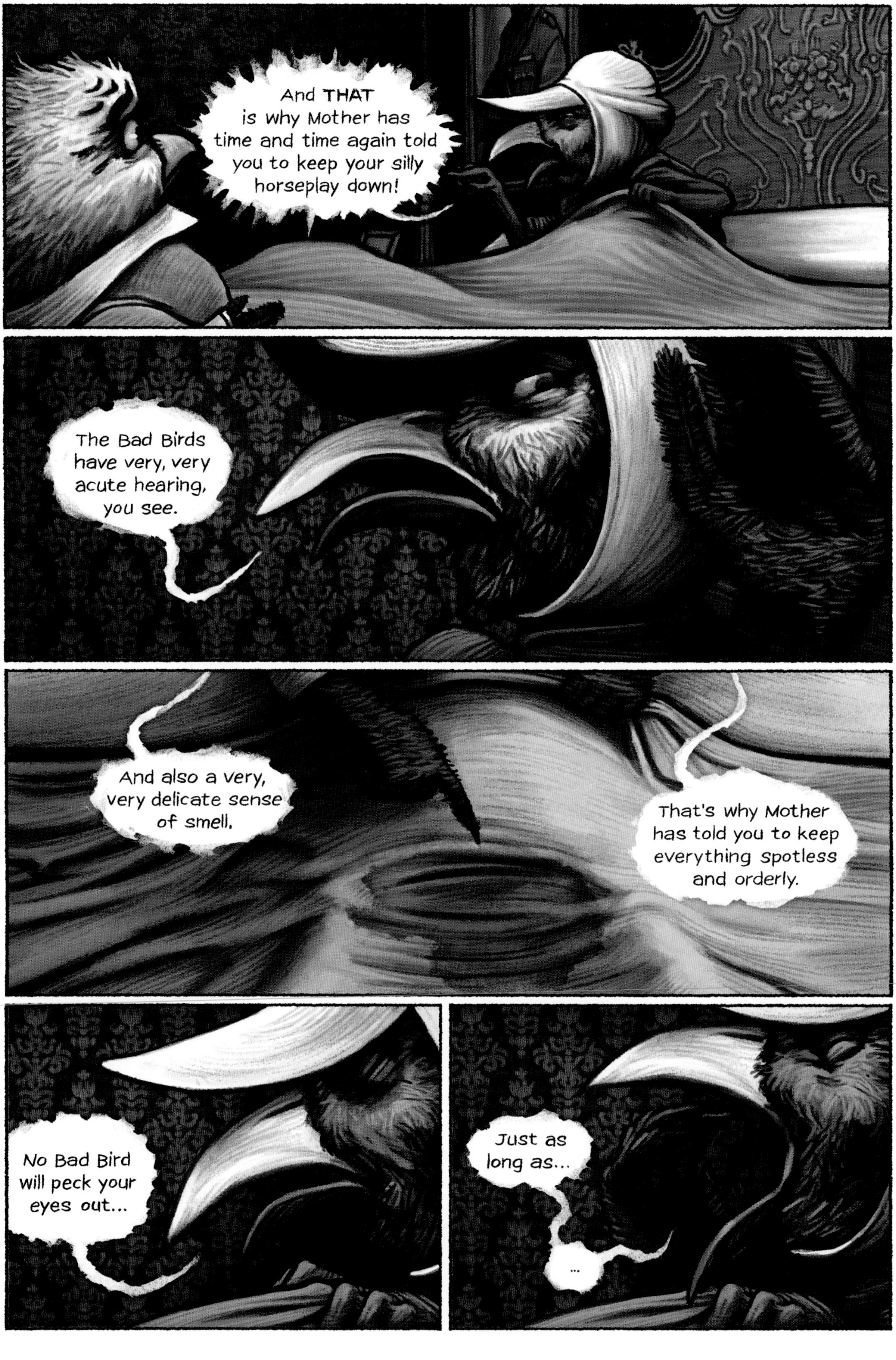
And THAT is why Mother has time and time again told you to keep your silly horseplay down!
The Bad Birds have very, very acute hearing, you see.
And also a very, very delicate sense of smell.
That's why Mother has told you to keep everything spotless and orderly.
No Bad Bird will peck your eyes out...
Just as long as...
...

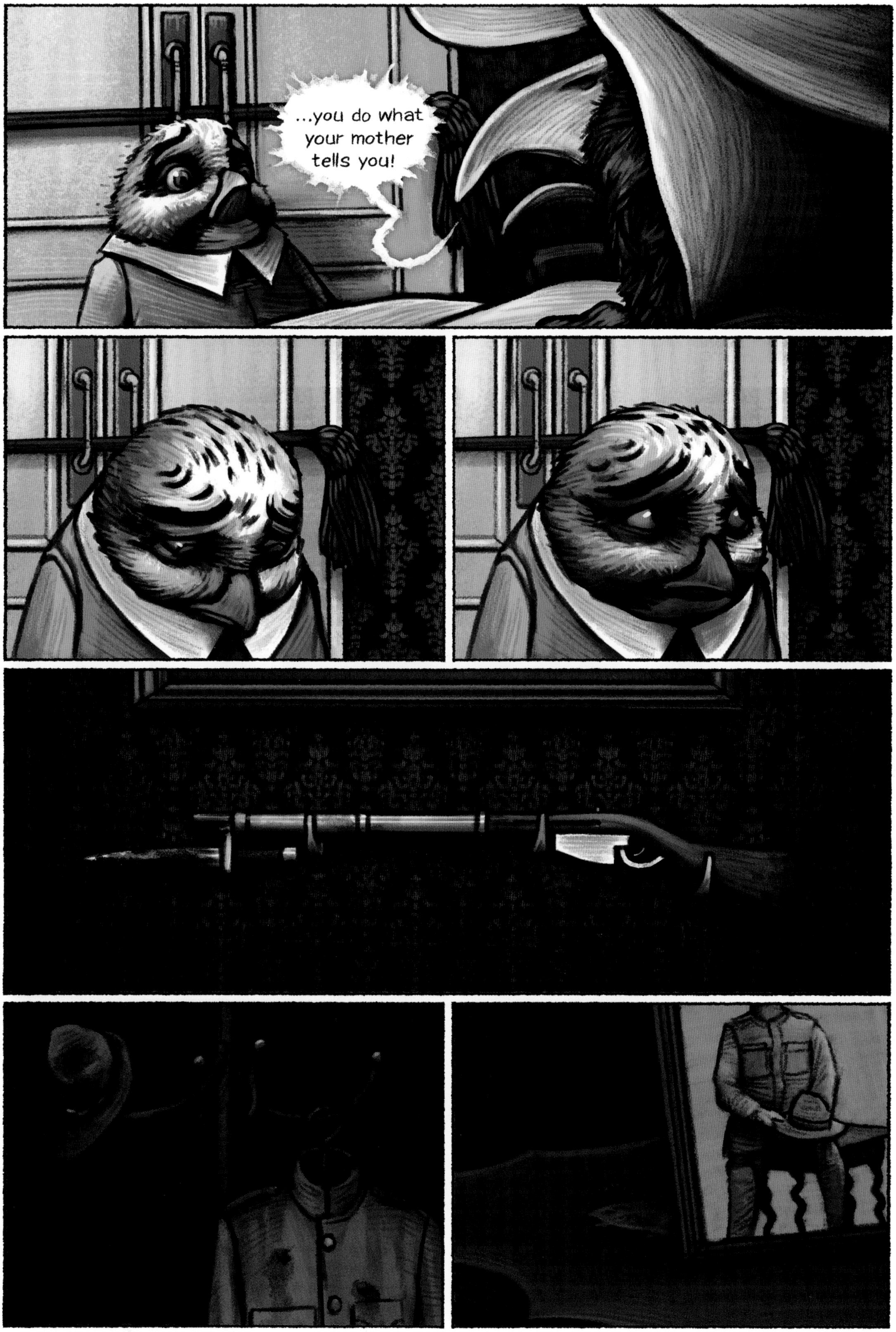
...you do what your mother tells you!

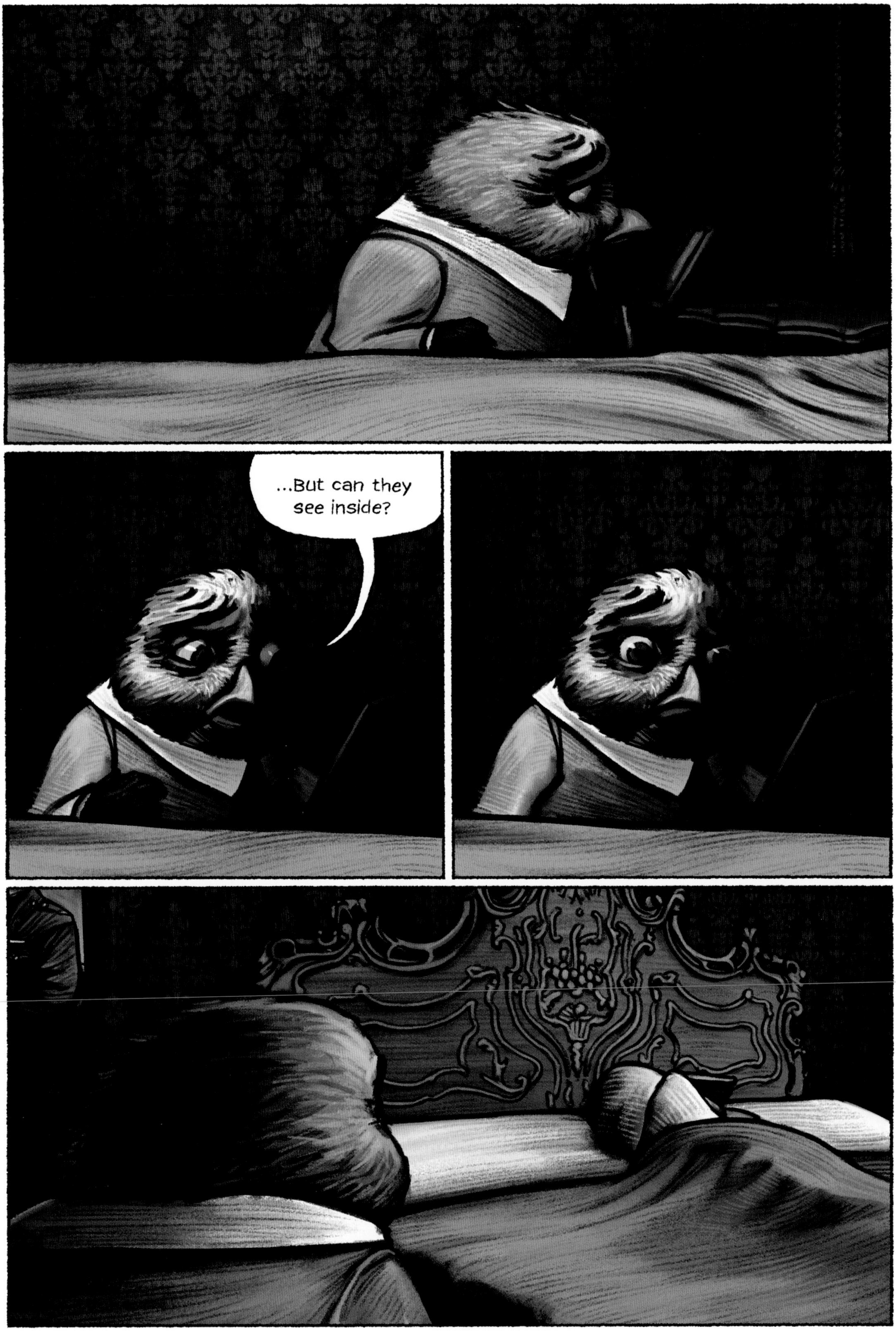
...But can they see inside?

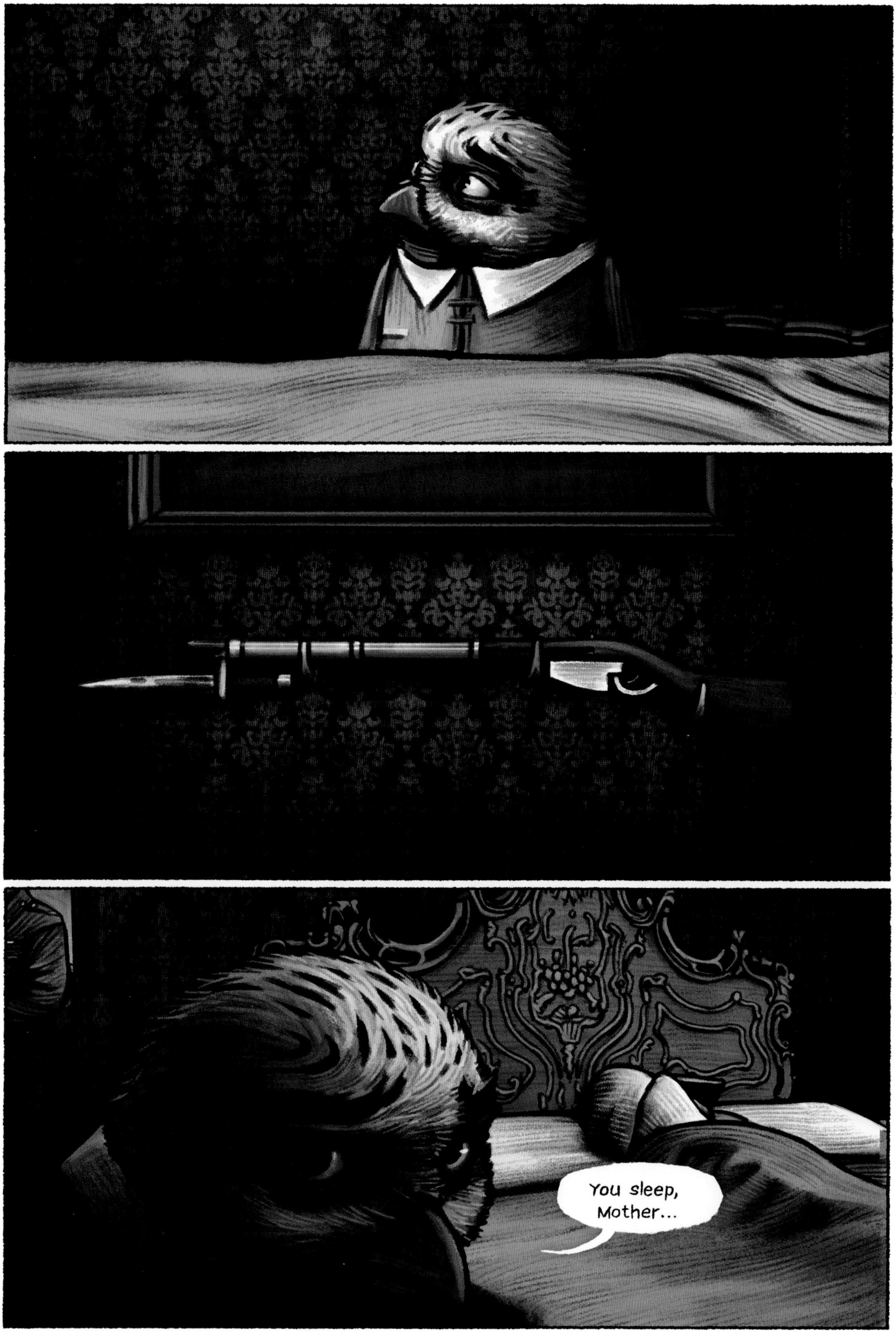
You sleep,
Mother...

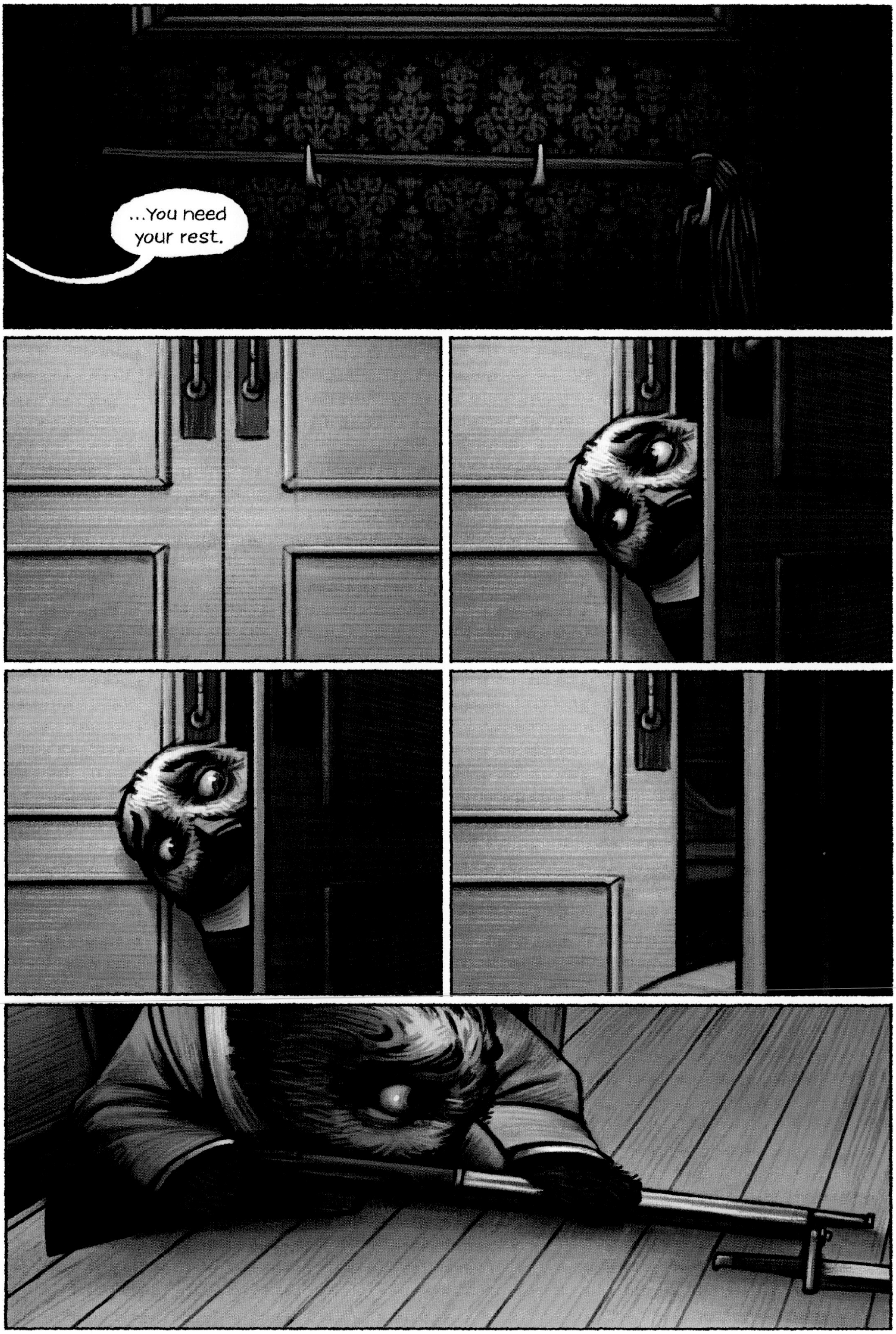
...You need your rest.

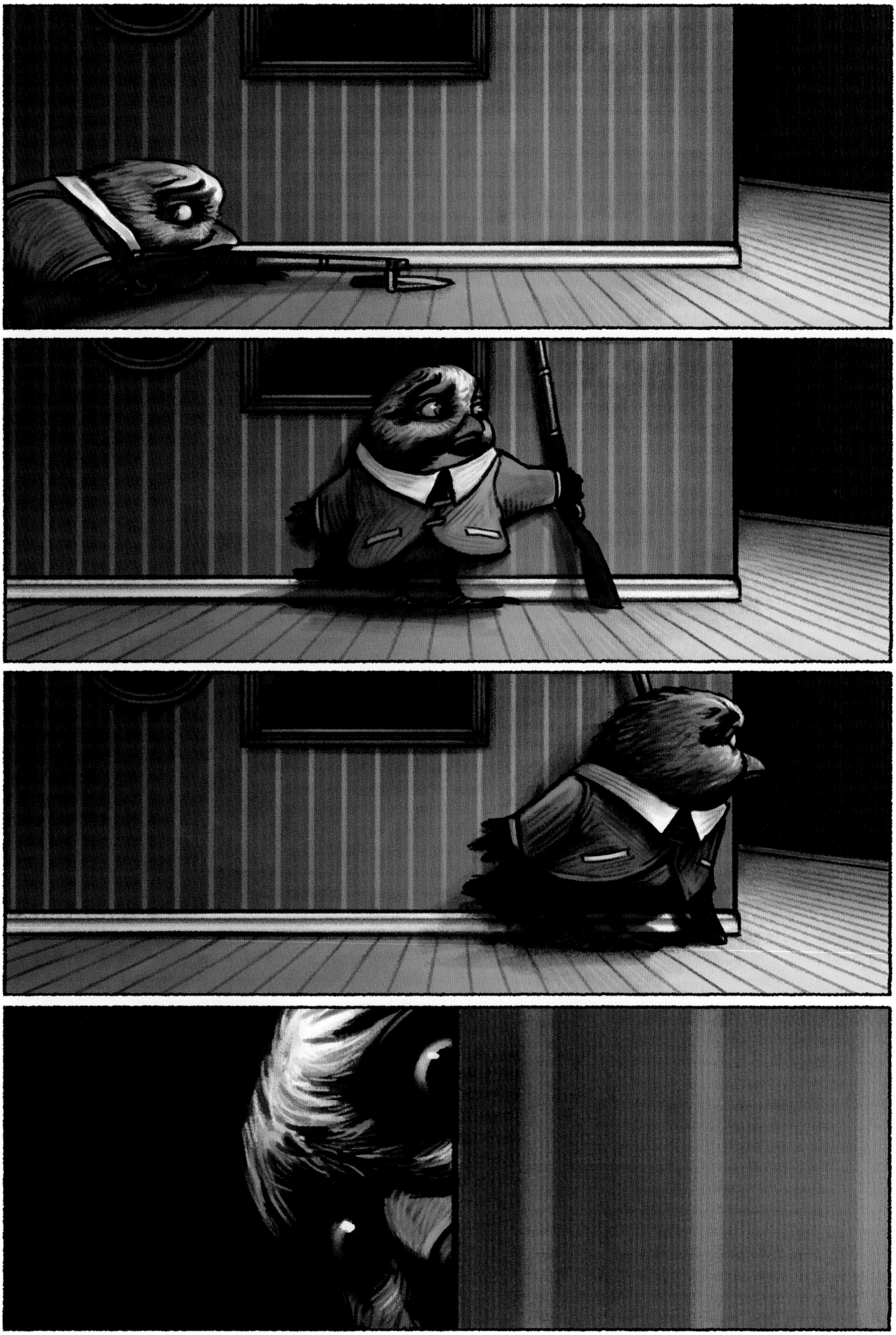

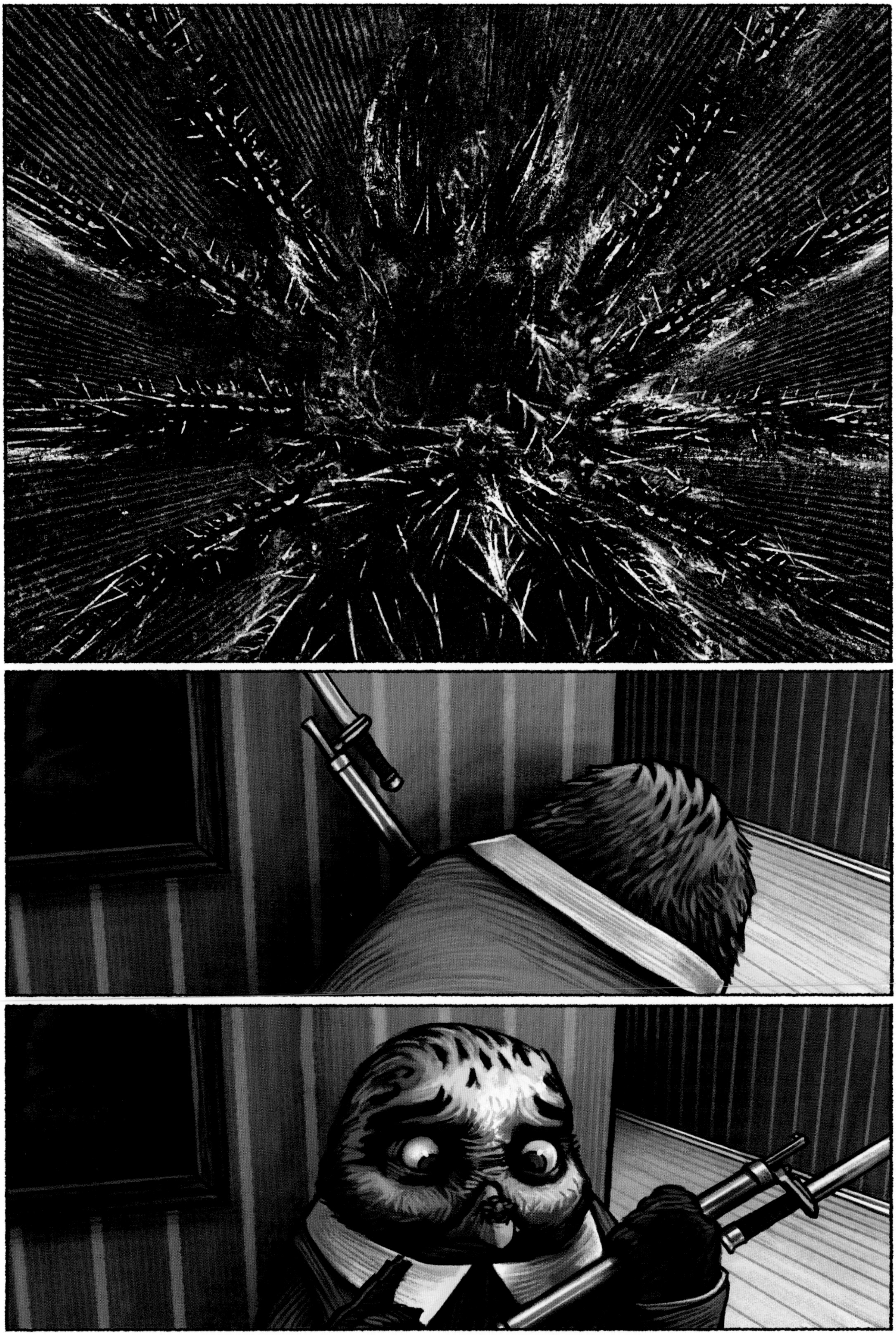

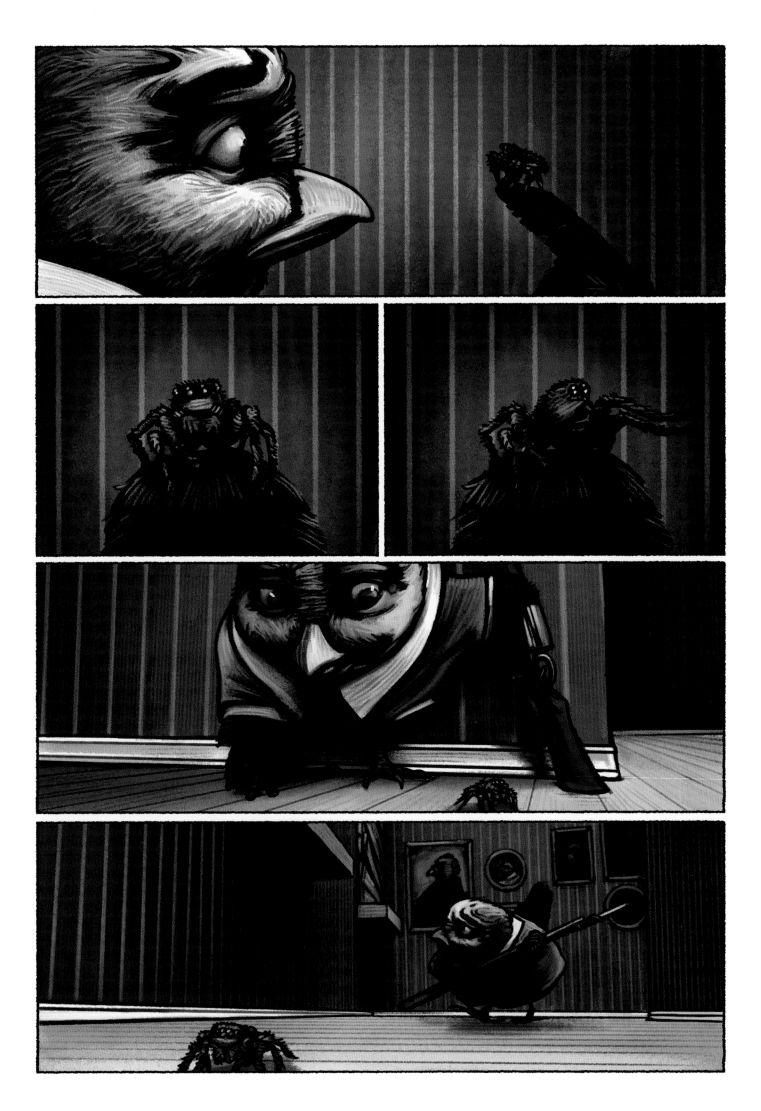

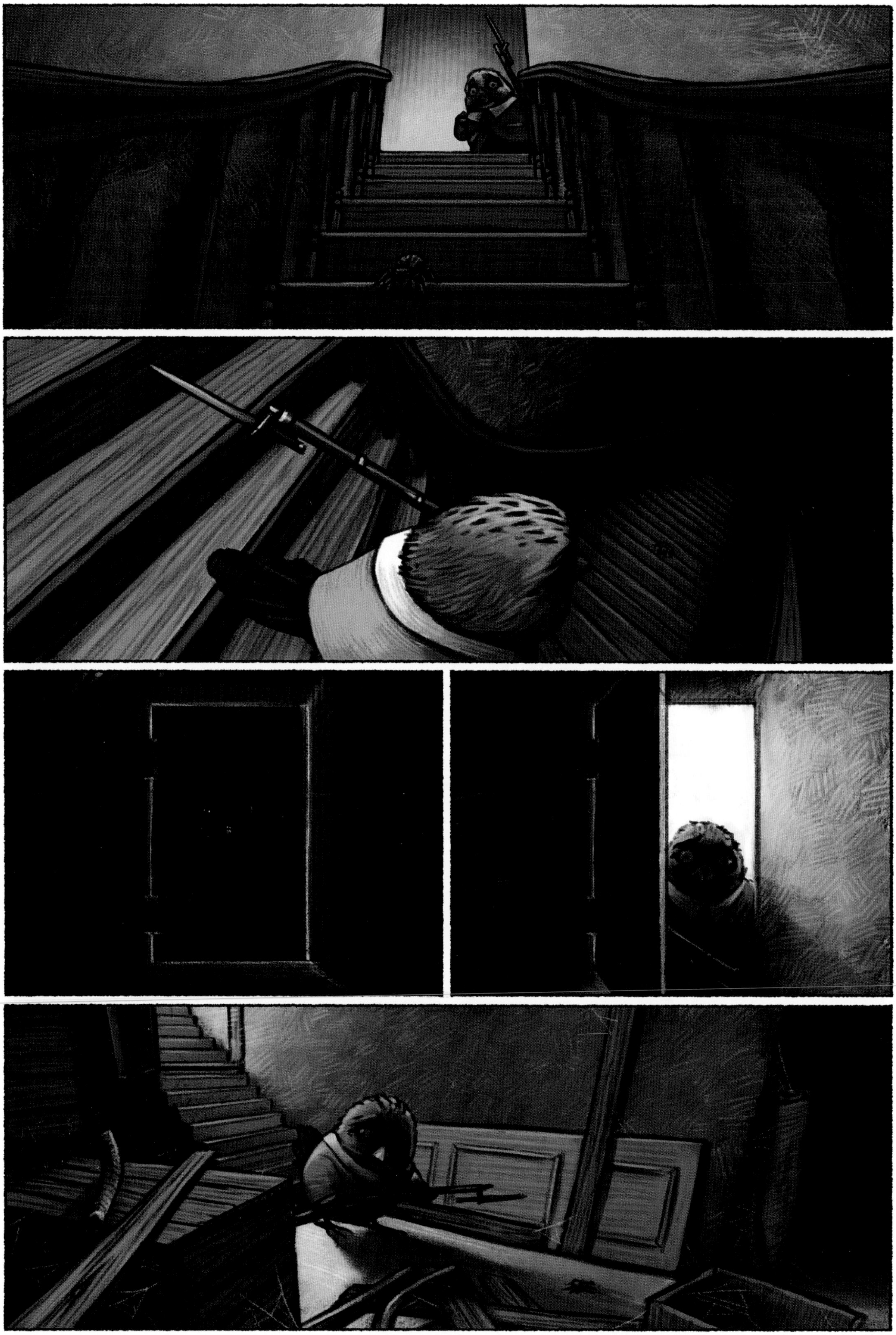

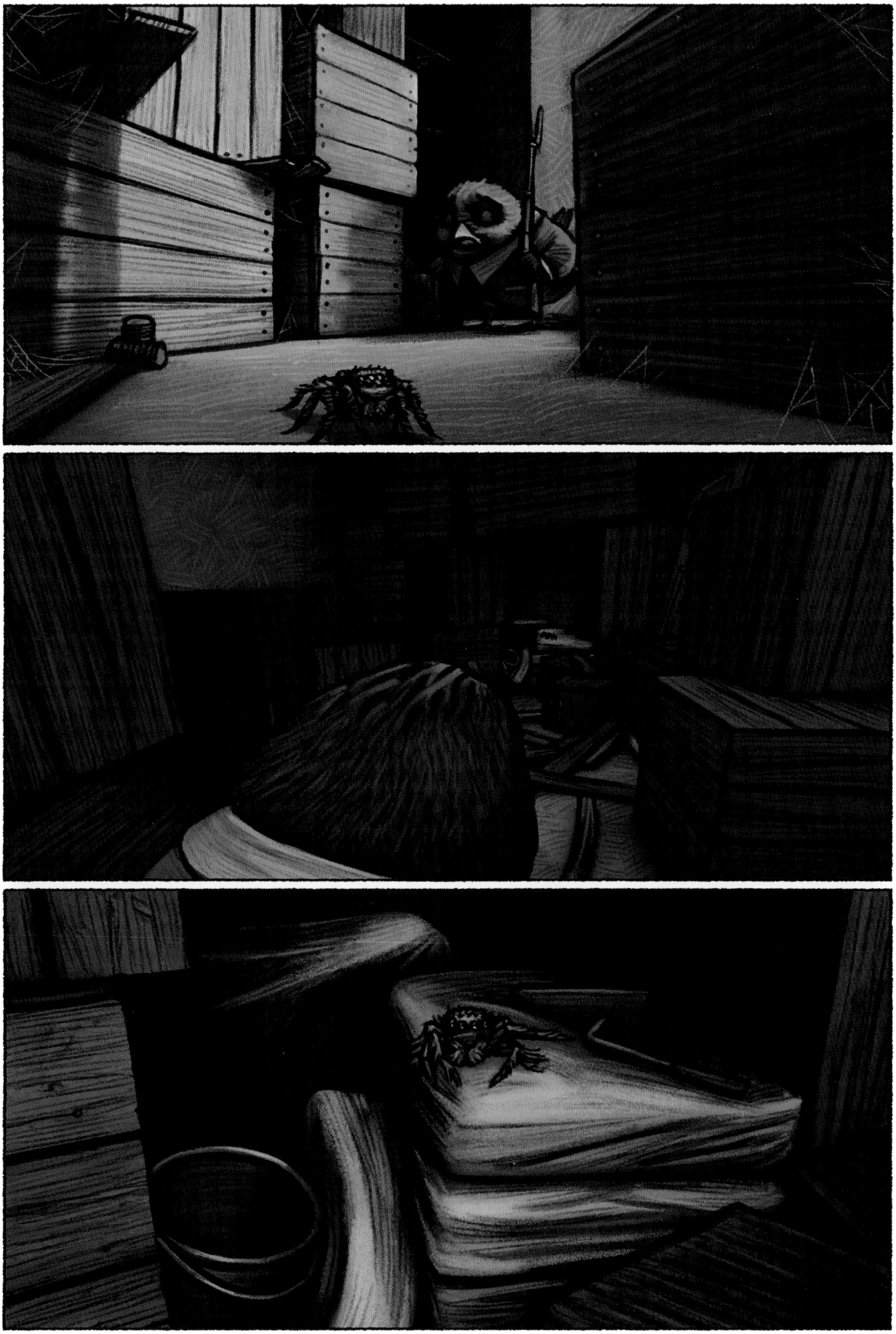

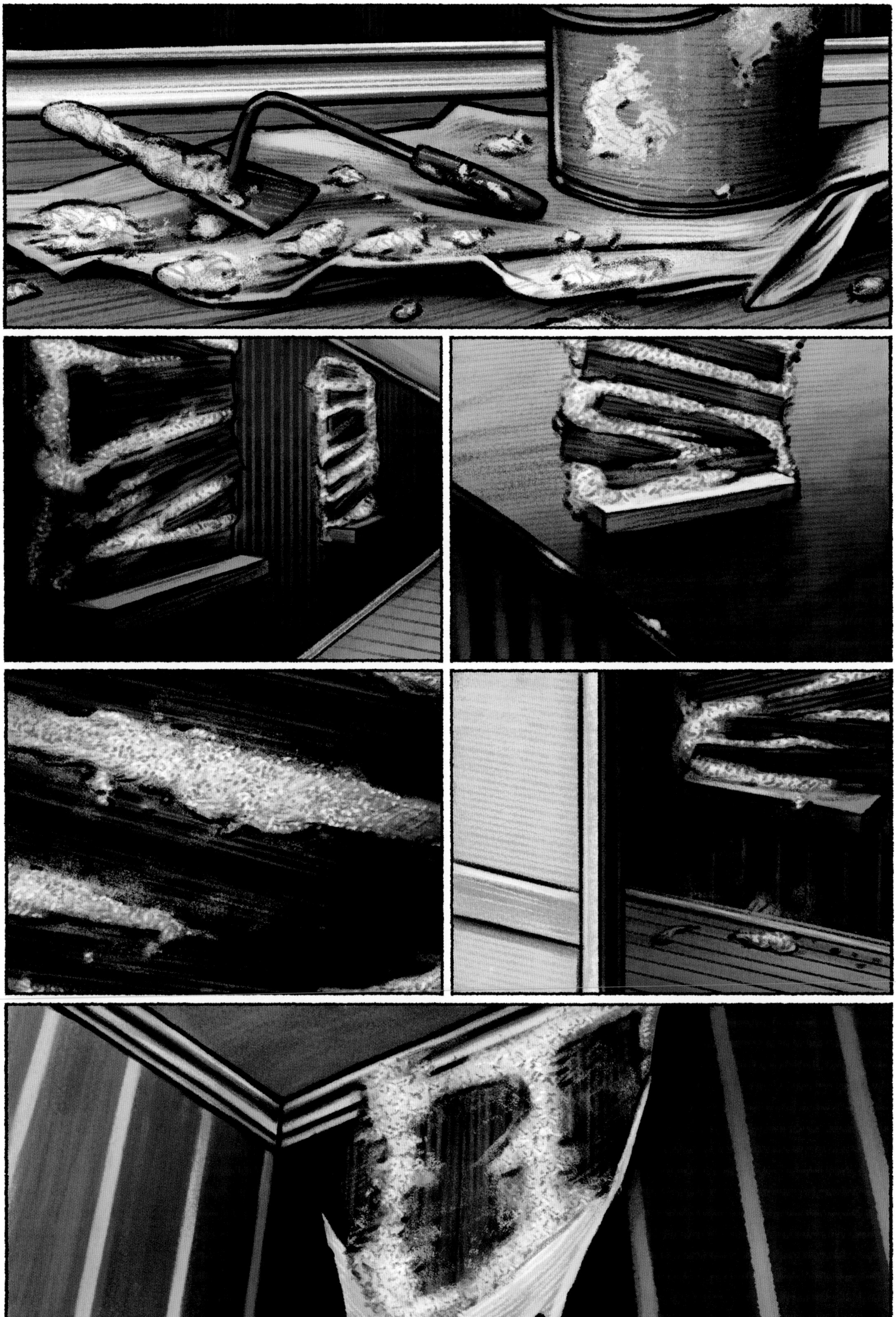

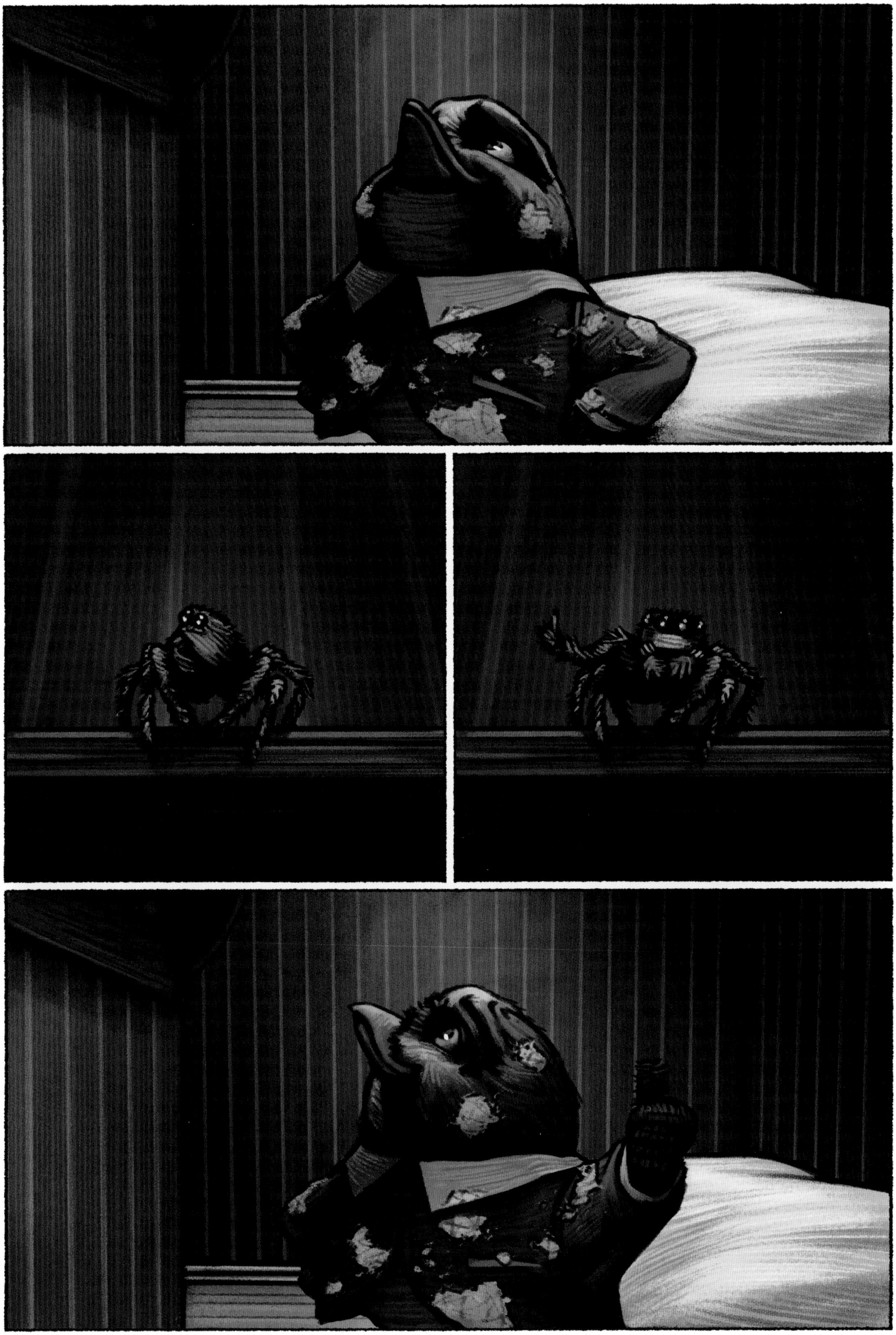

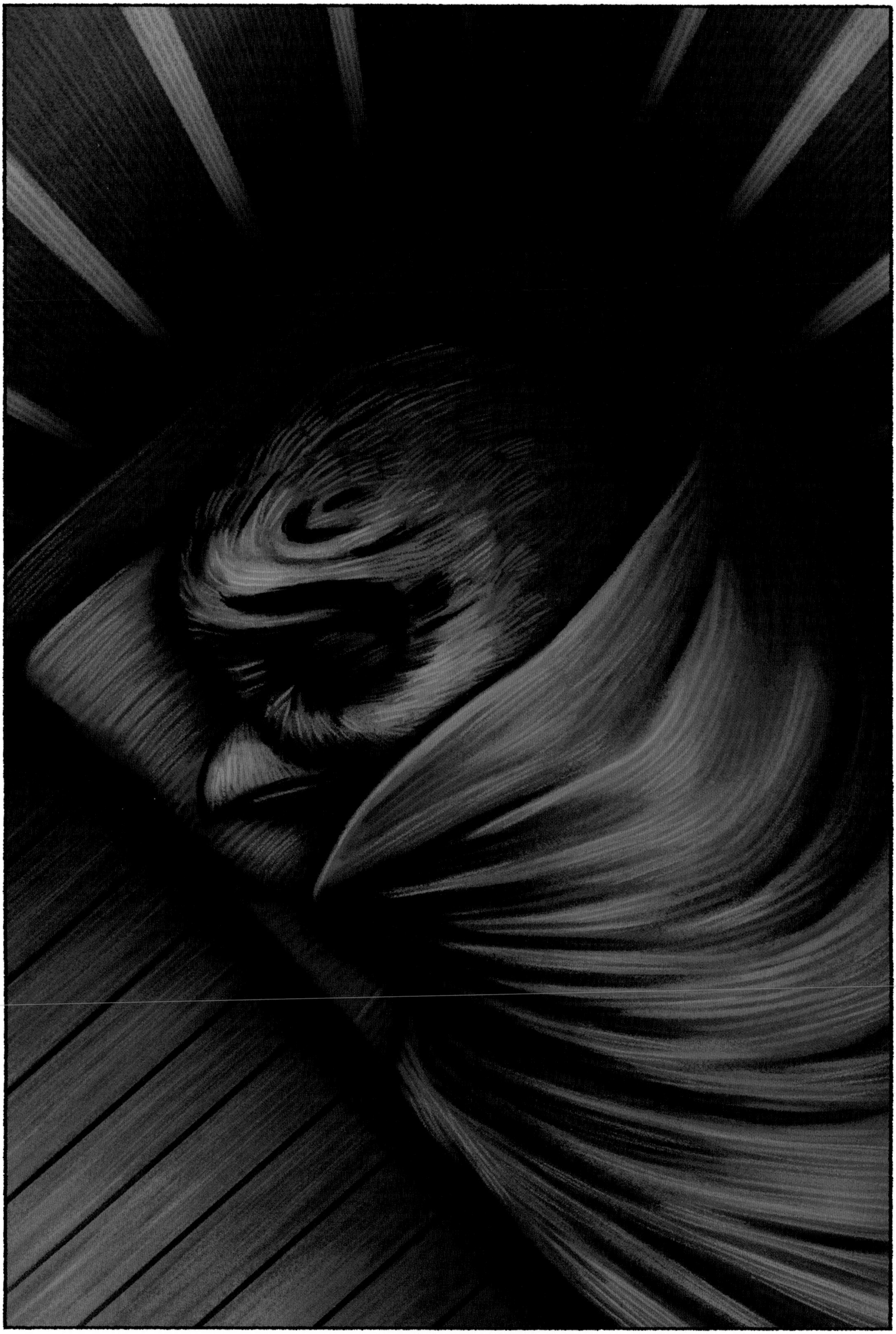

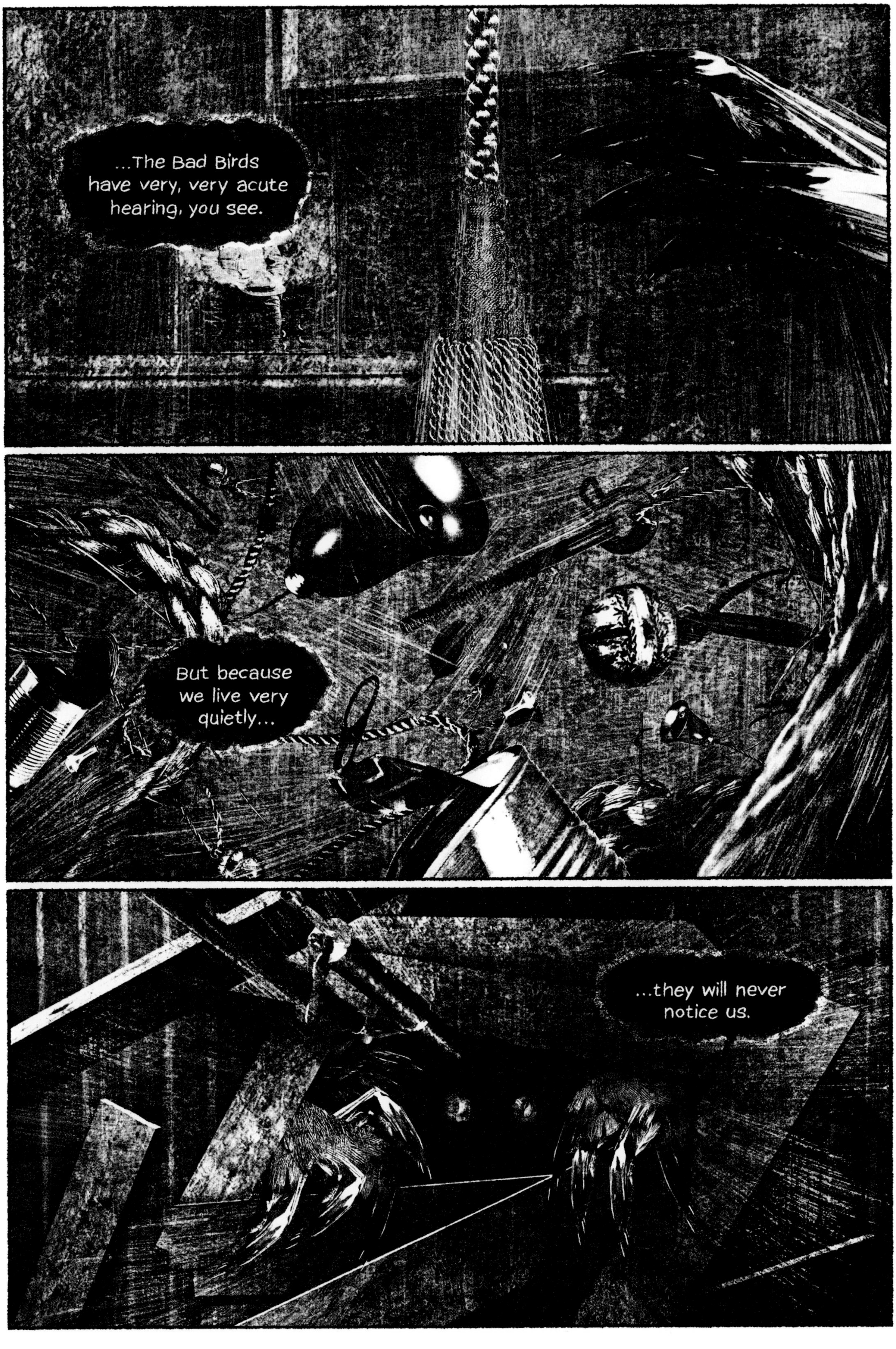
...The Bad Birds have very, very acute hearing, you see.
But because we live very quietly...
...they will never notice us.

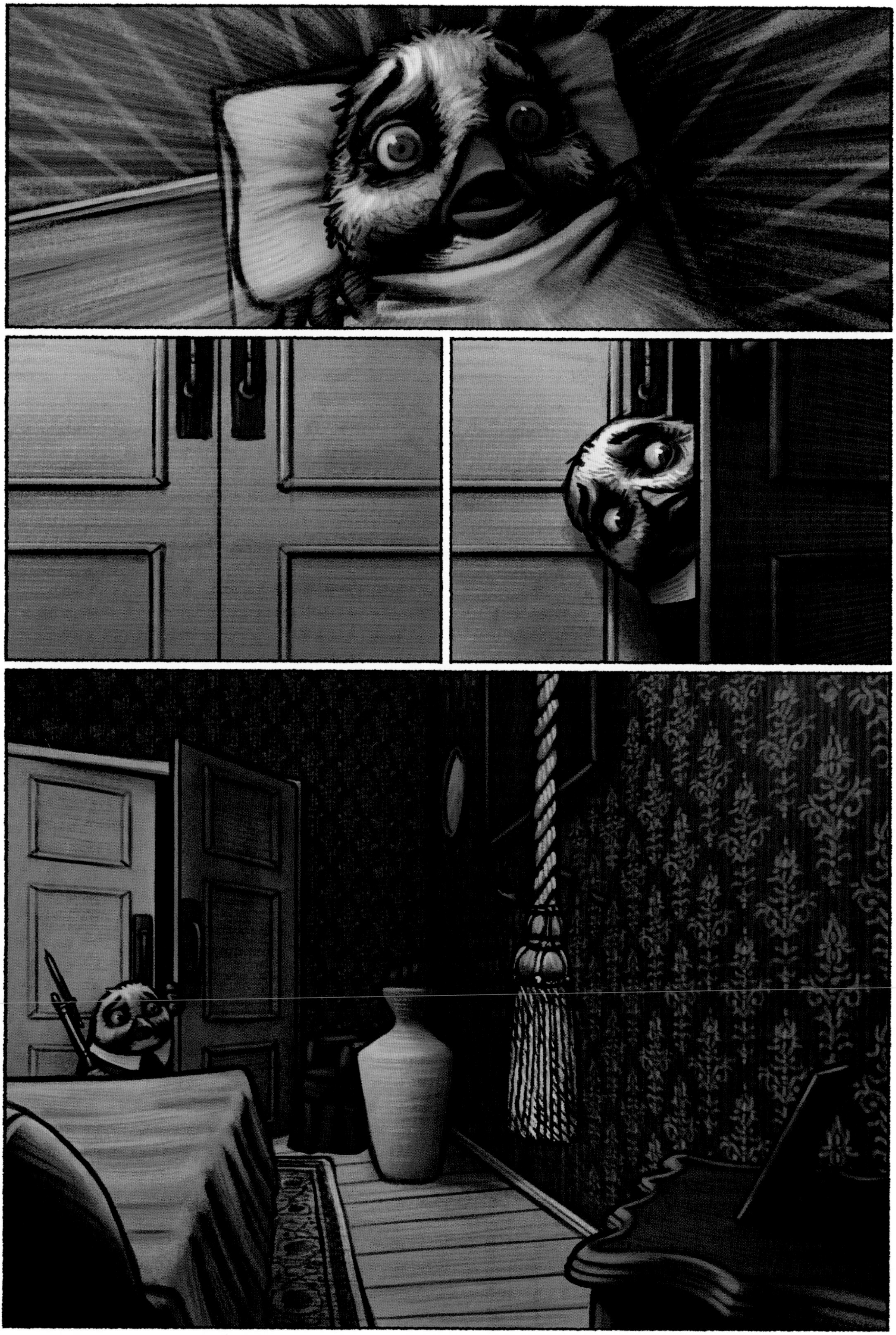

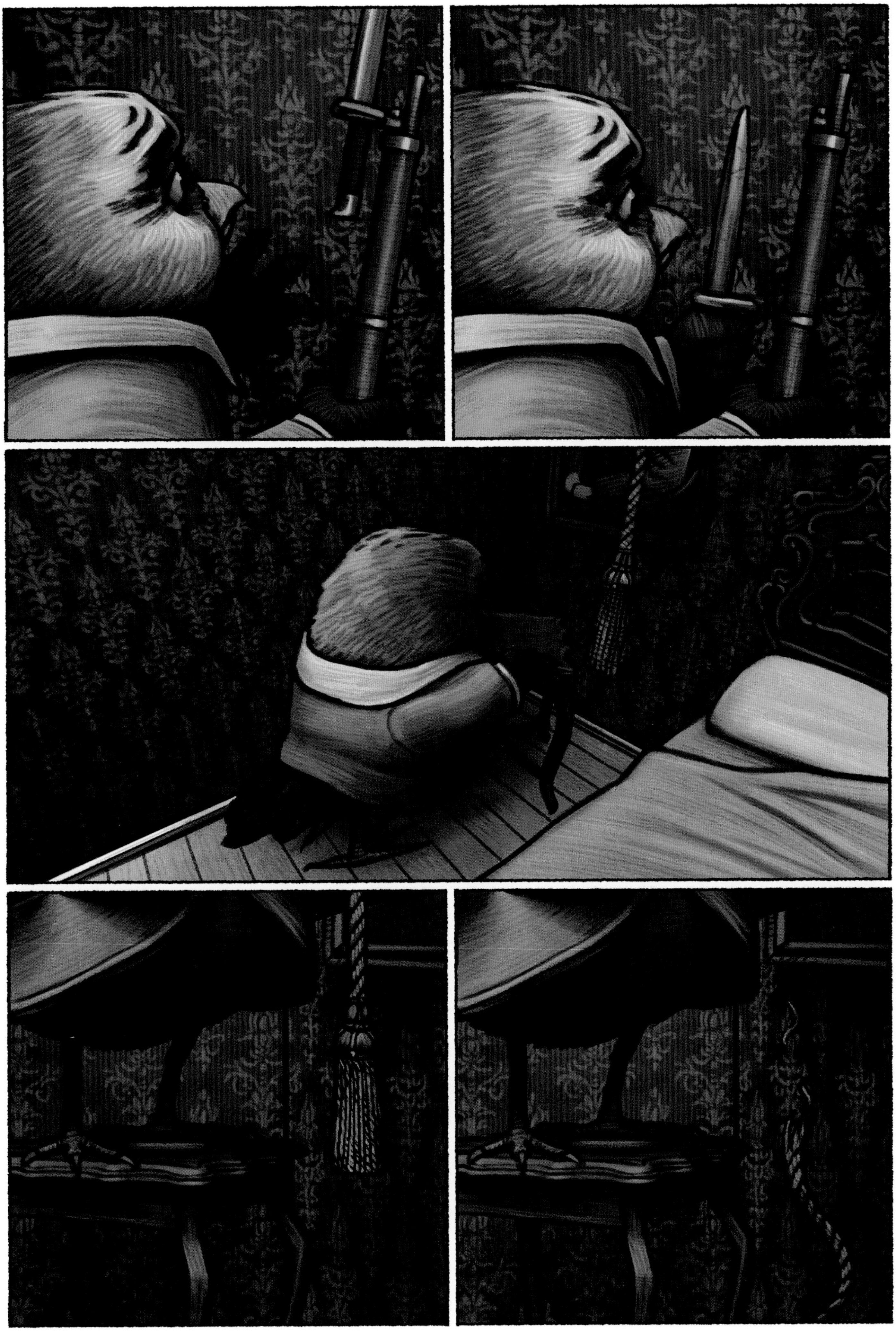

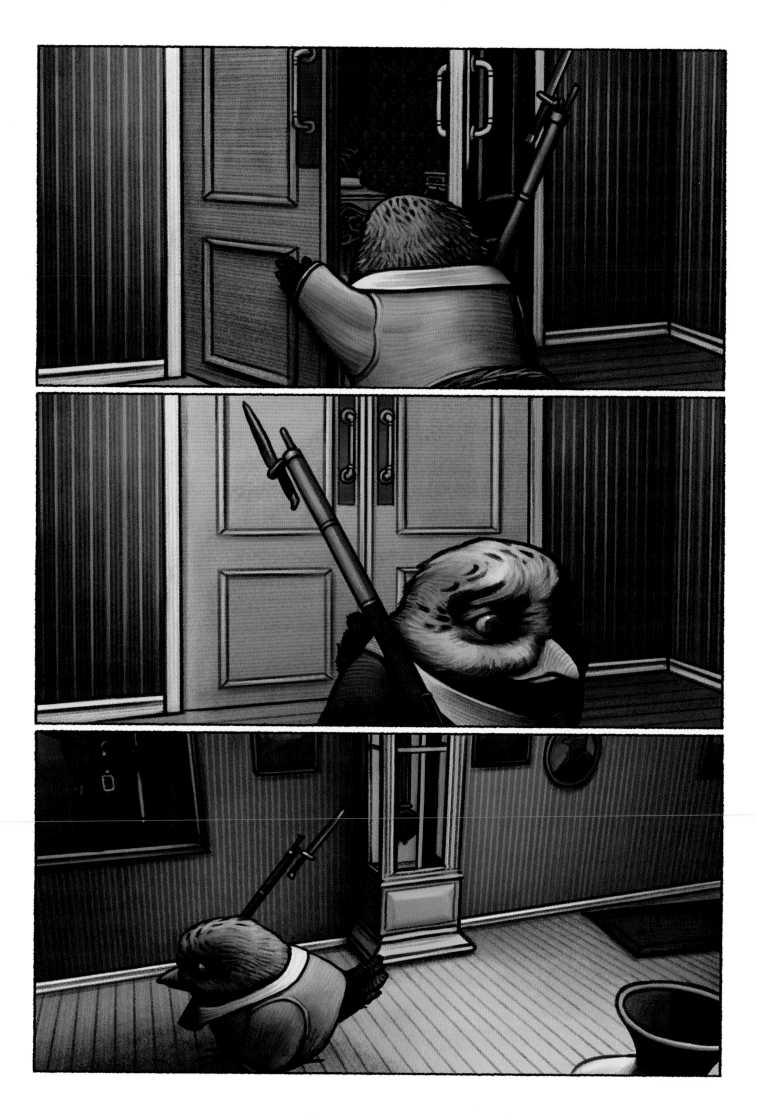

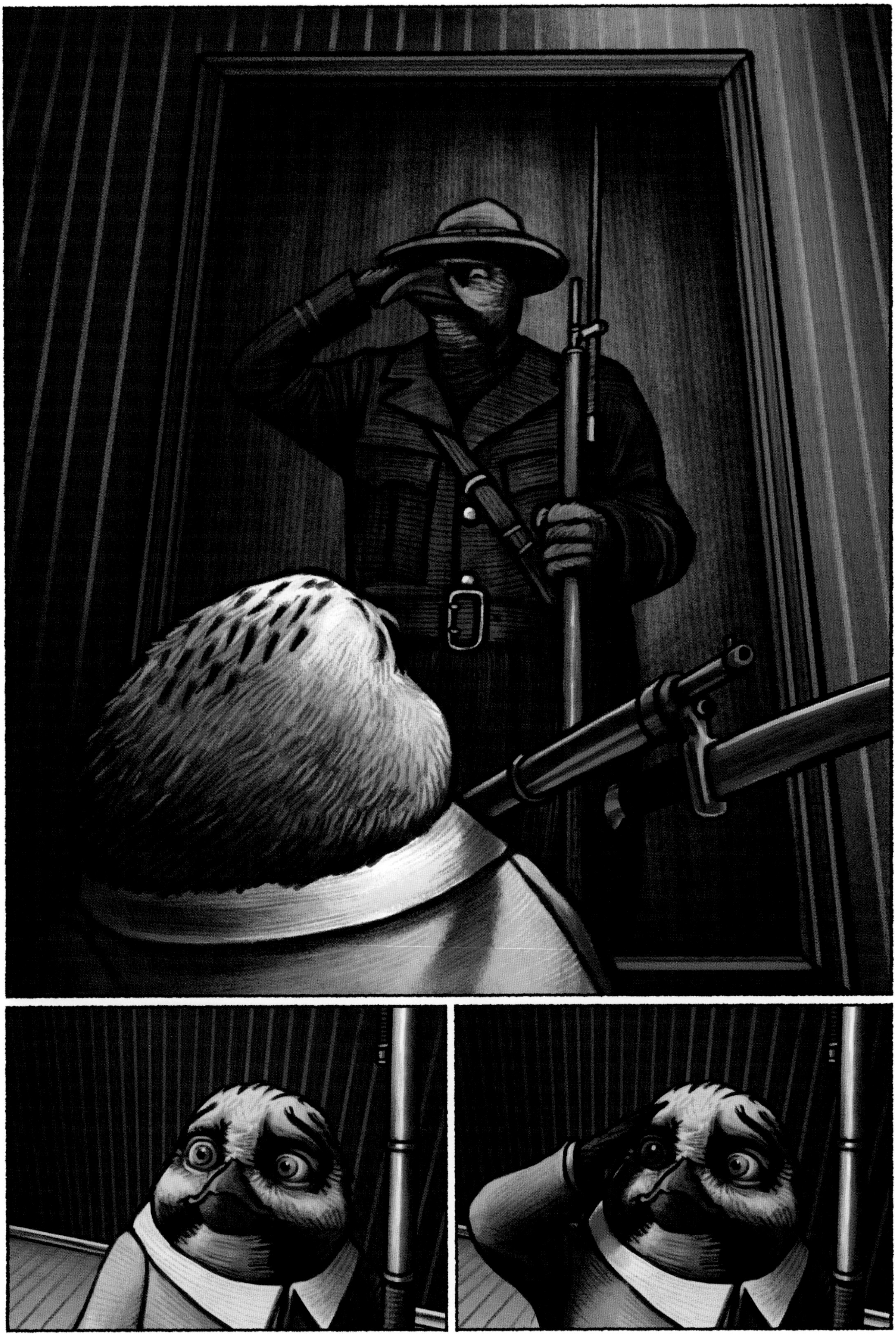

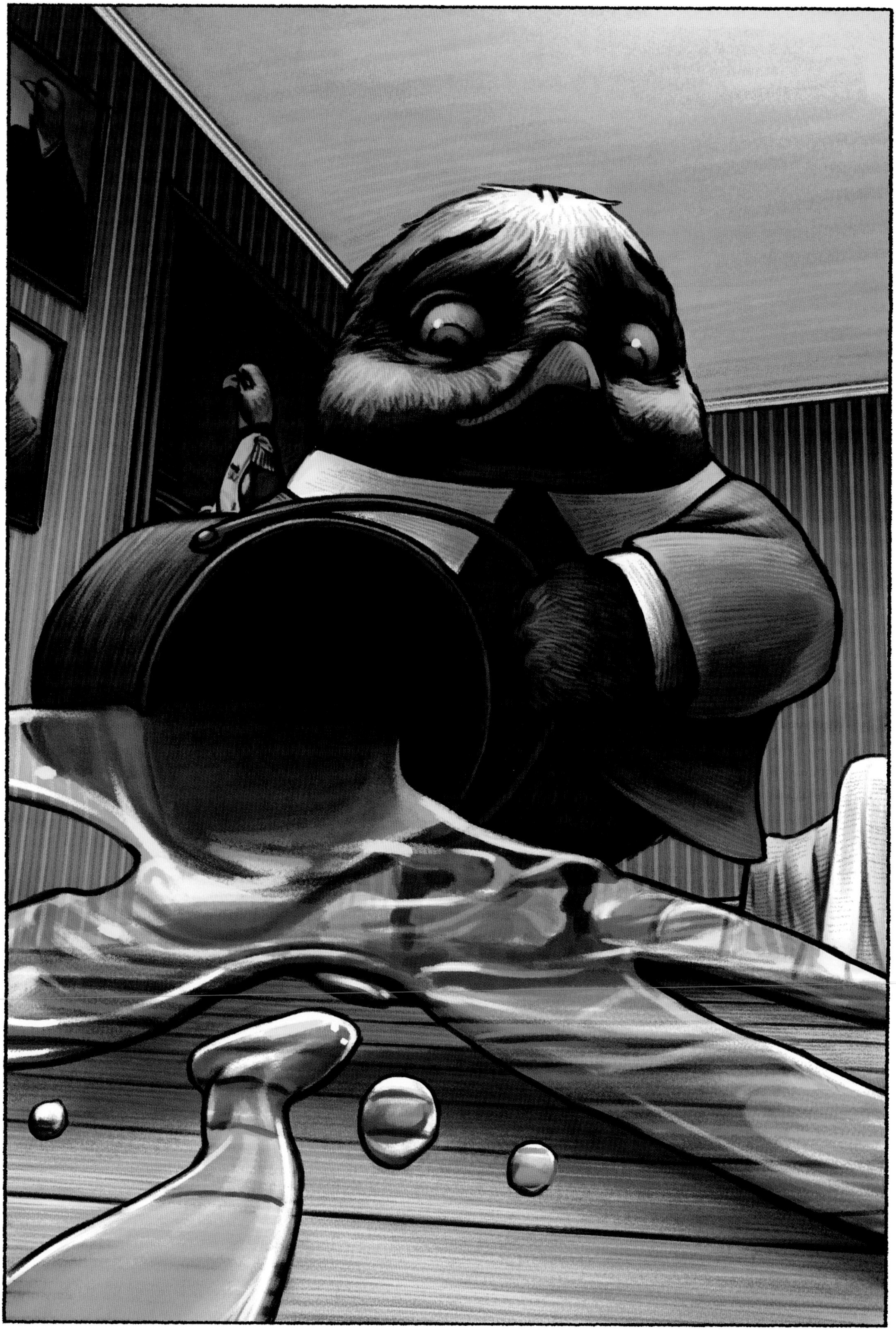

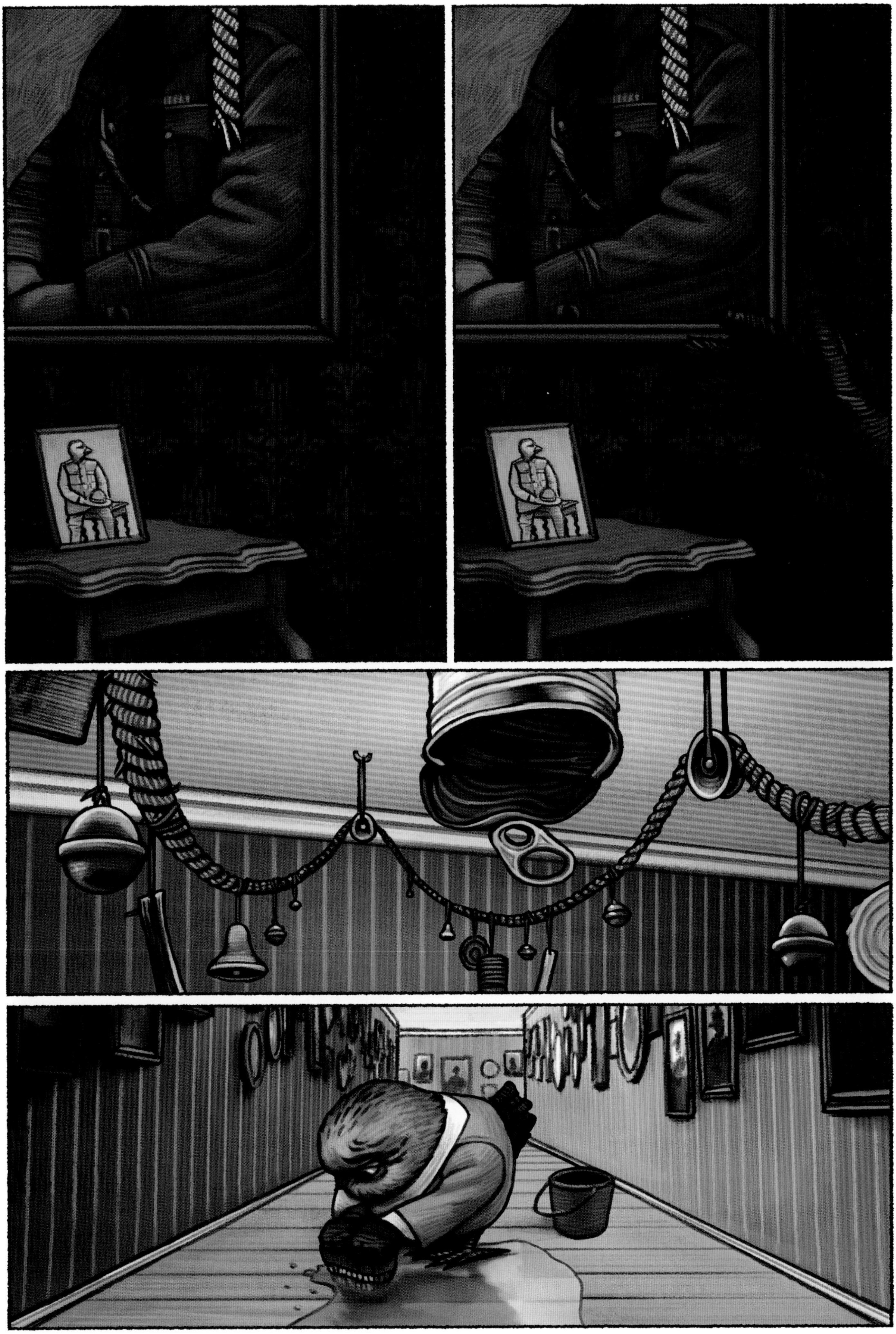

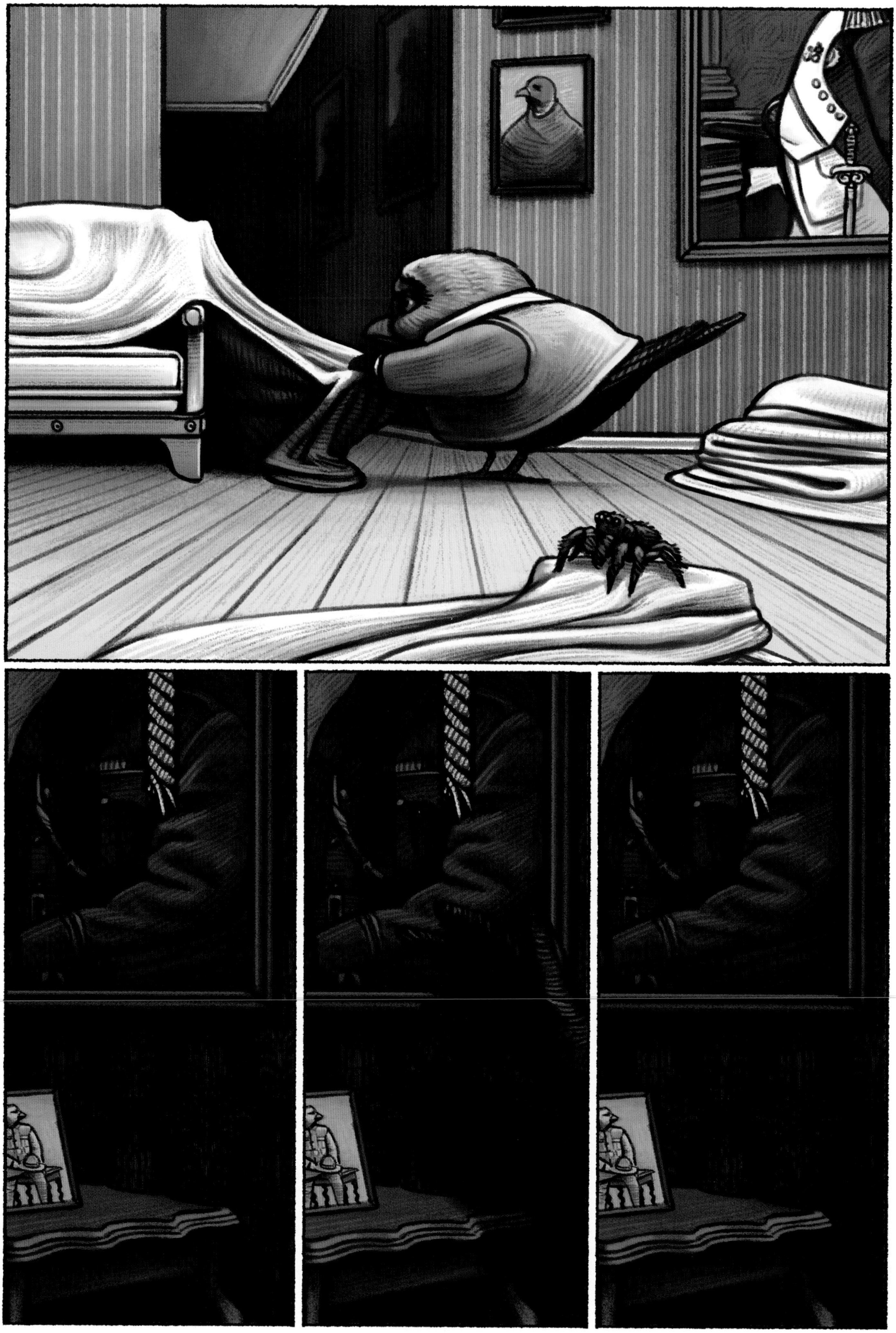

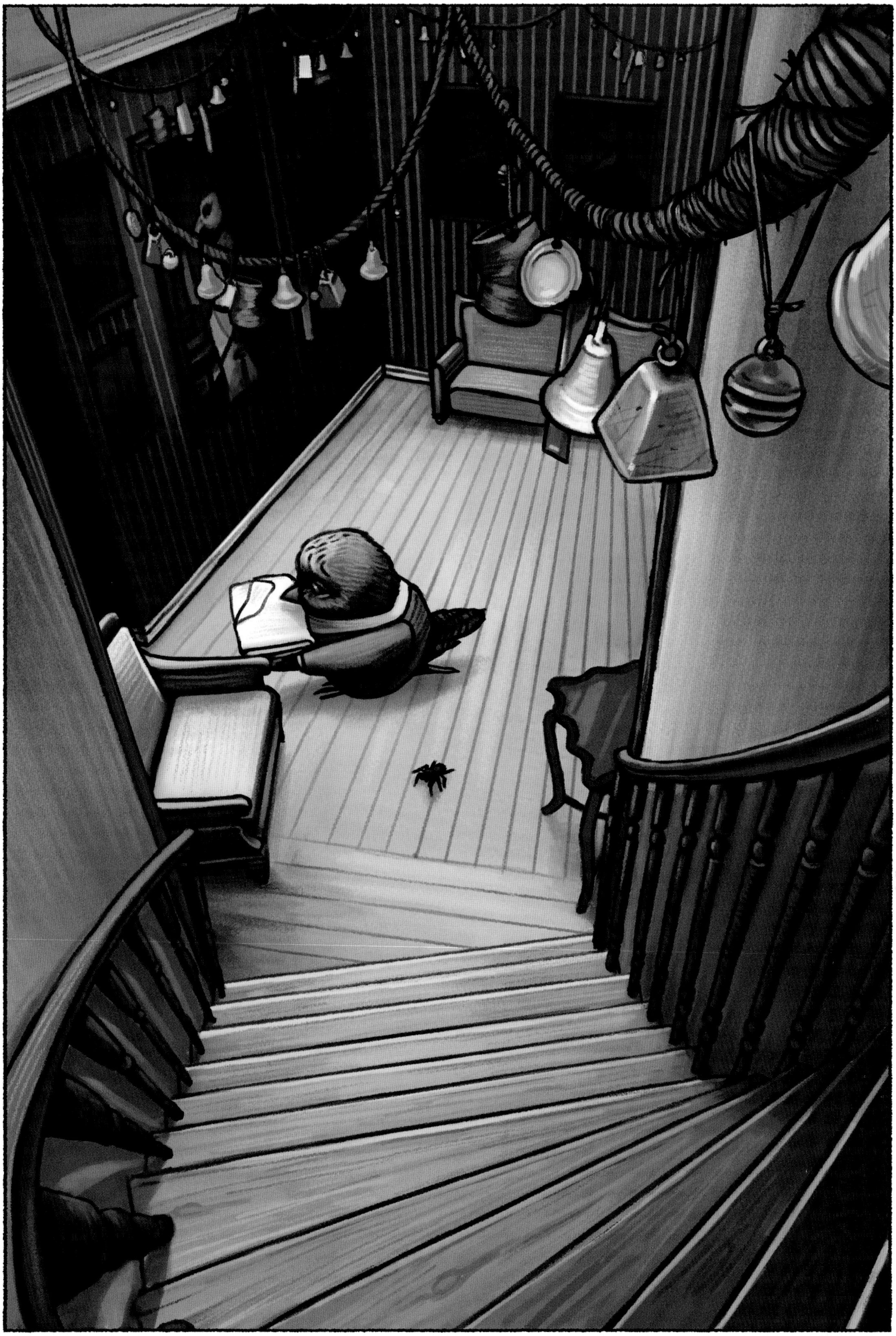

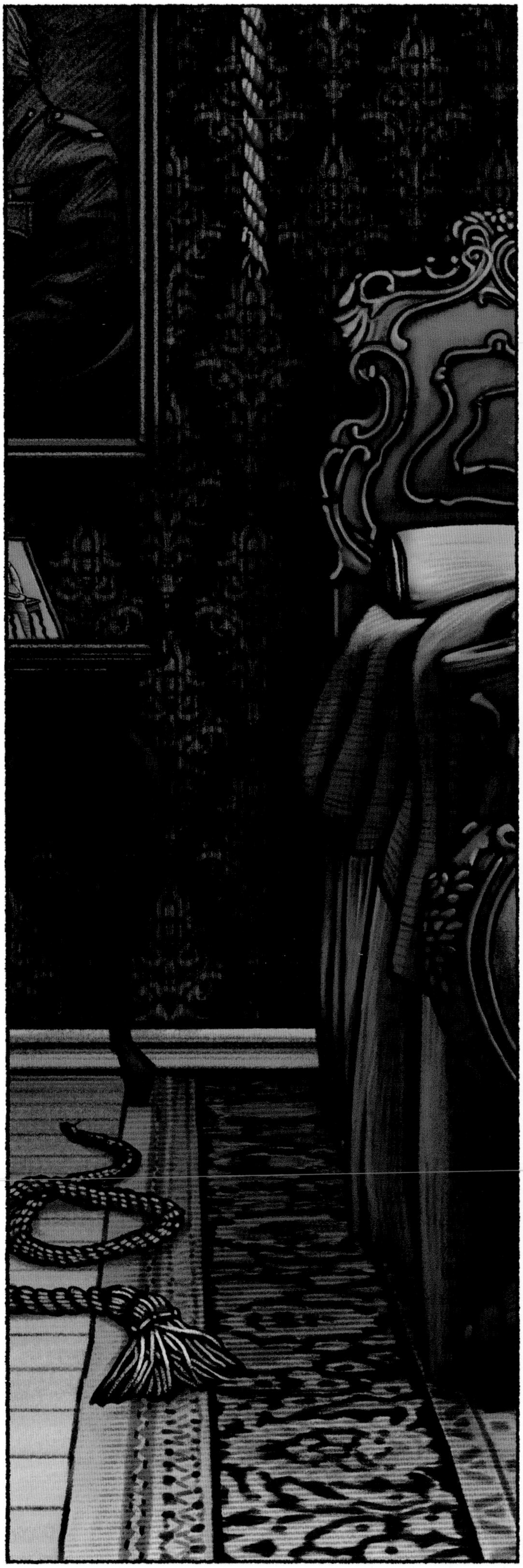
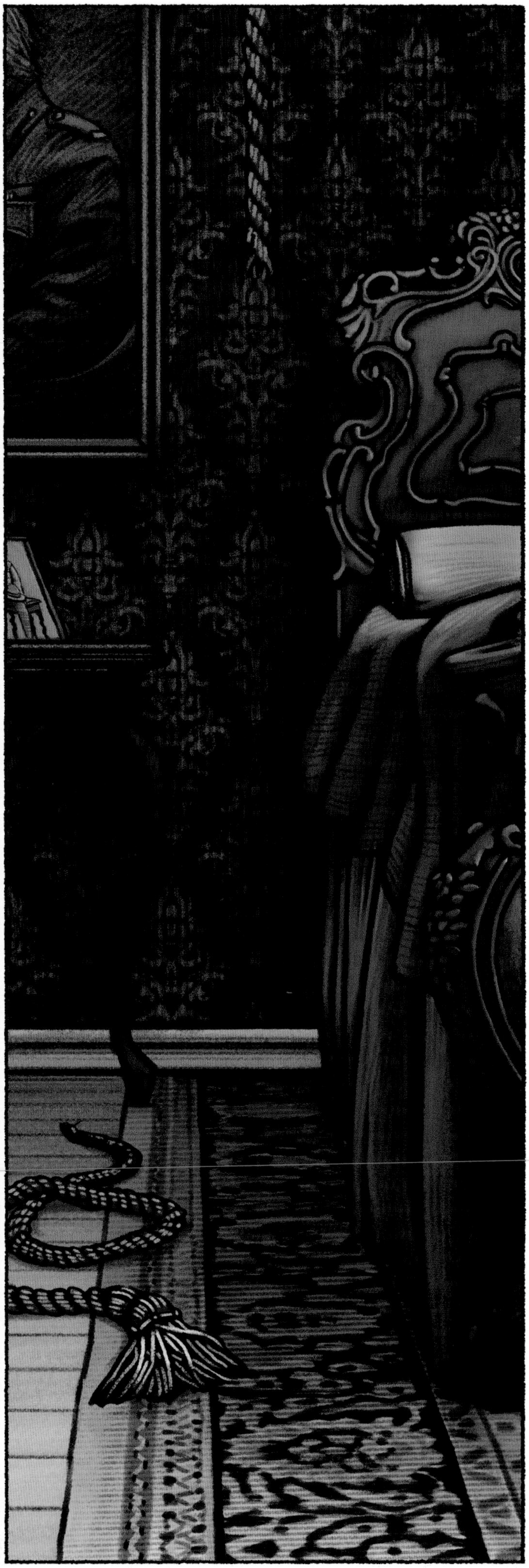

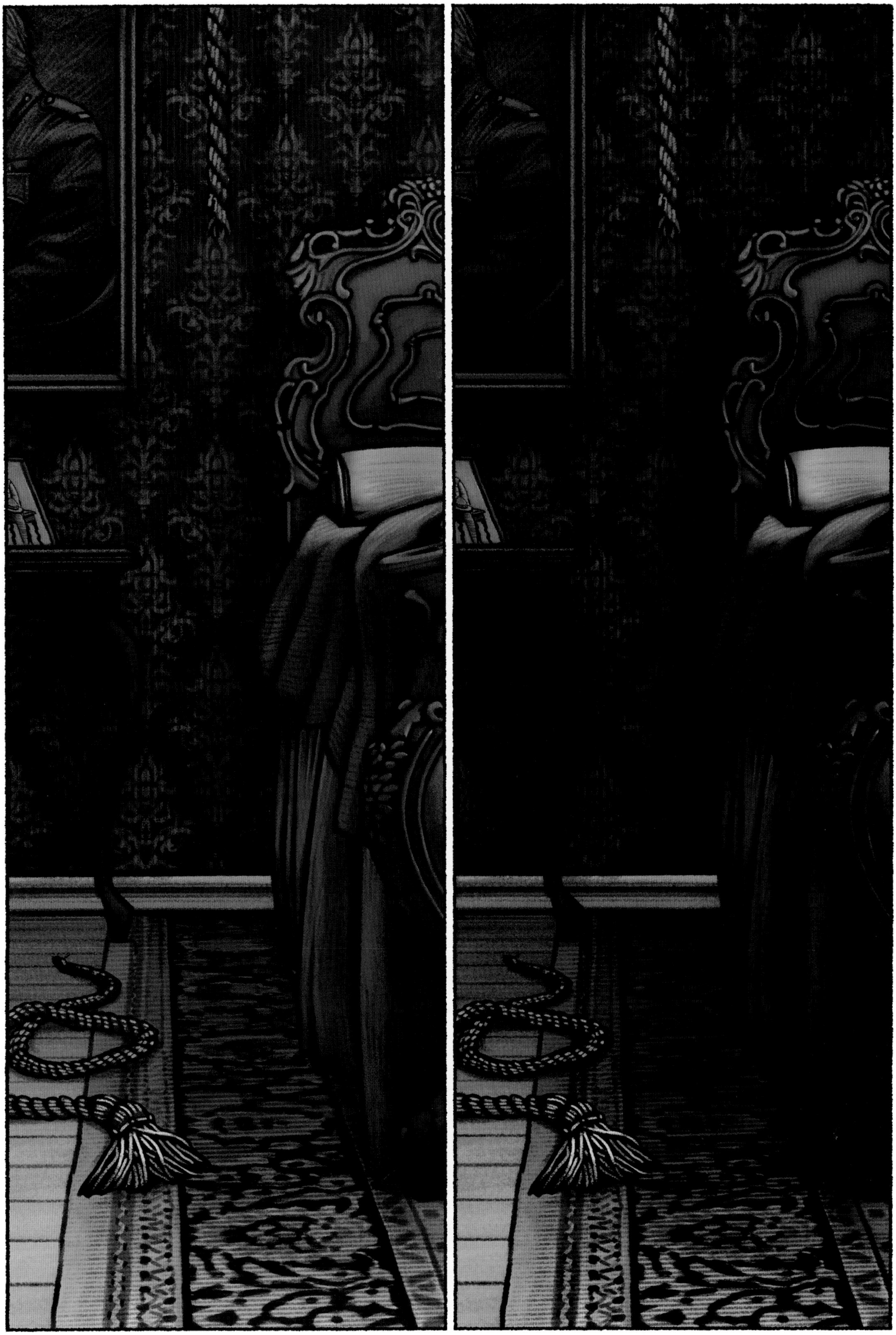

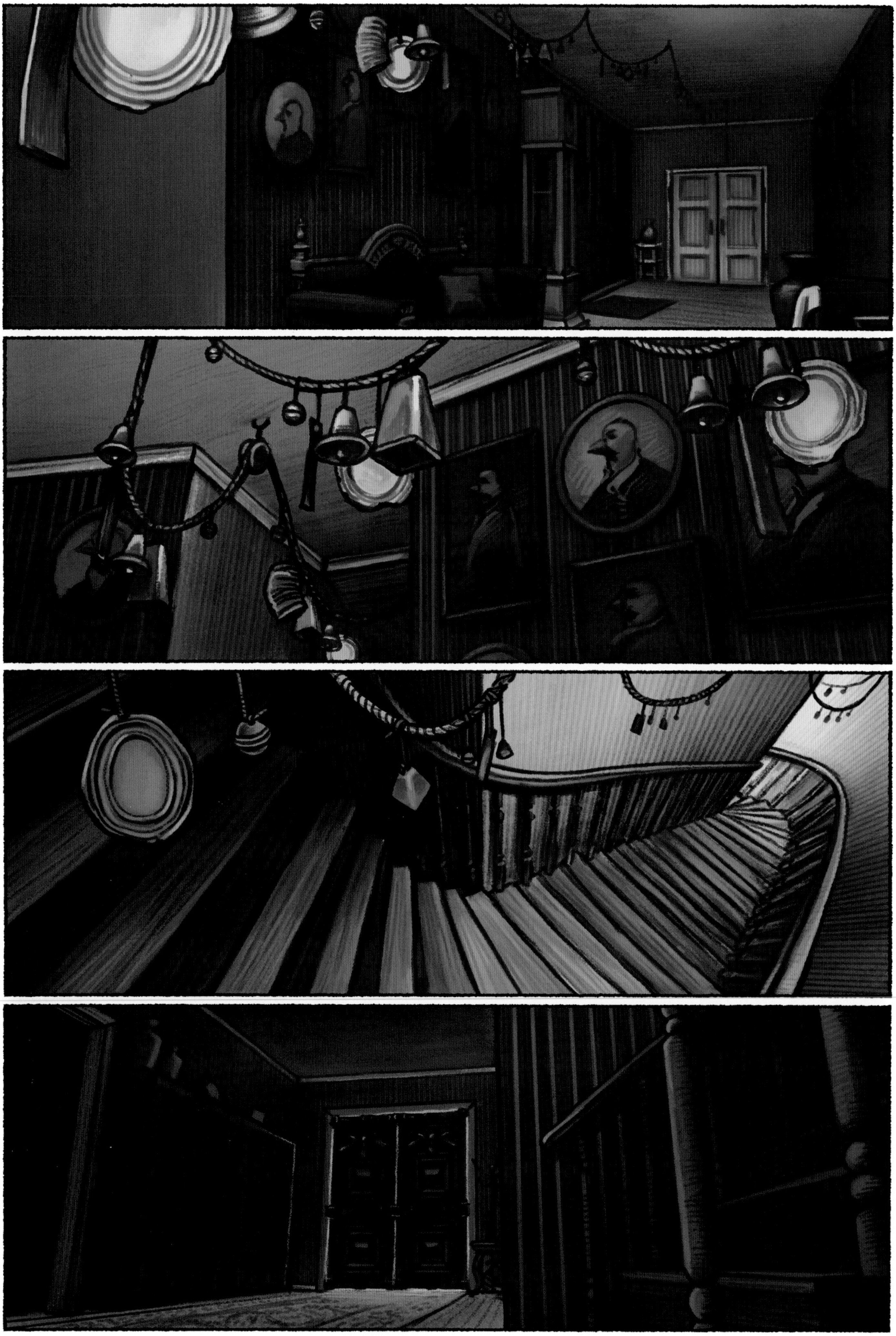

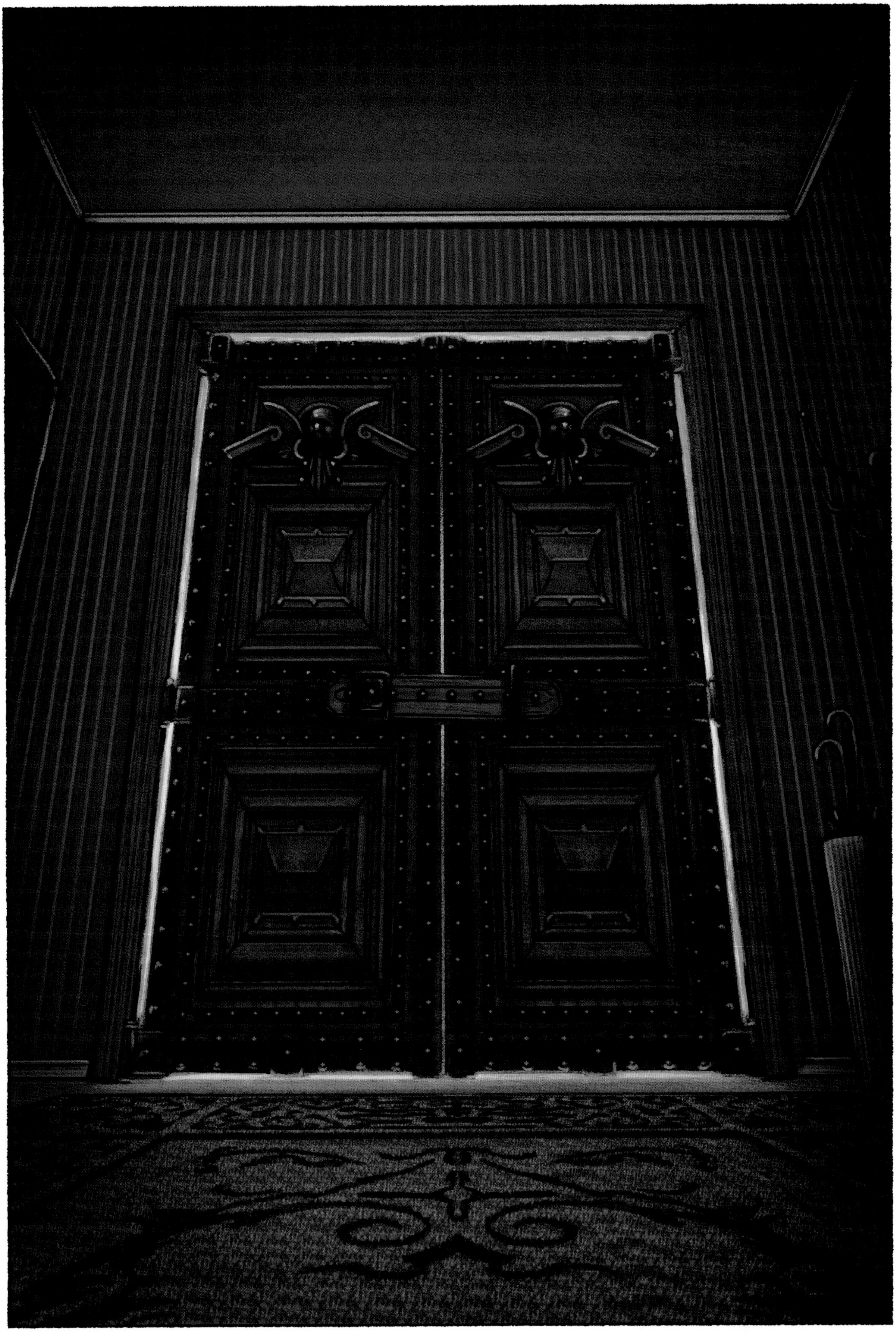

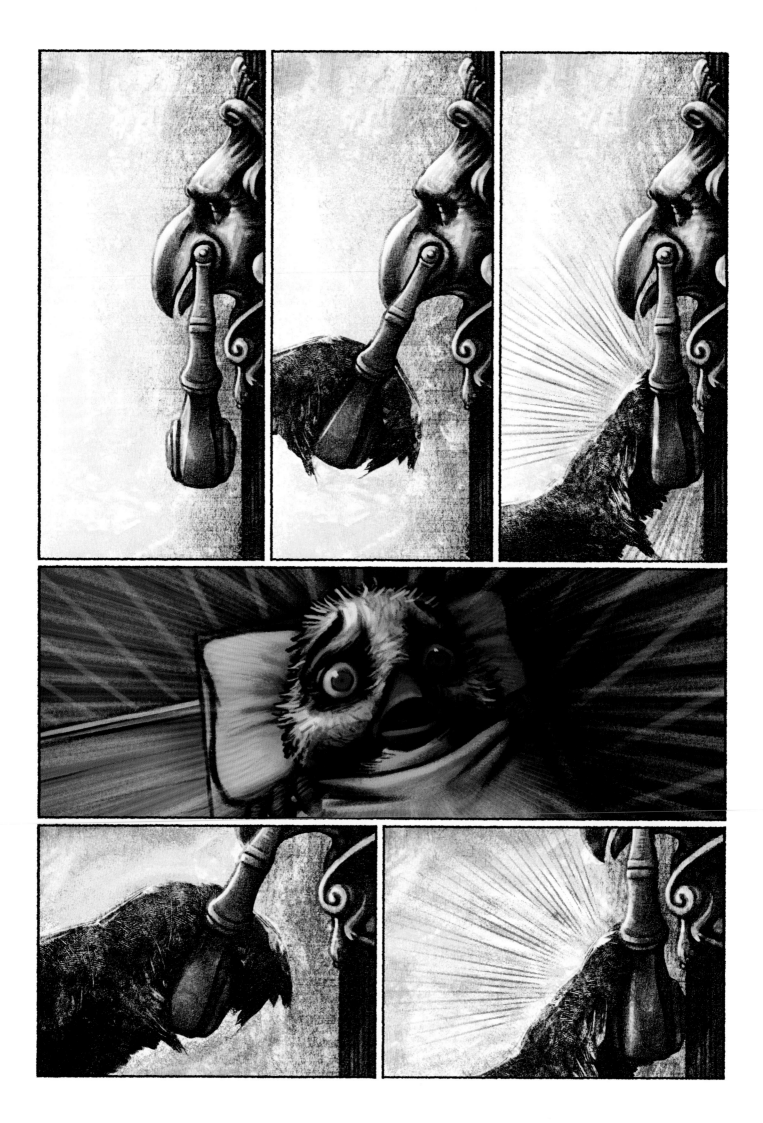

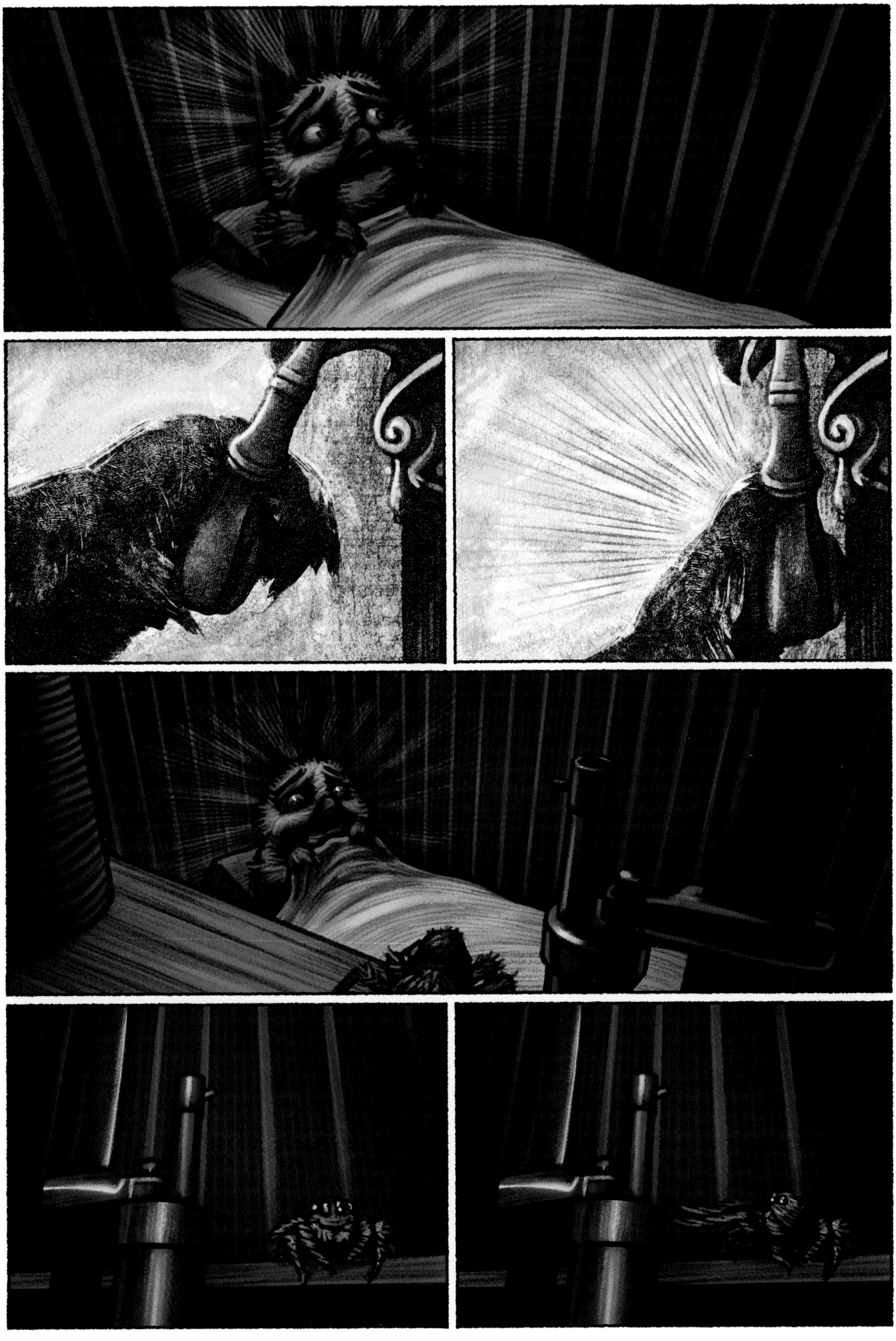

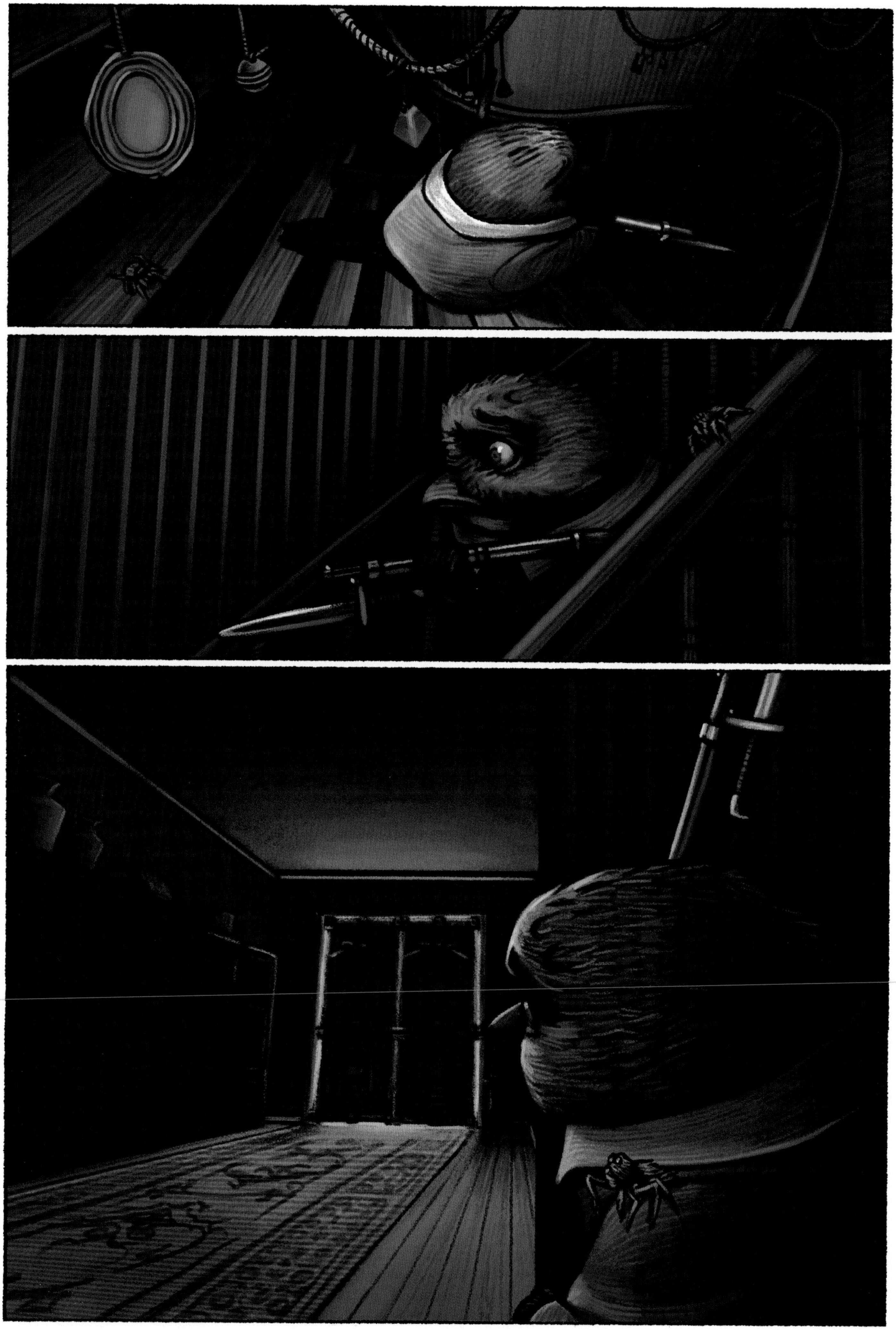

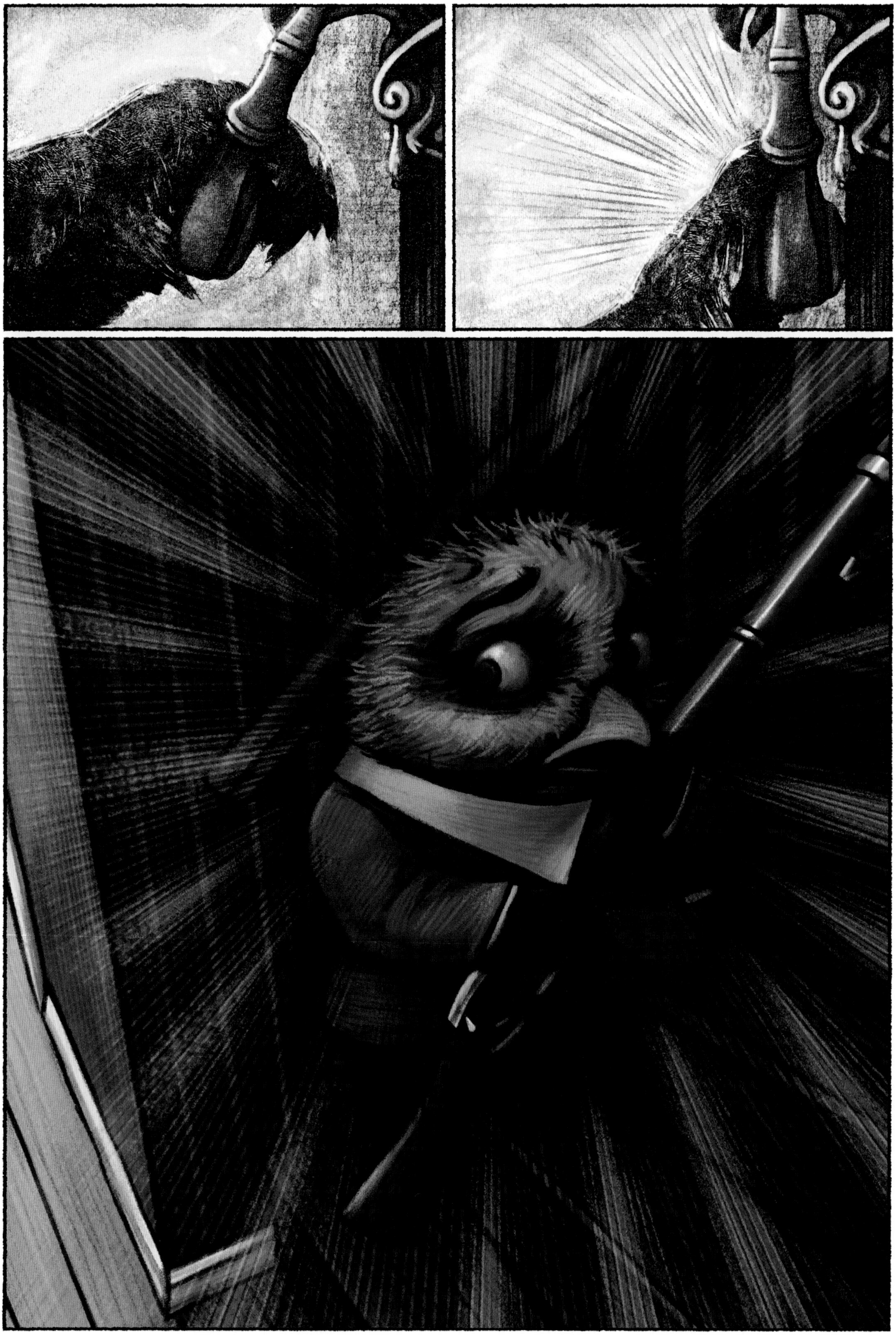

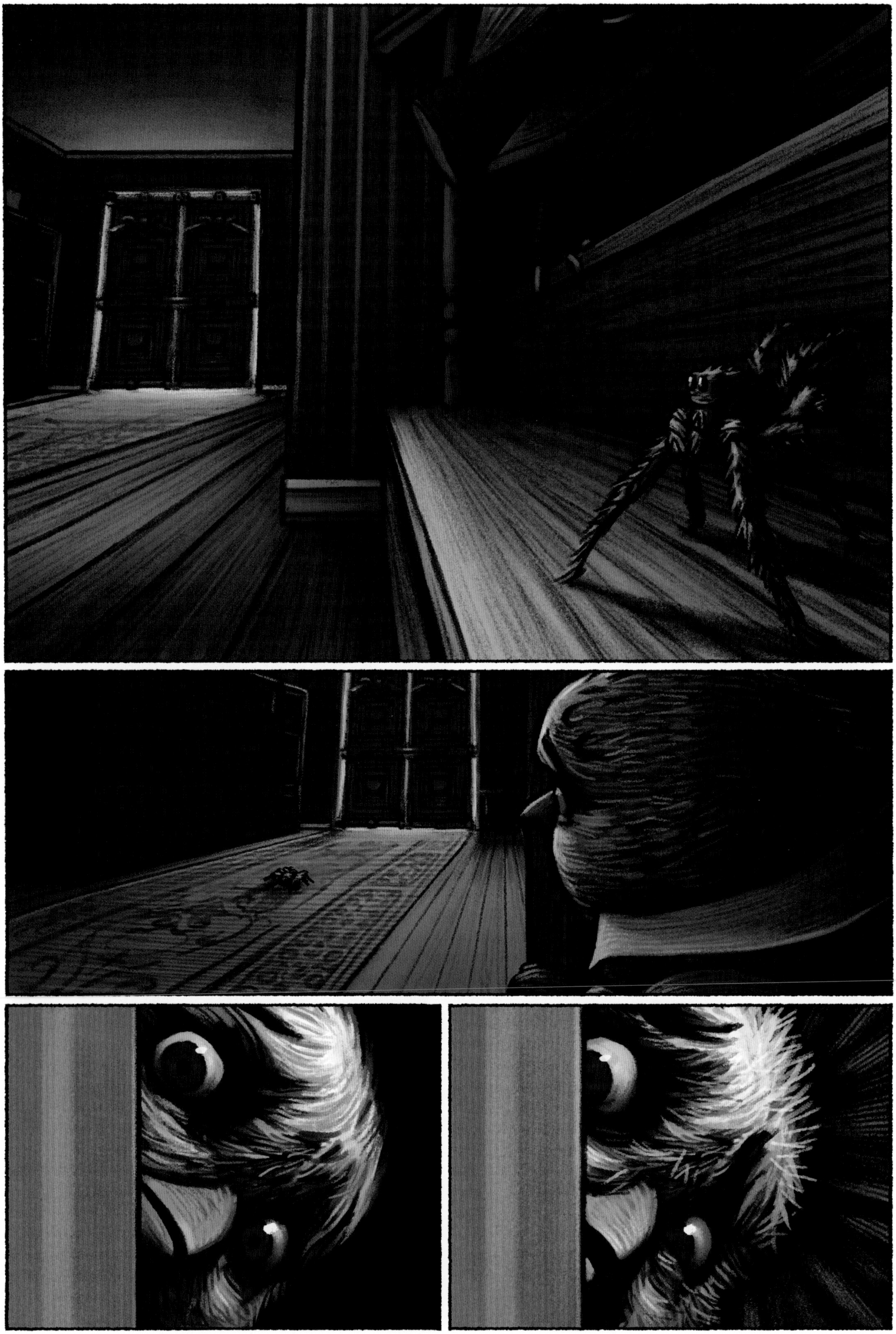

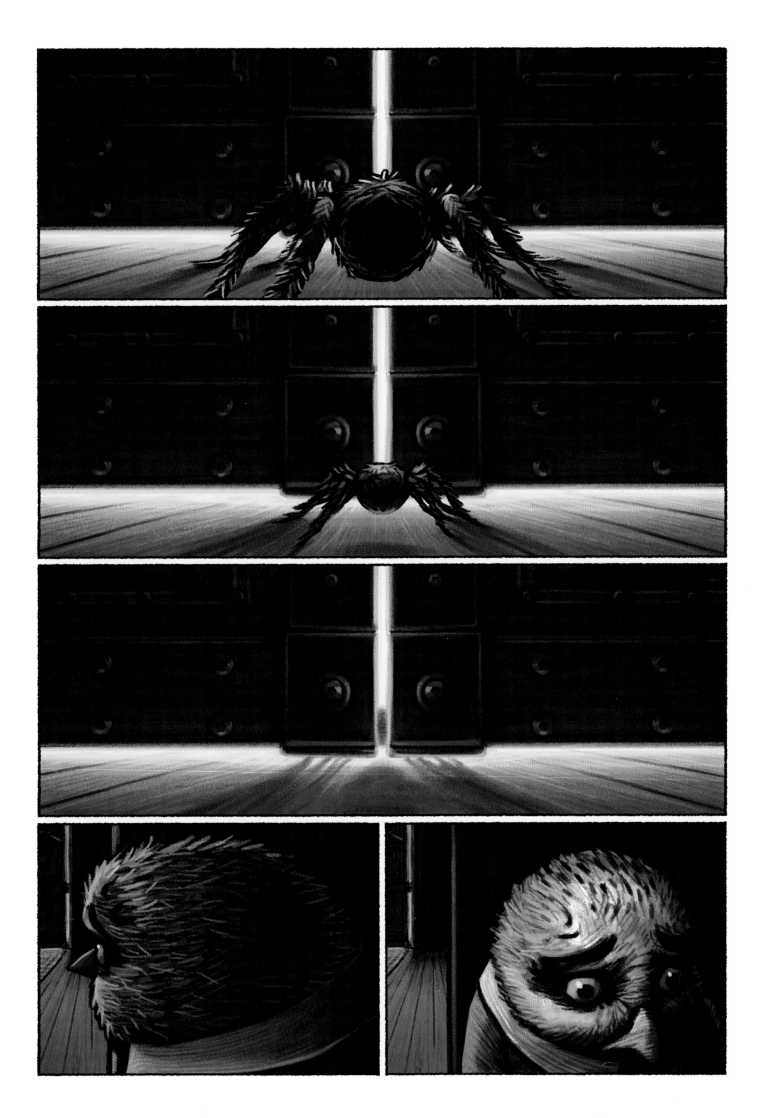

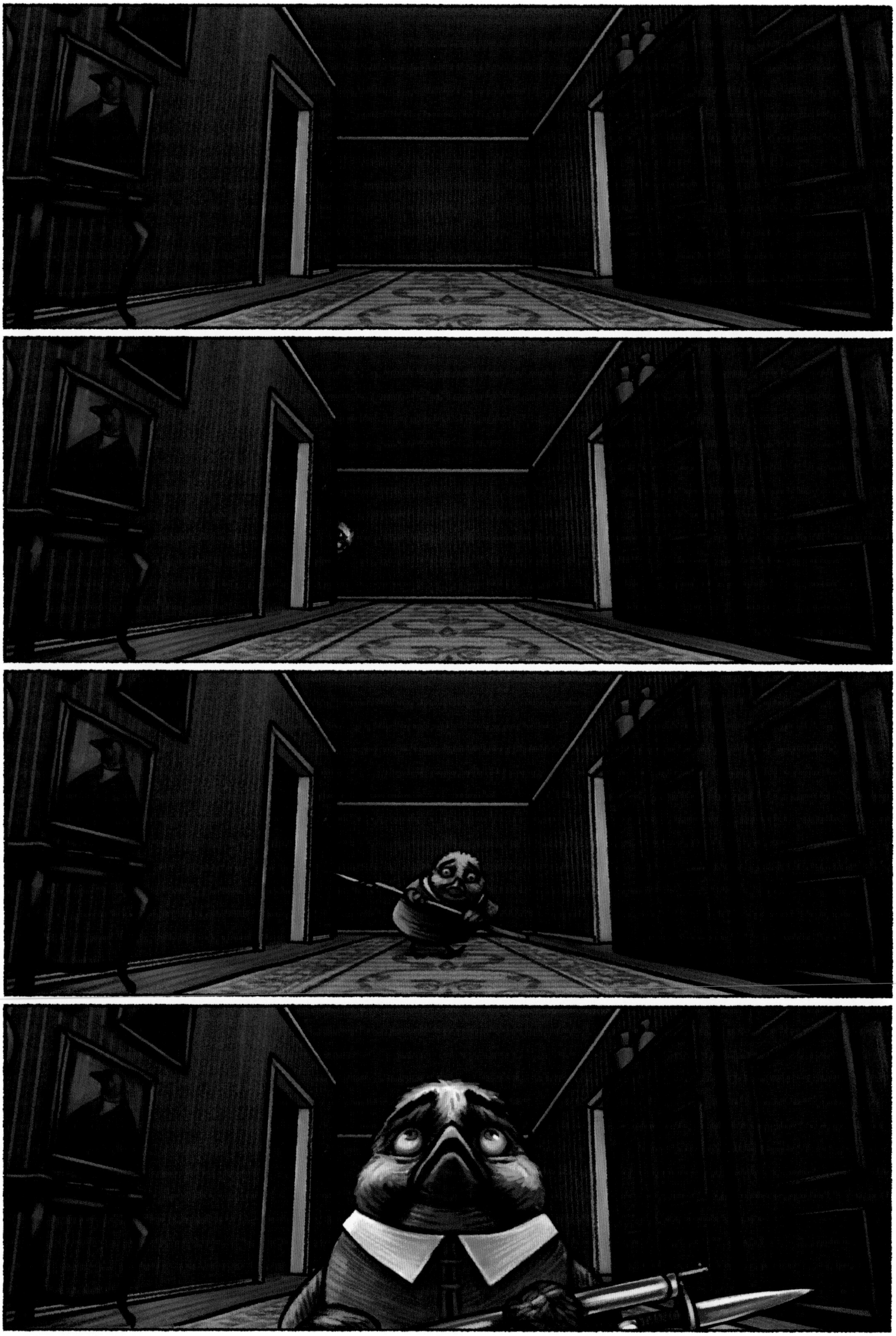

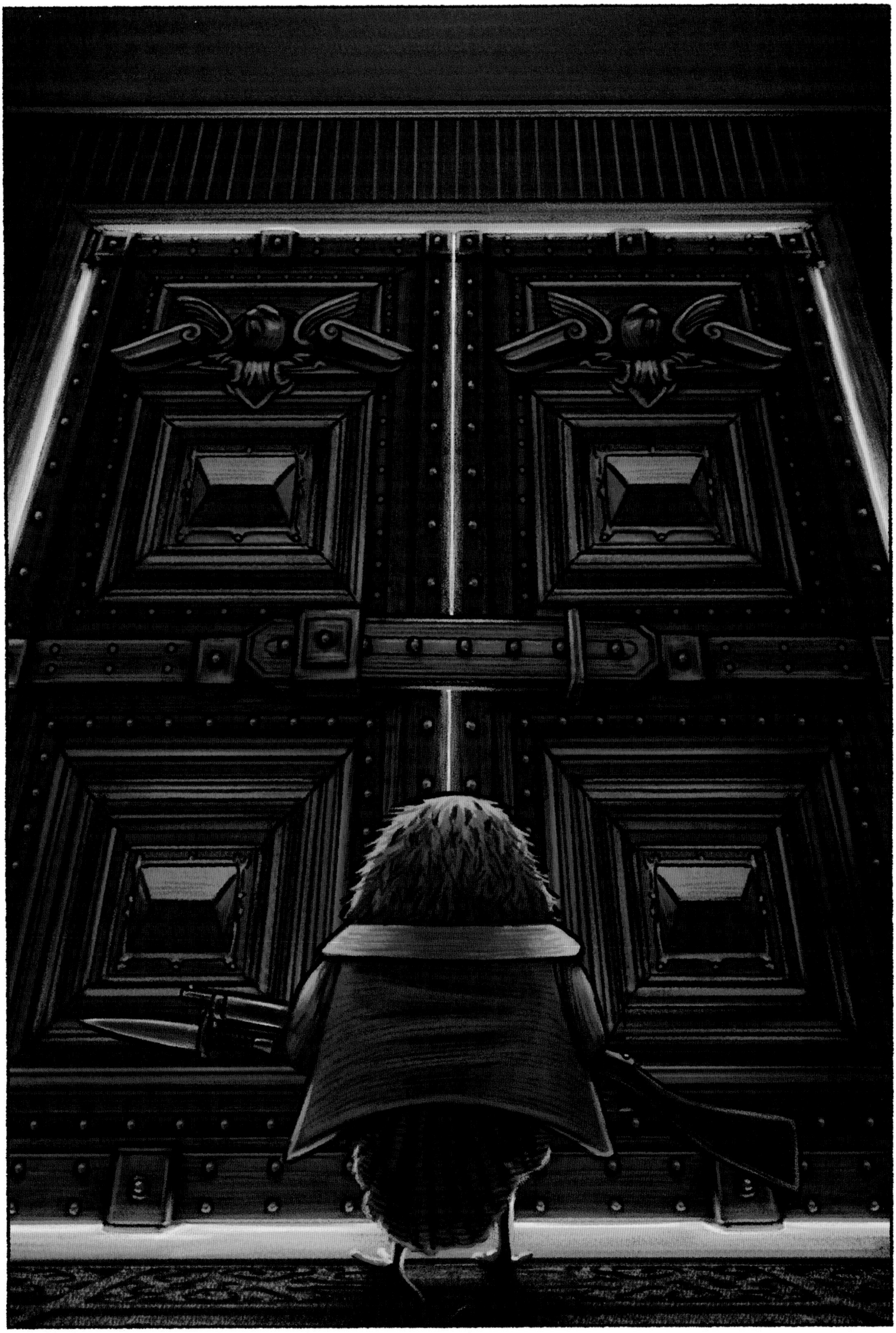

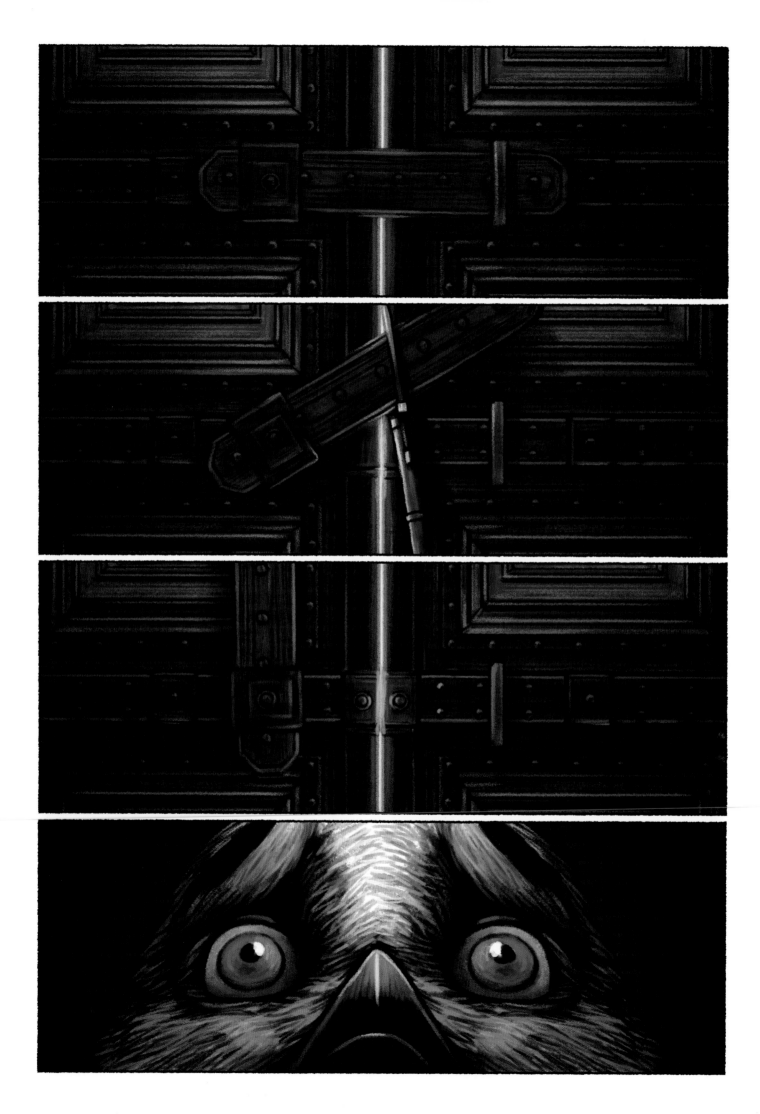

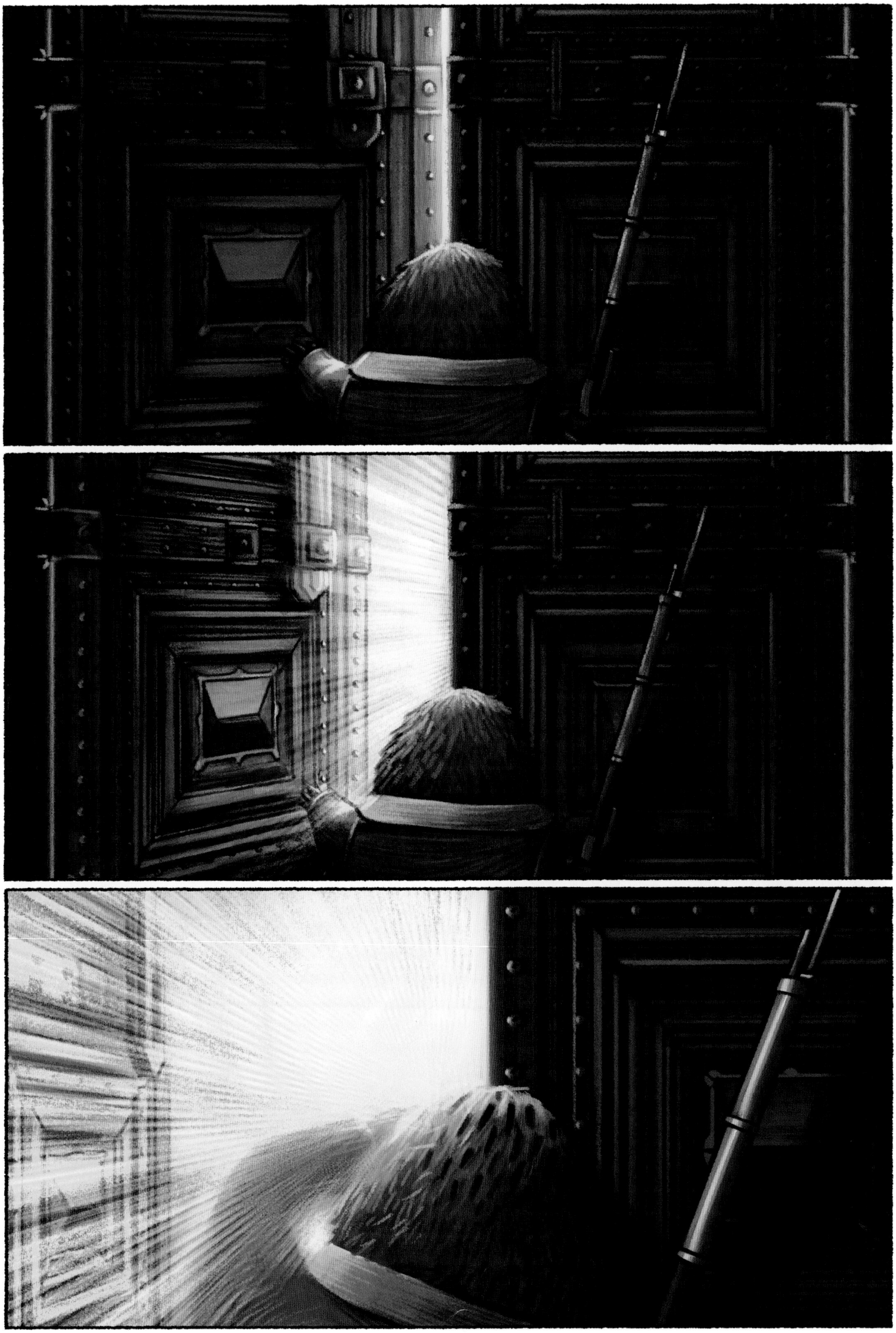

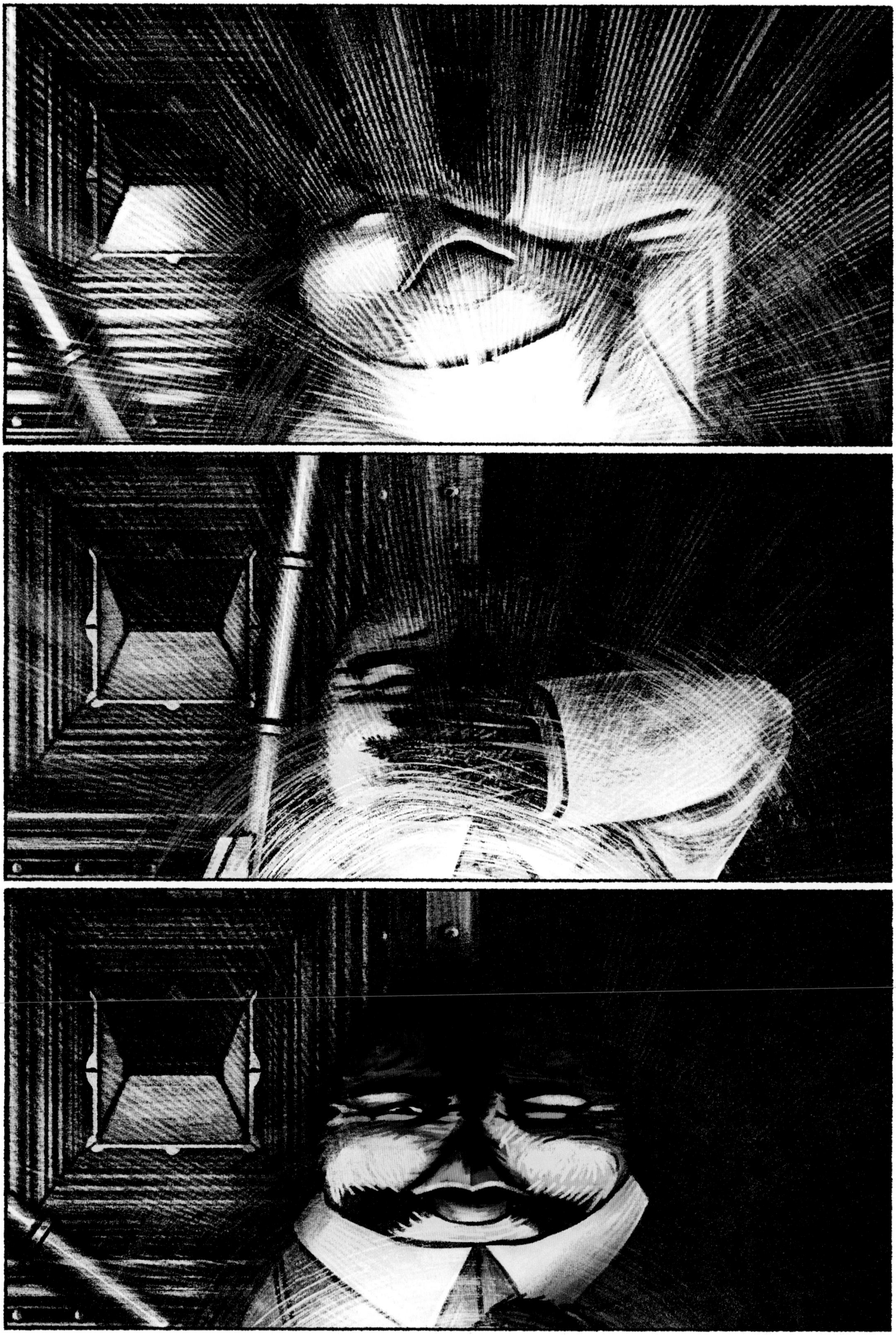

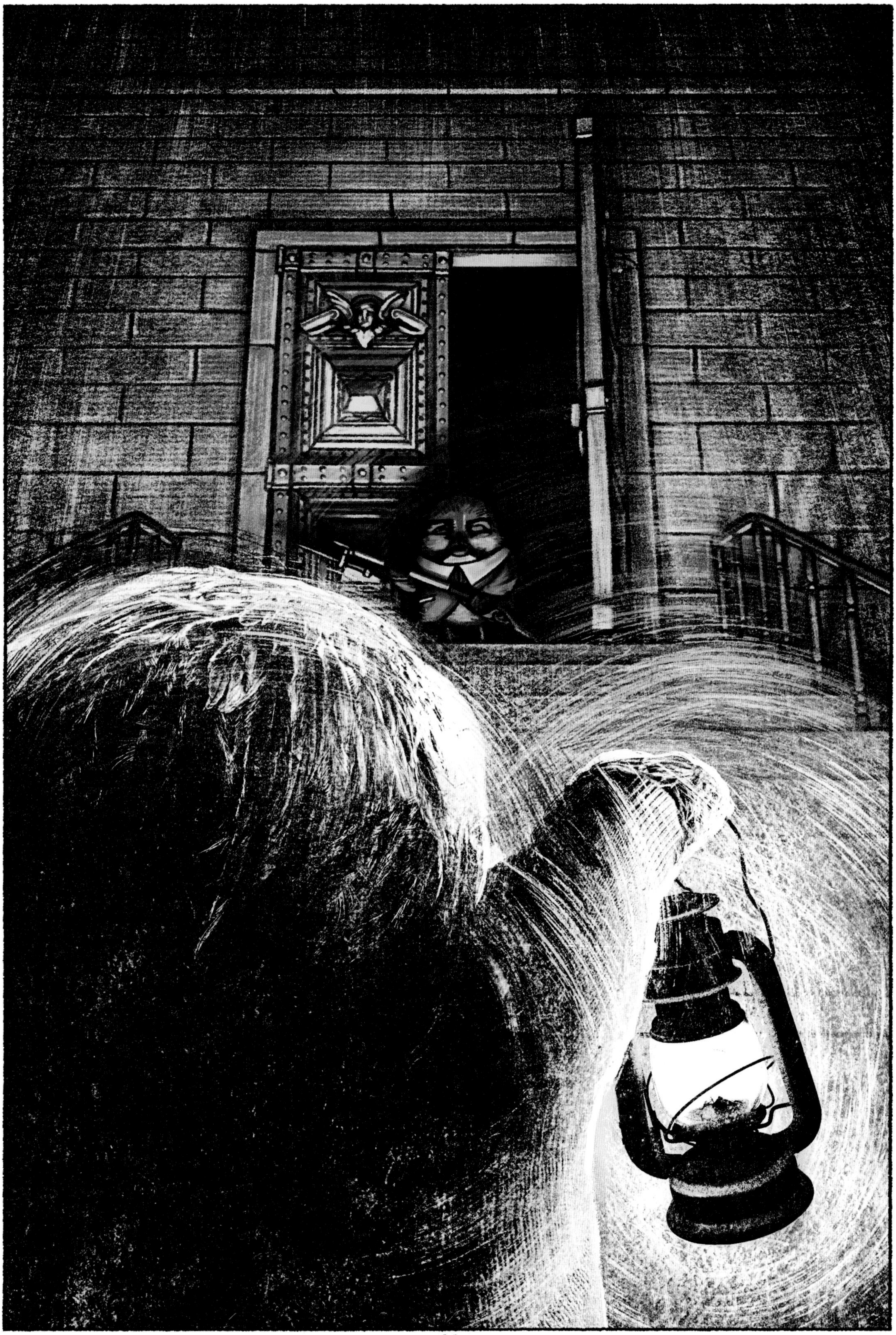

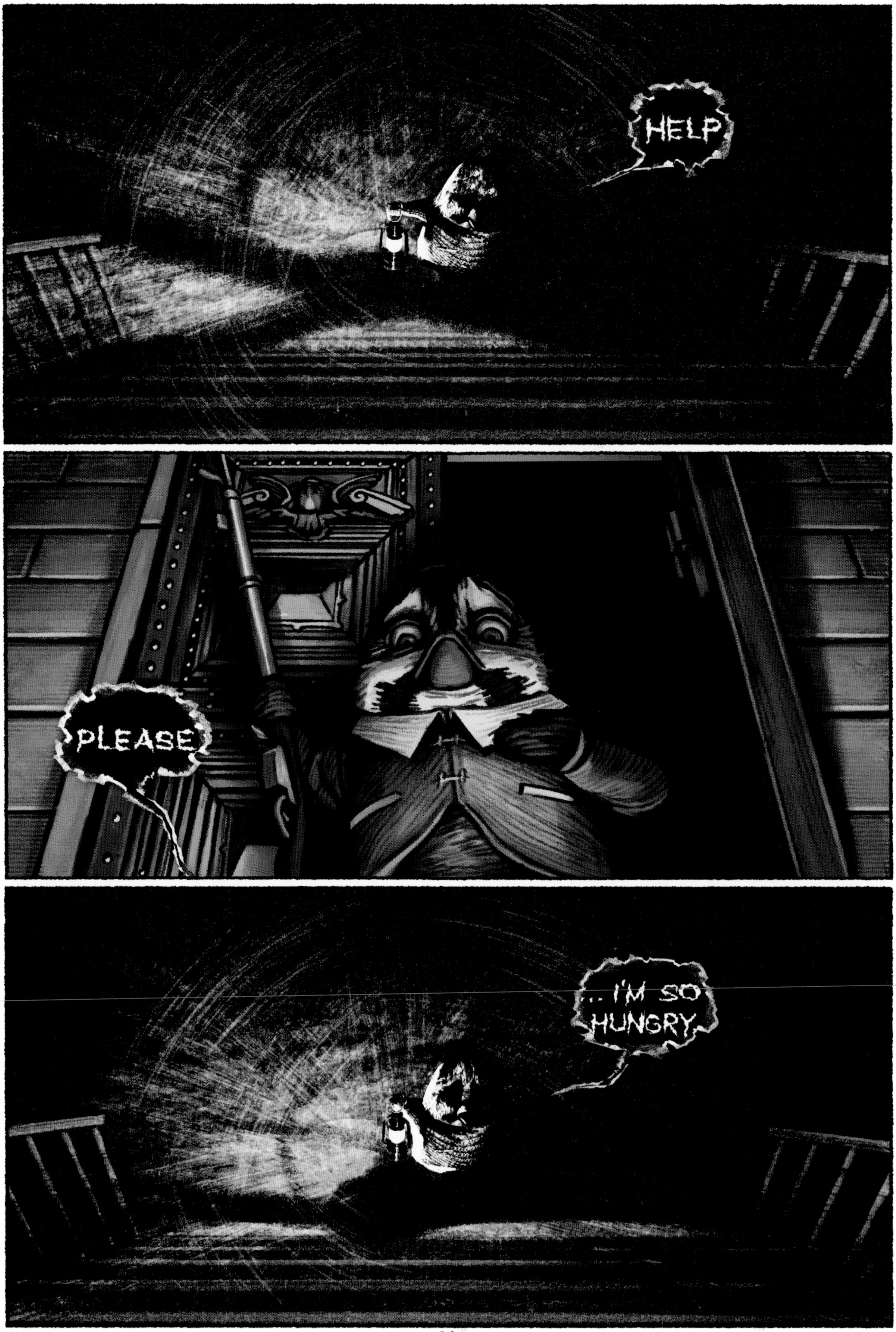
HELP
PLEASE
...I'M SO HUNGRY

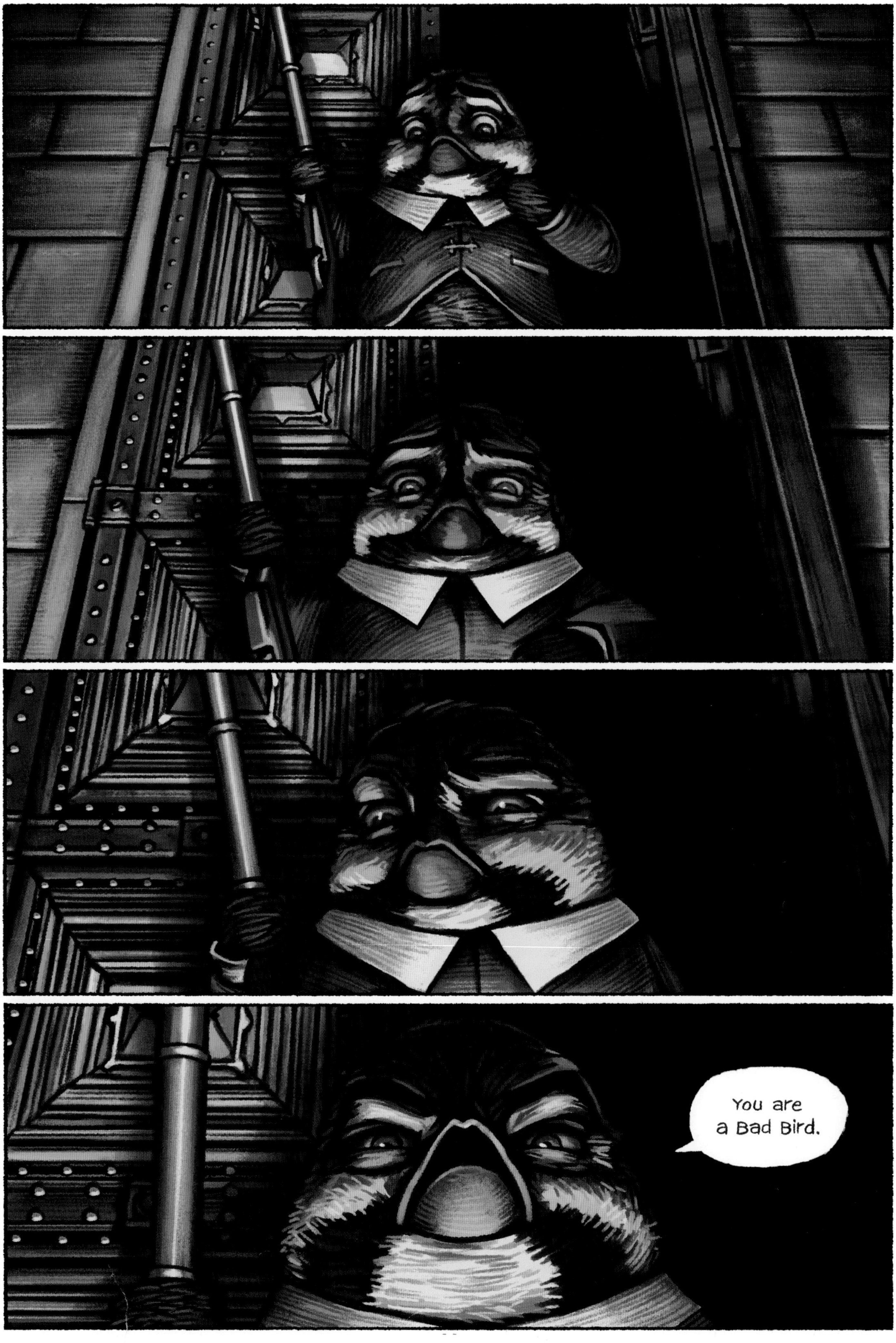
You are
a Bad Bird.

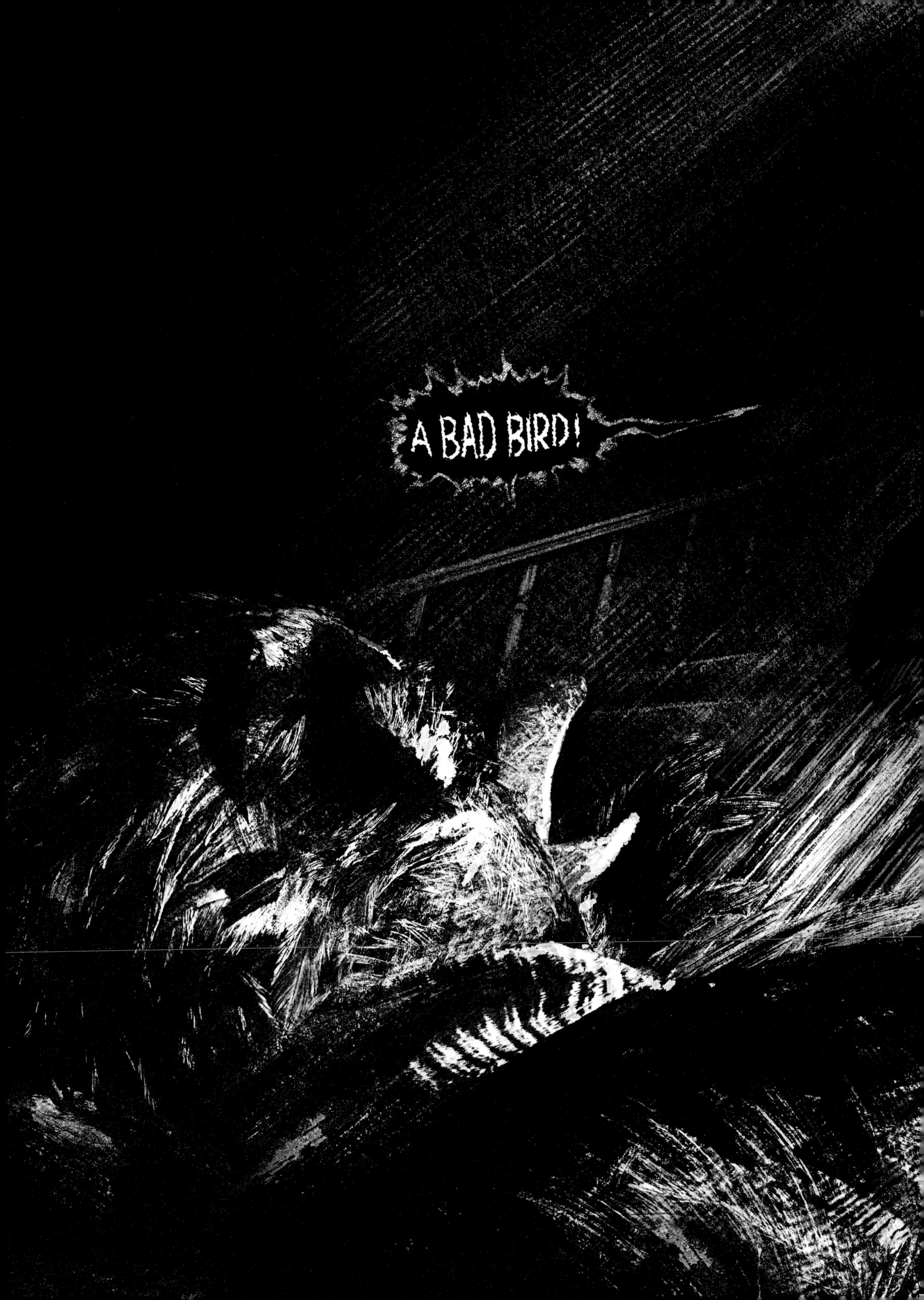
A BAD BIRD!

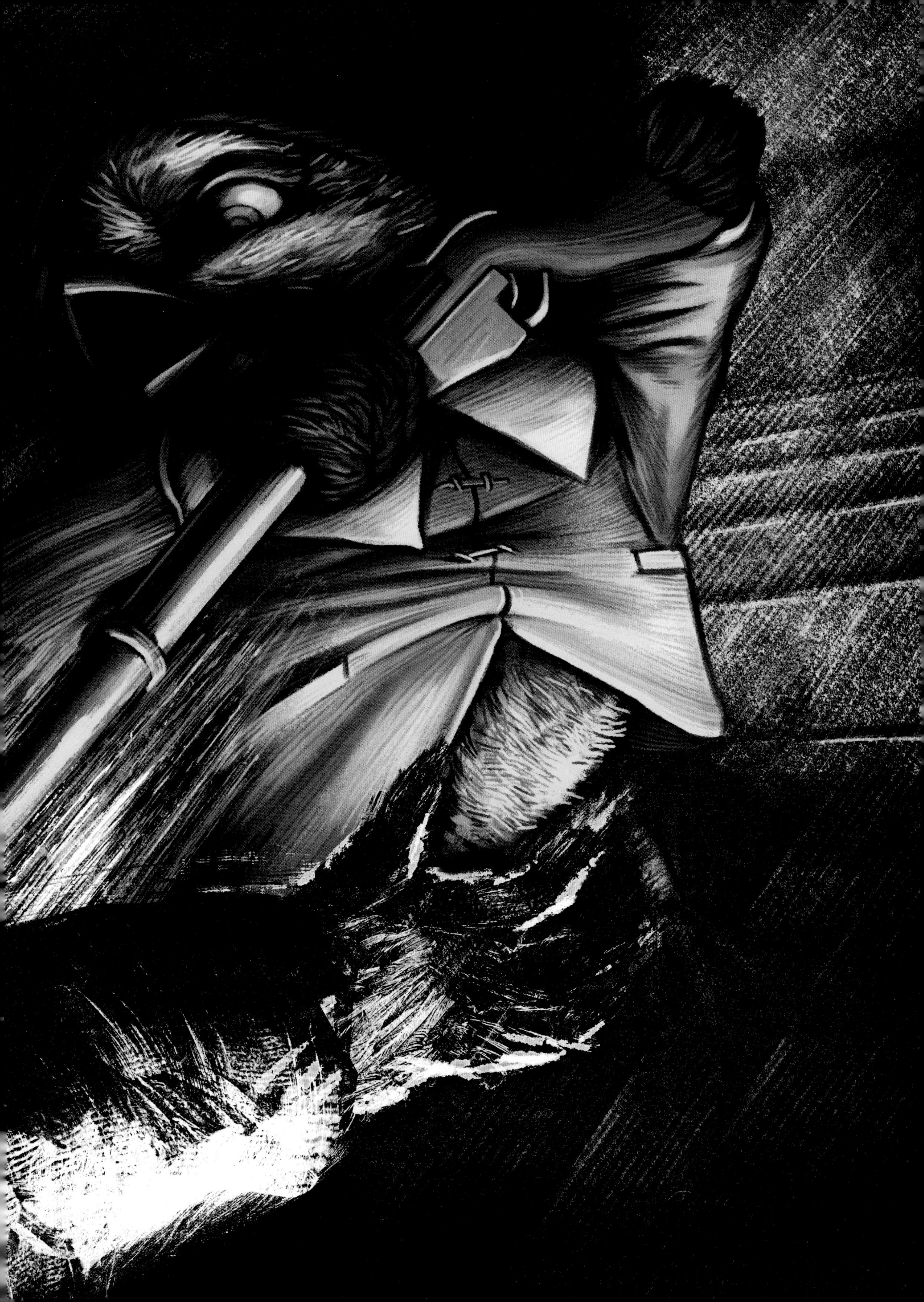

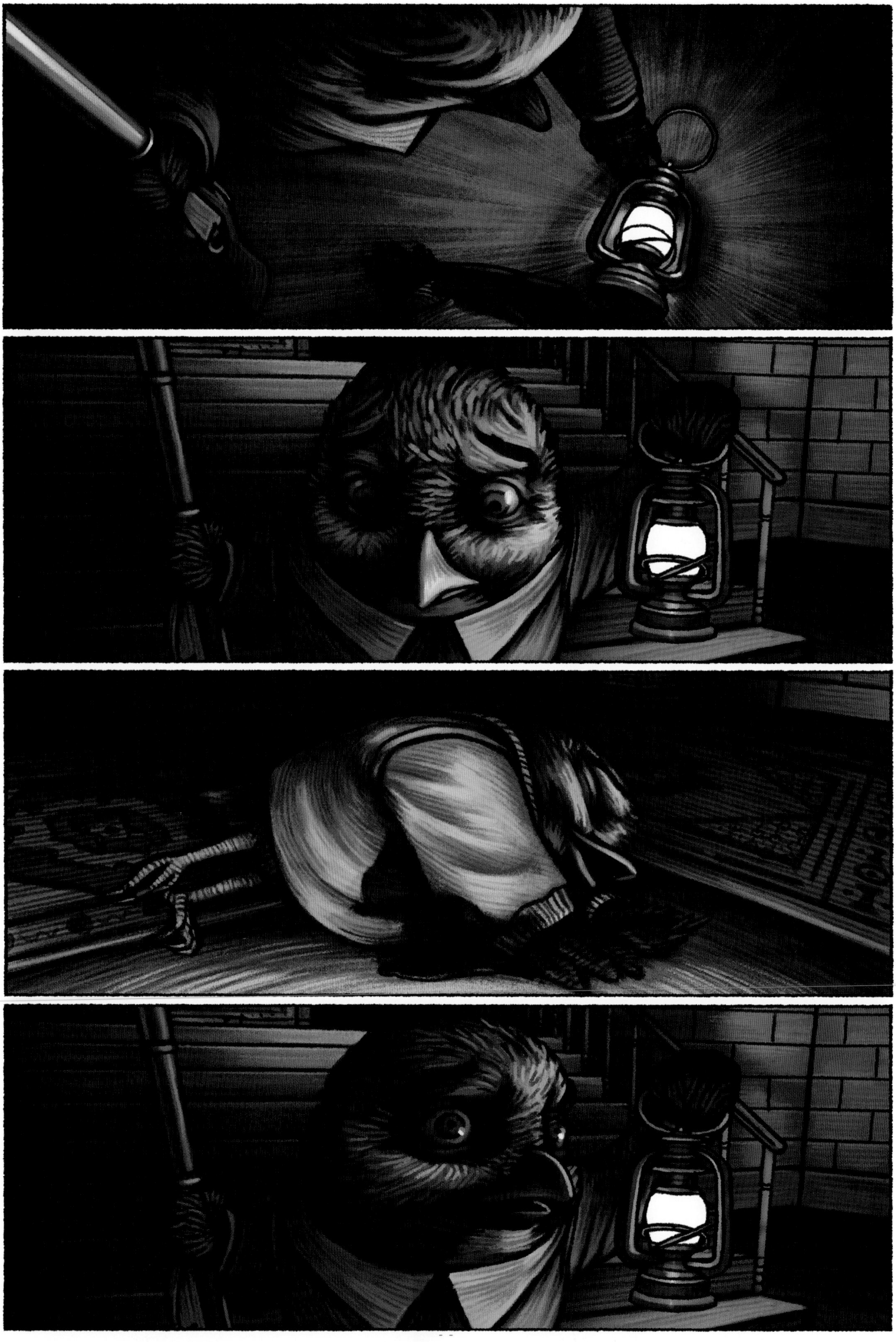

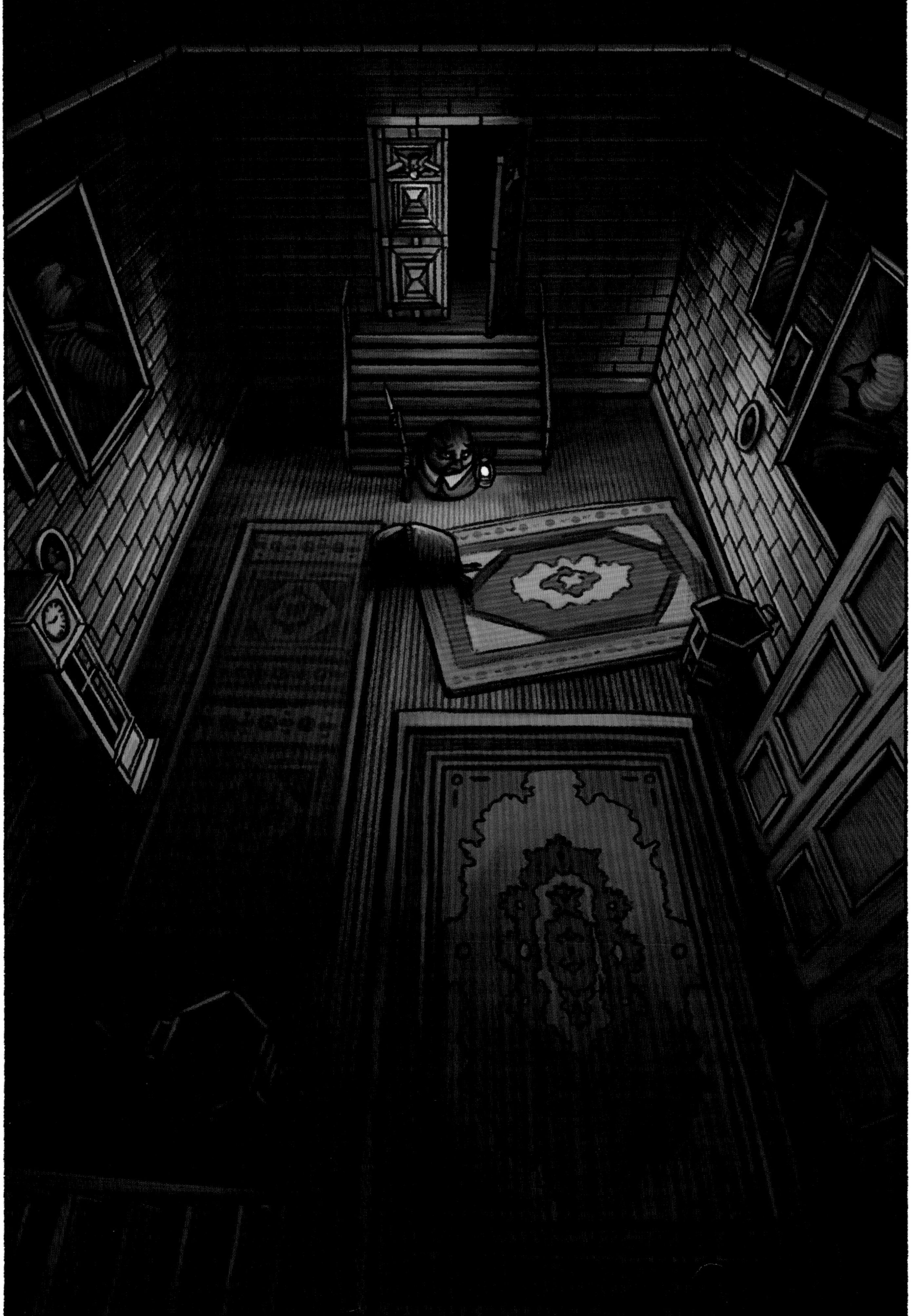

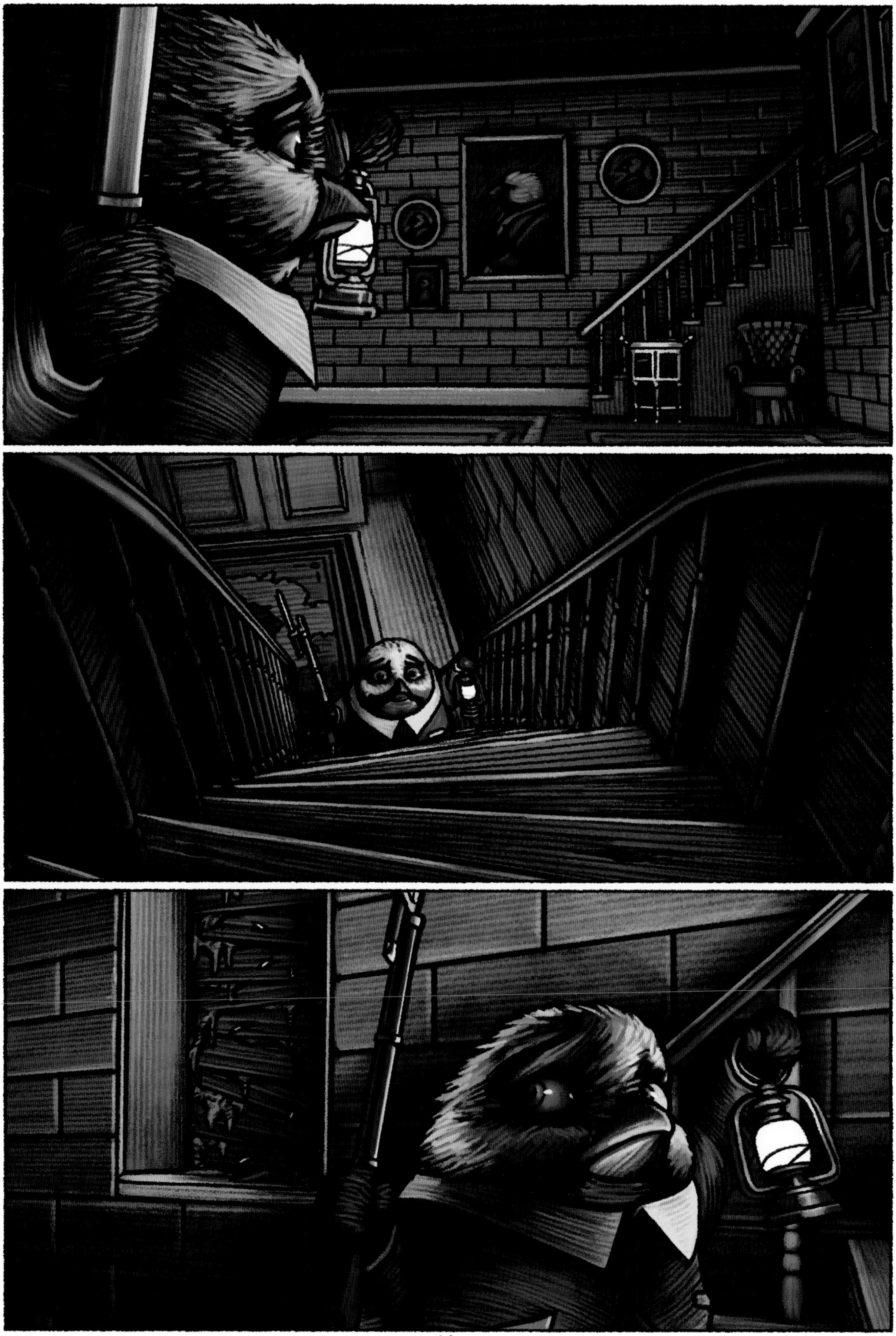

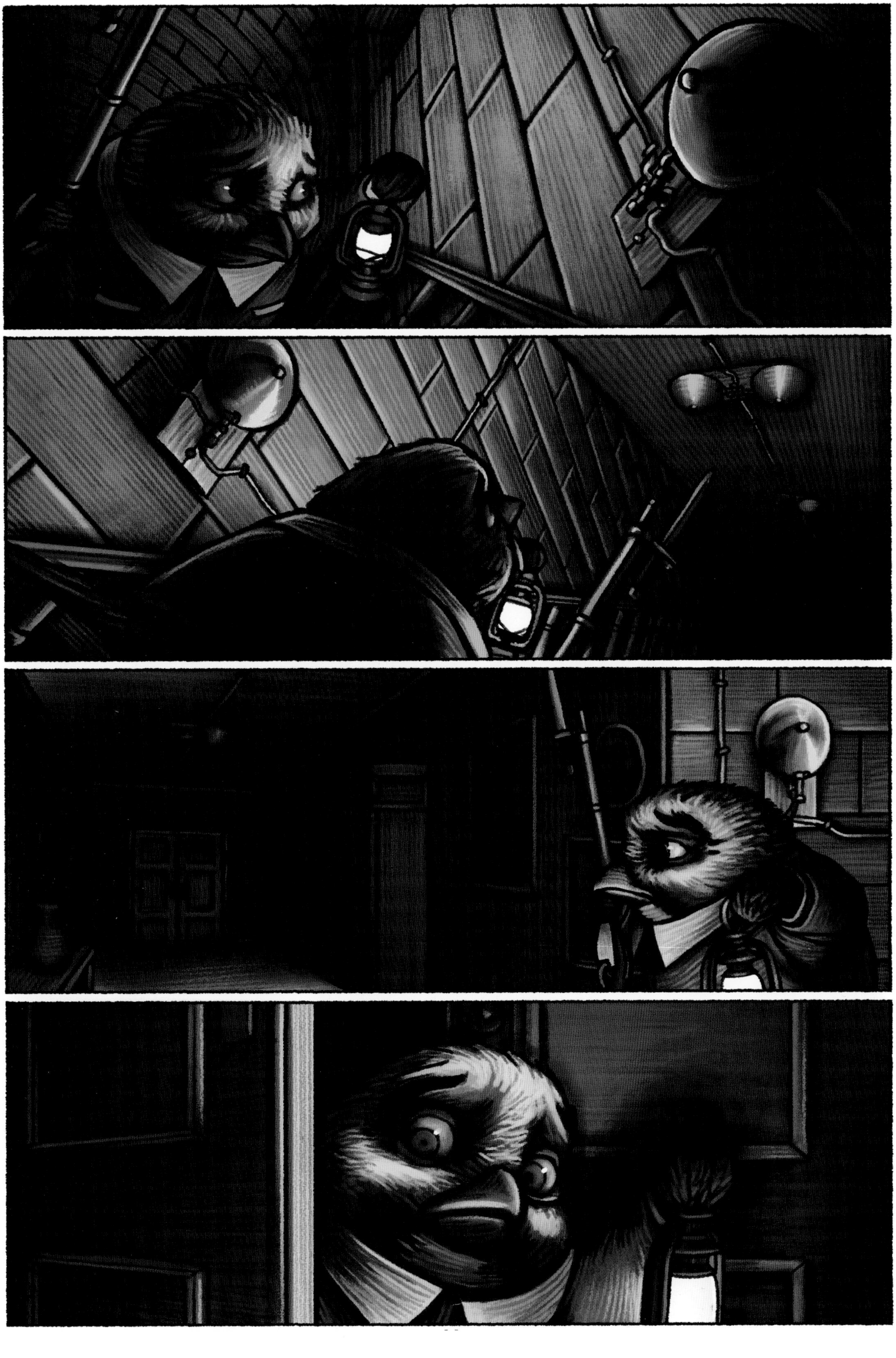

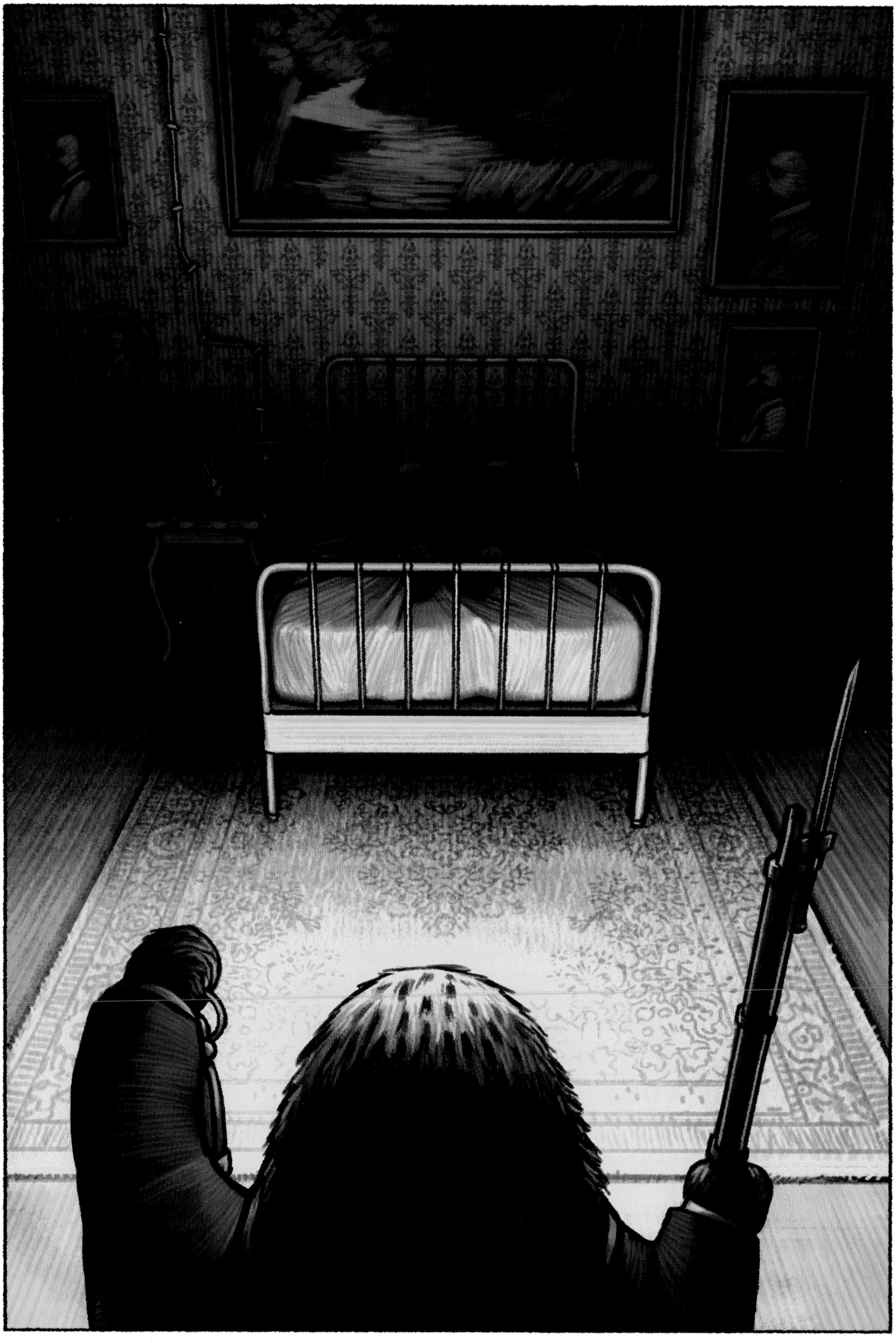

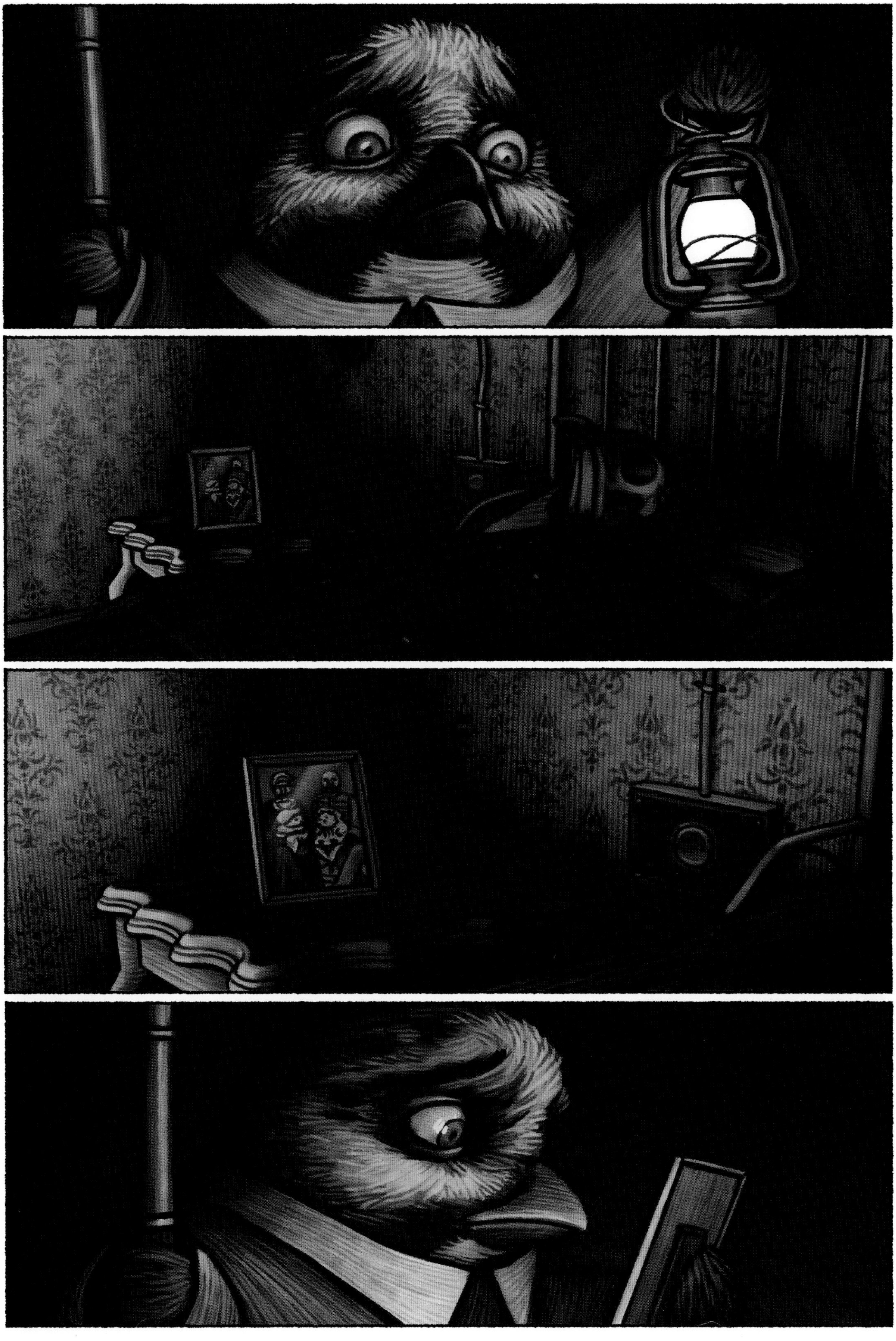

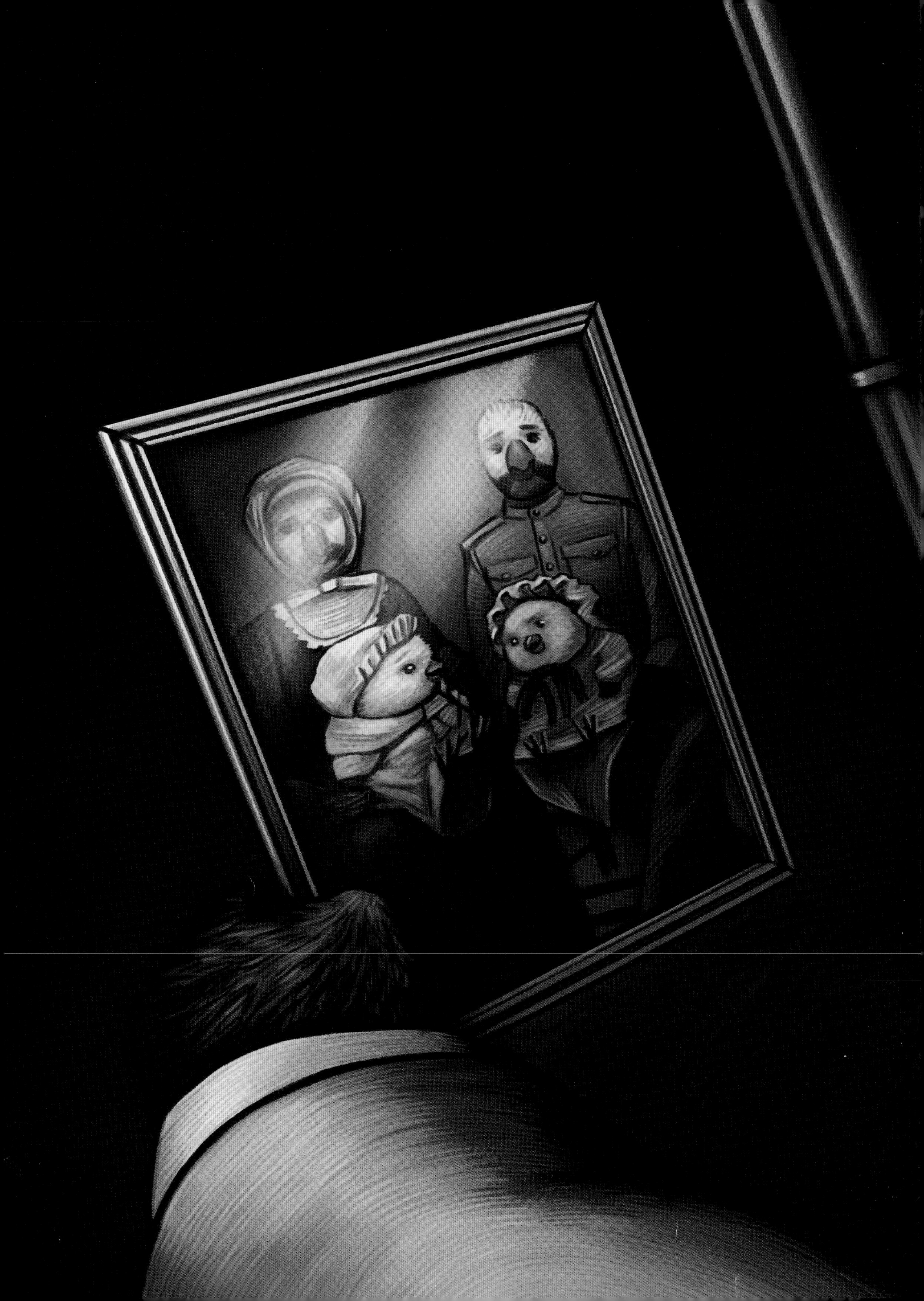

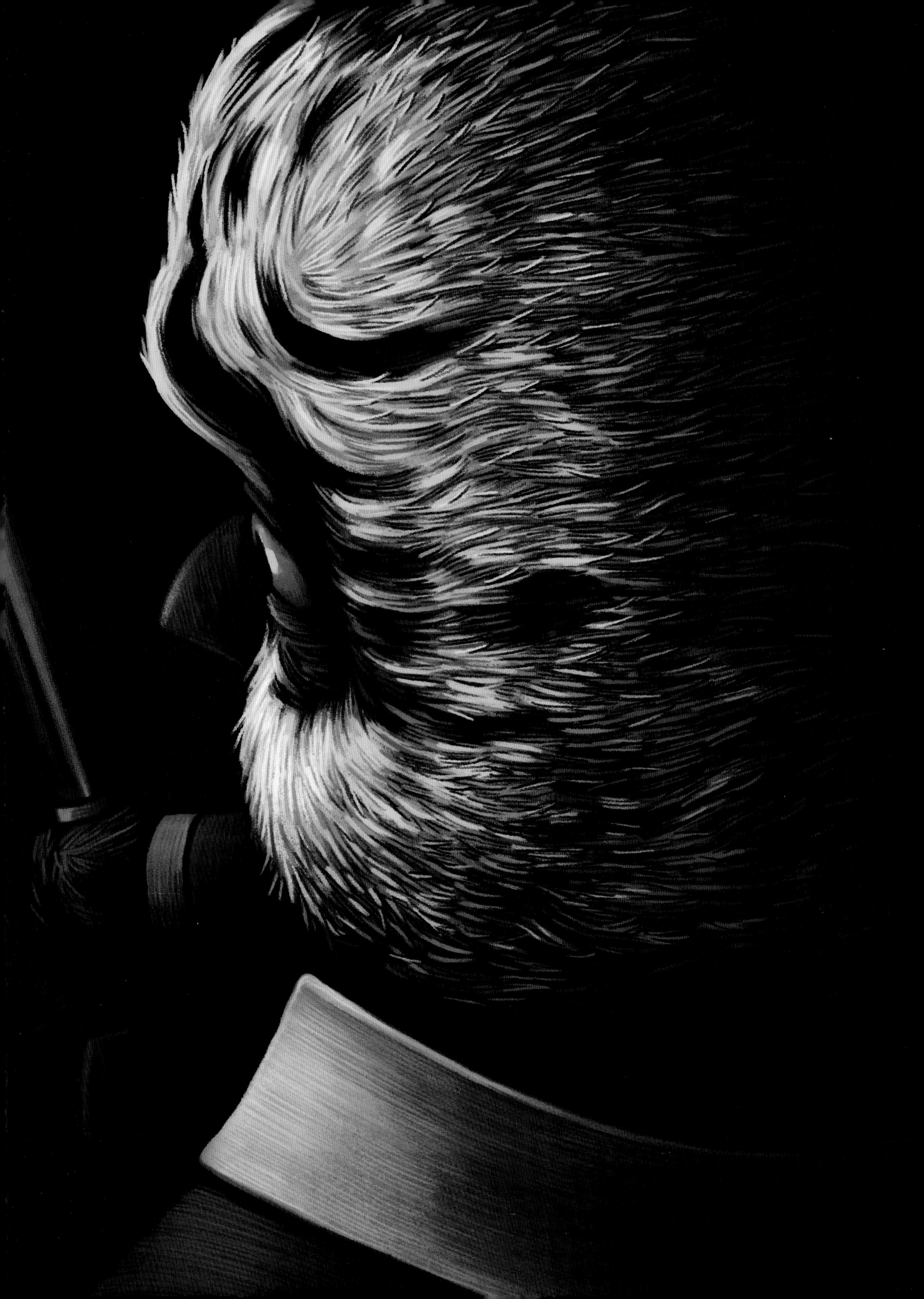

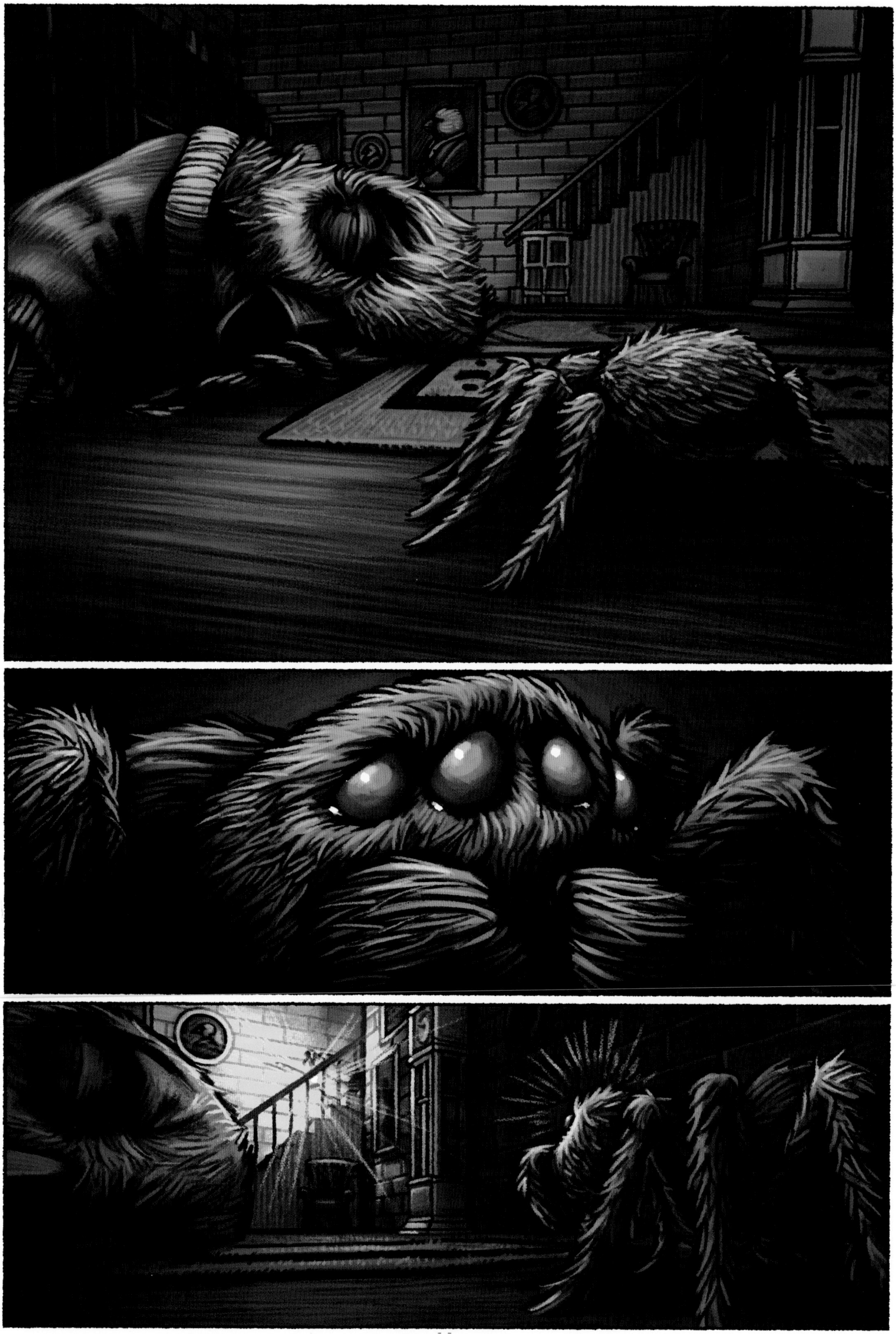

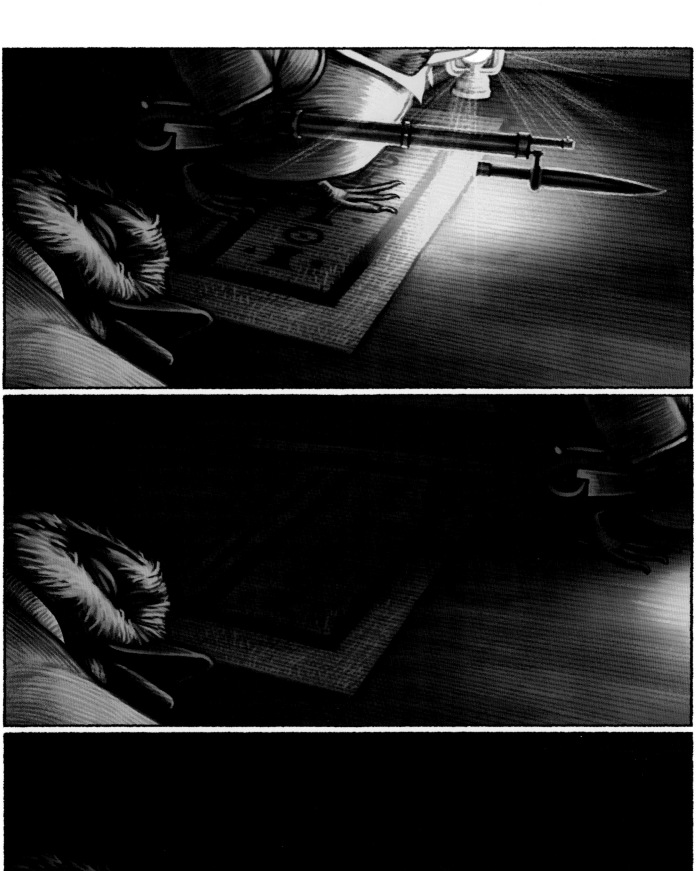

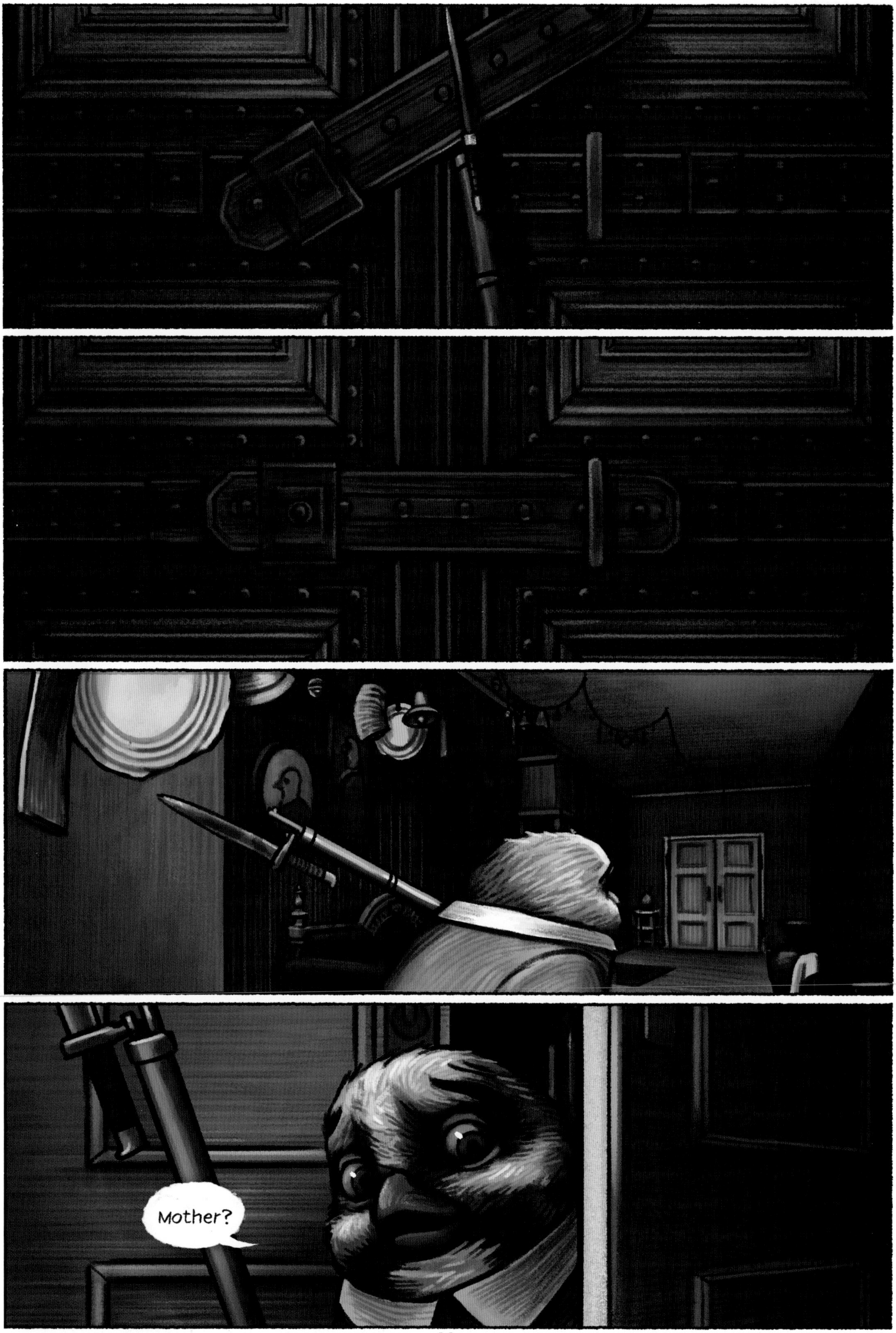
Mother?

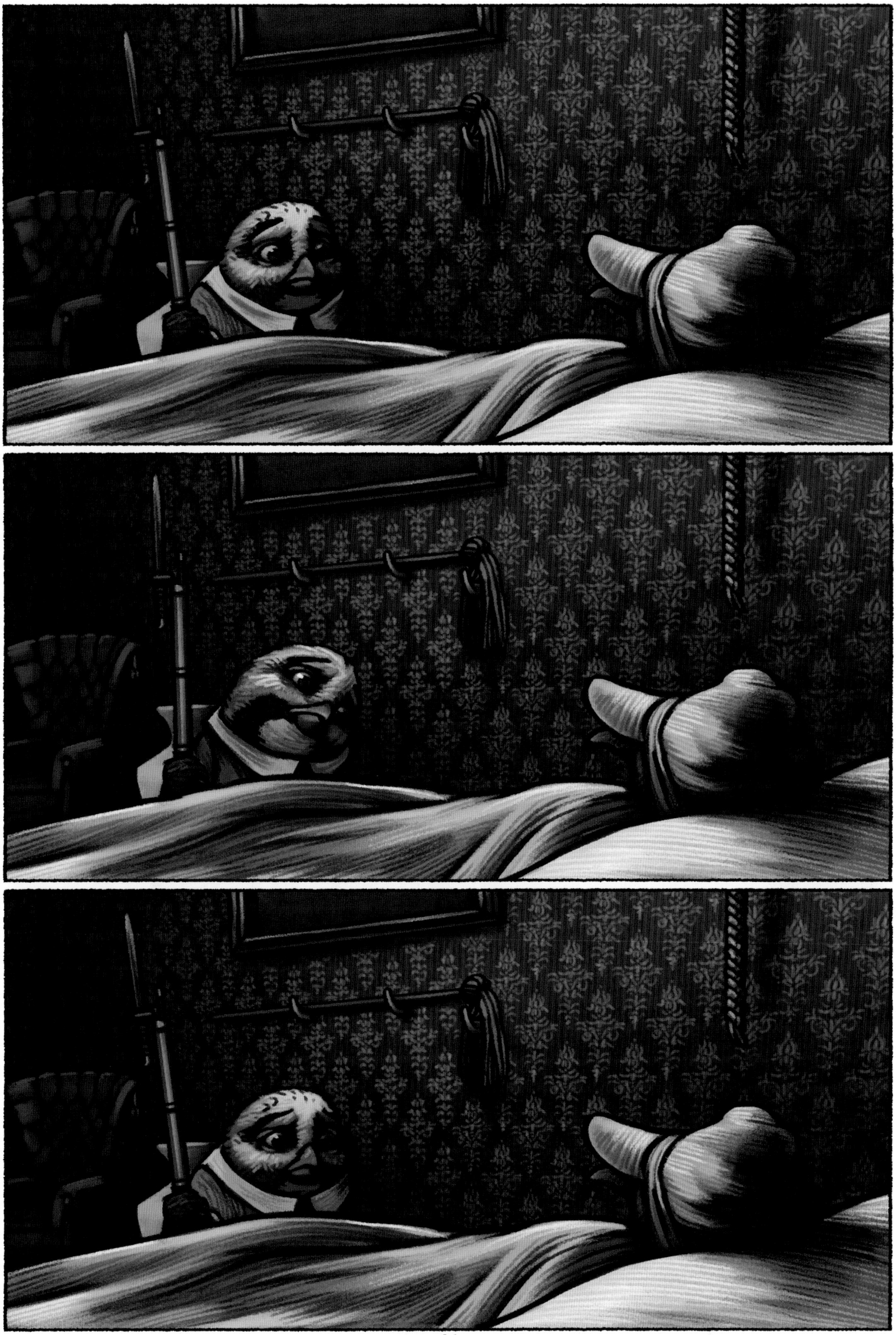

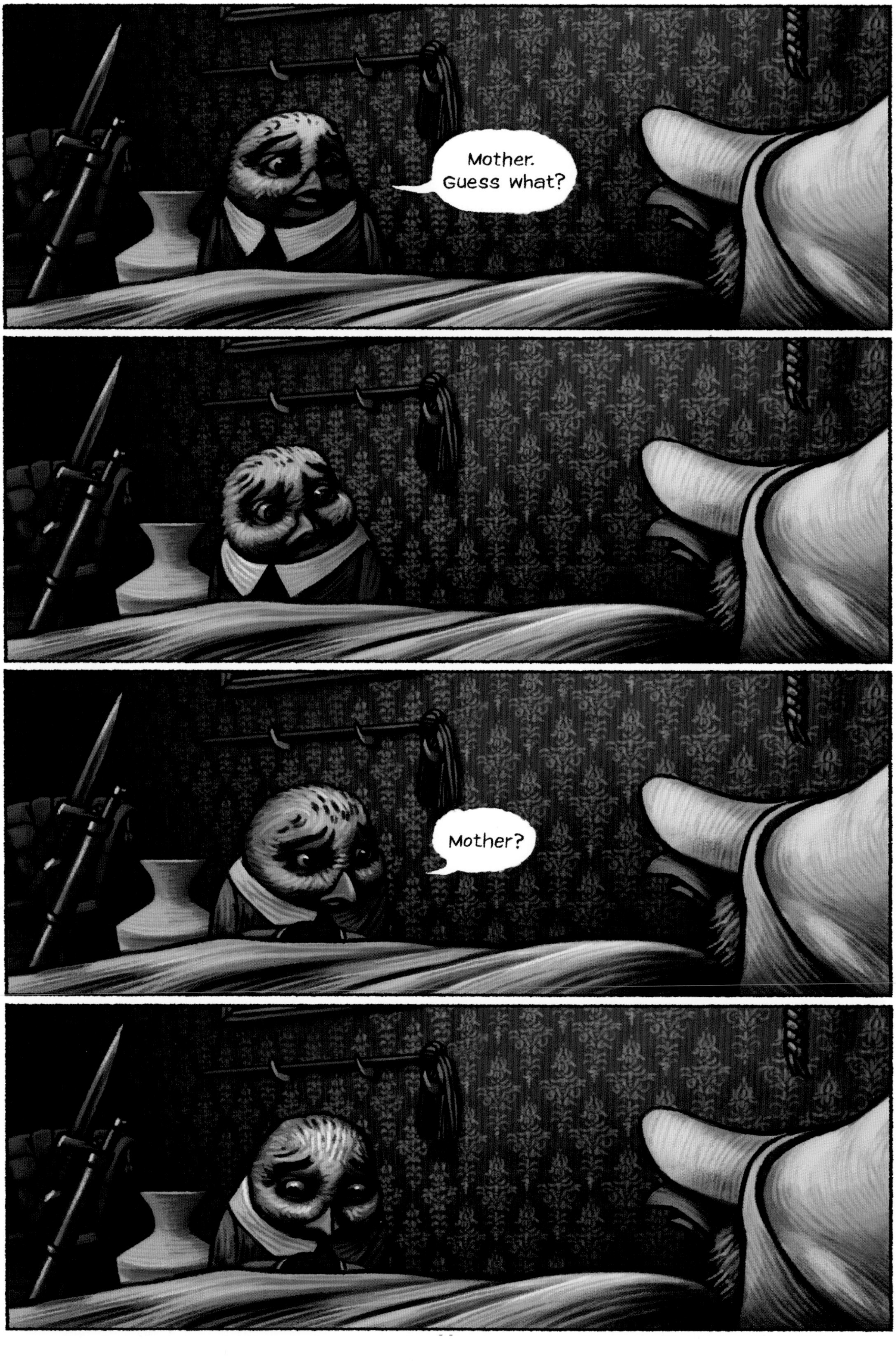
Mother. Guess what?
Mother?

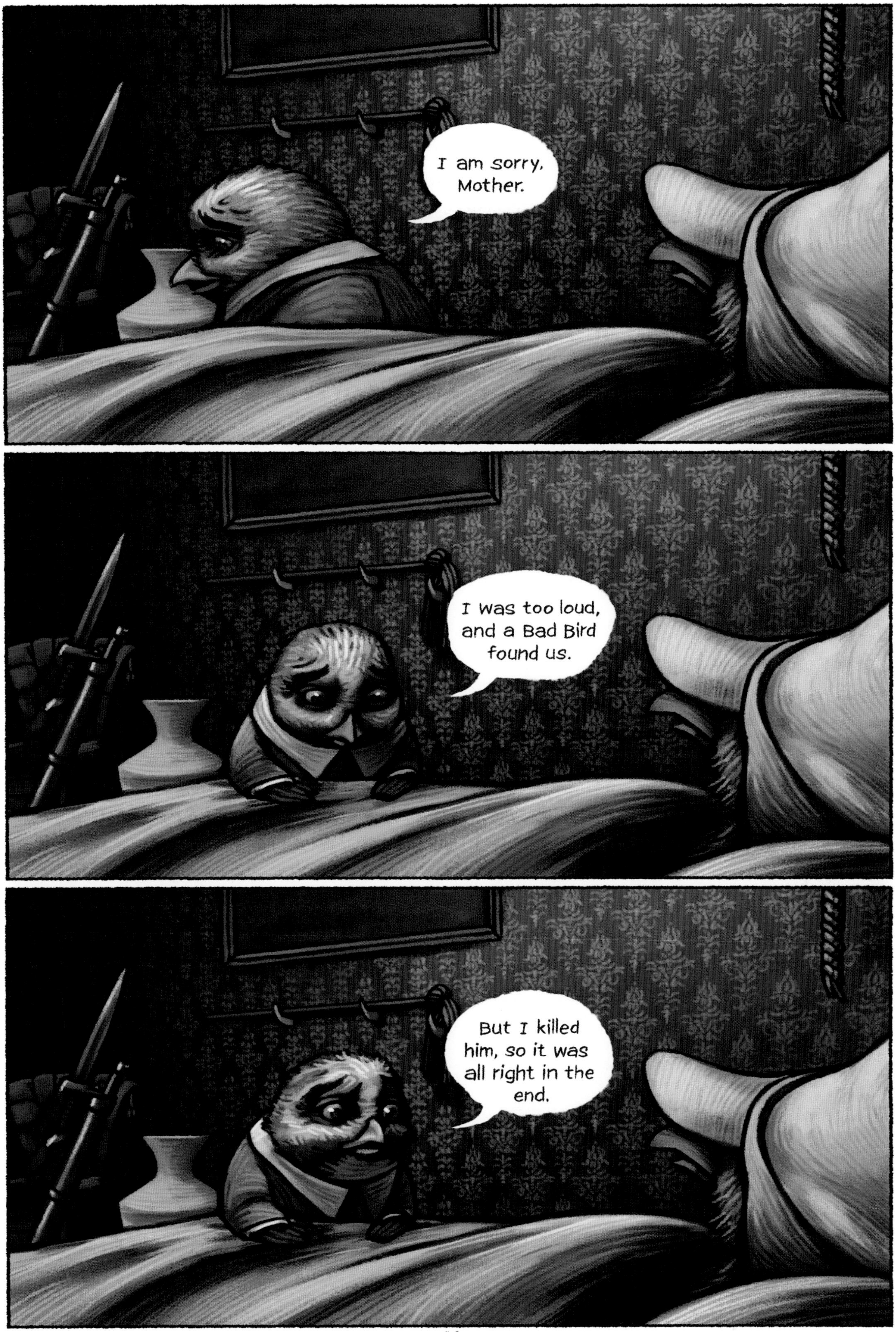
I am sorry, Mother.
I was too loud, and a Bad Bird found us.
But I killed him, so it was all right in the end.

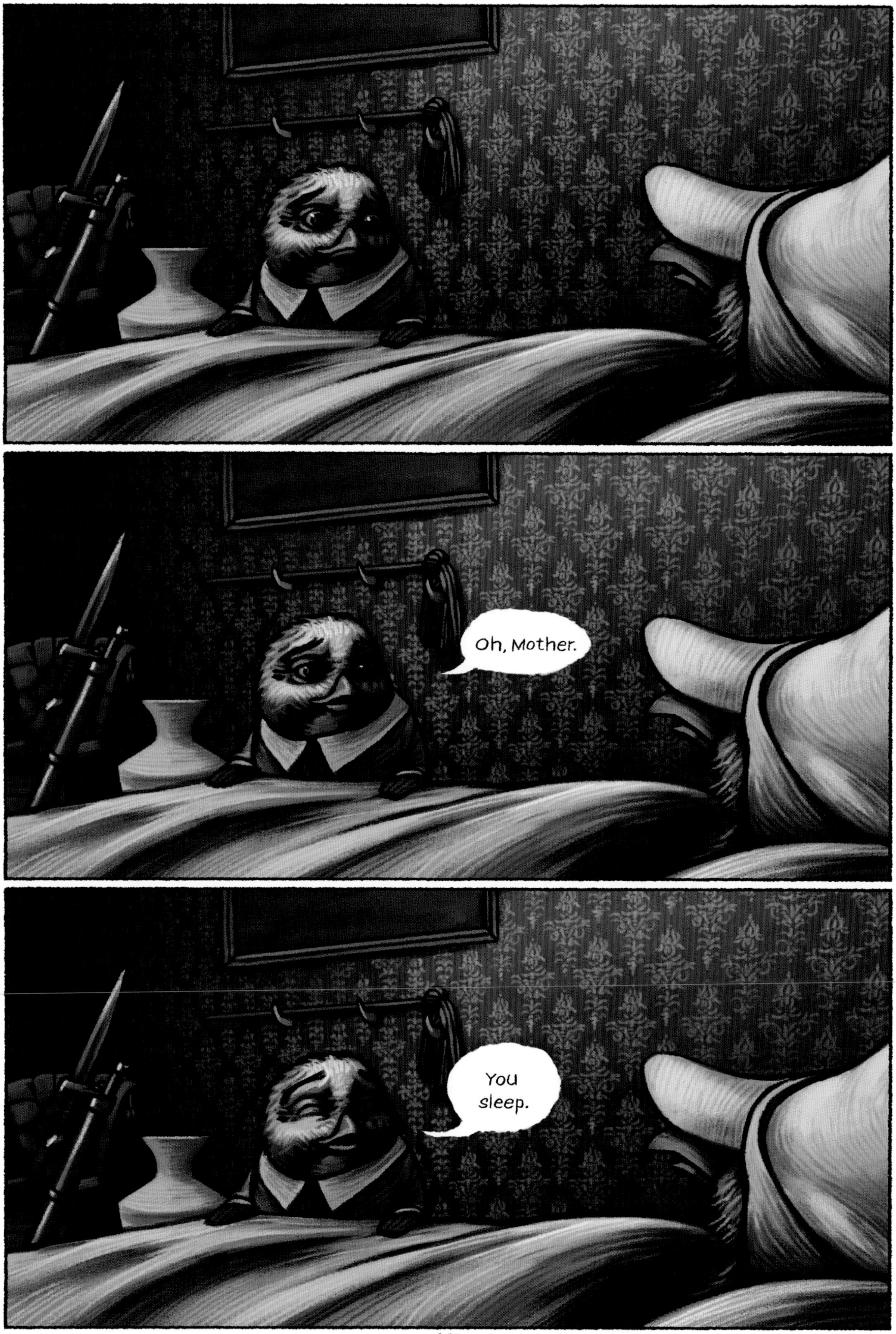
Oh, Mother.
You sleep.

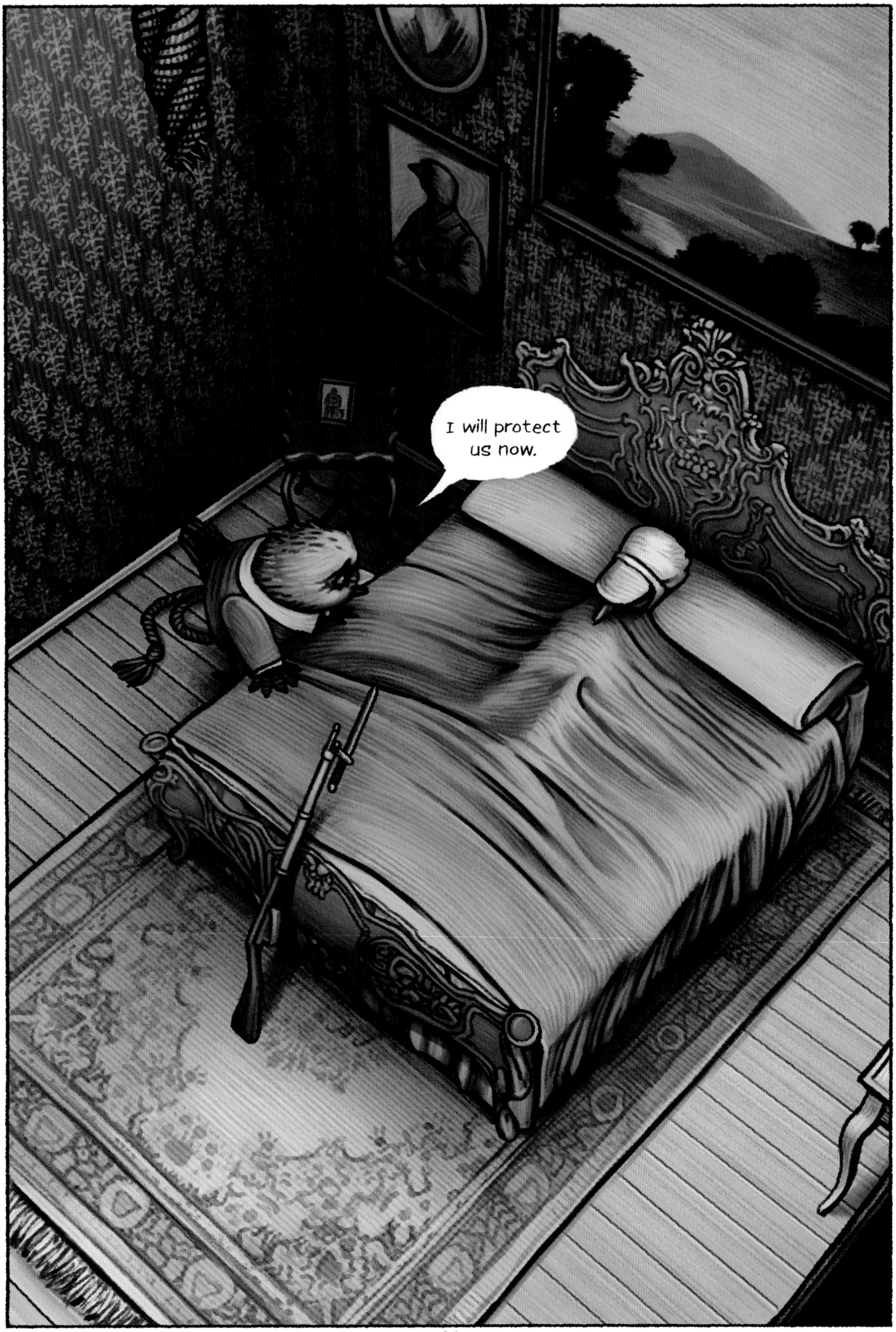
I will protect us now.

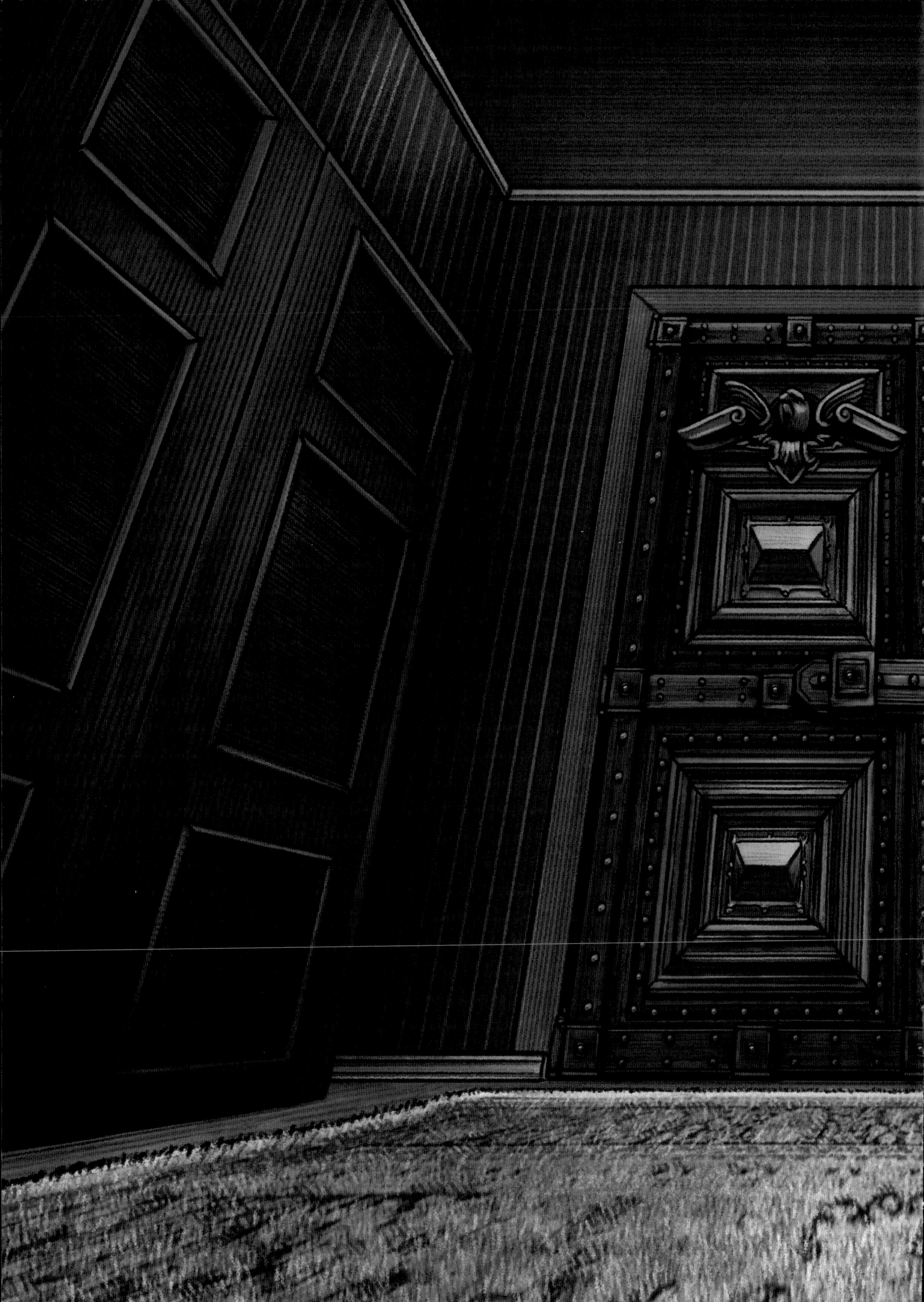

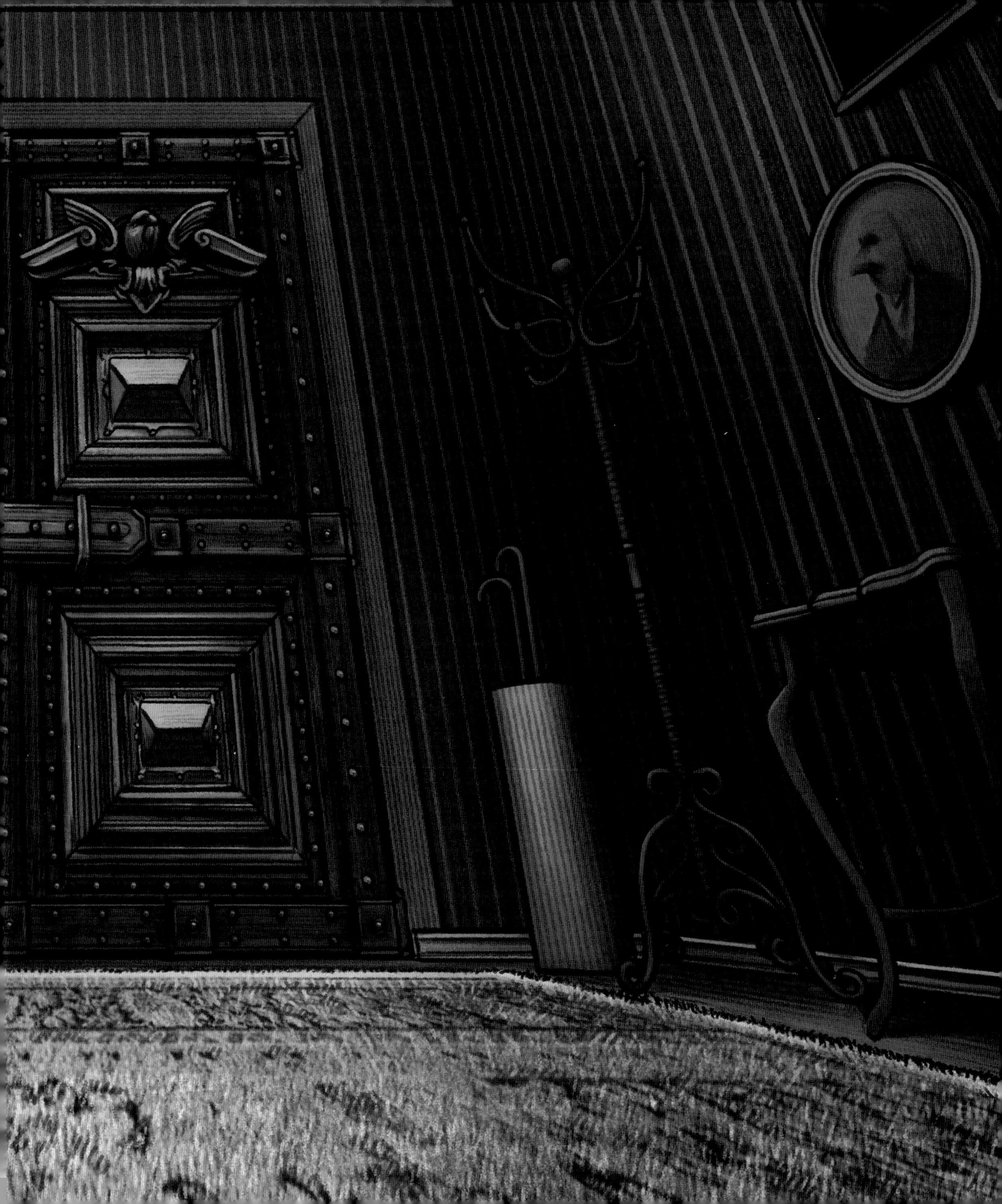

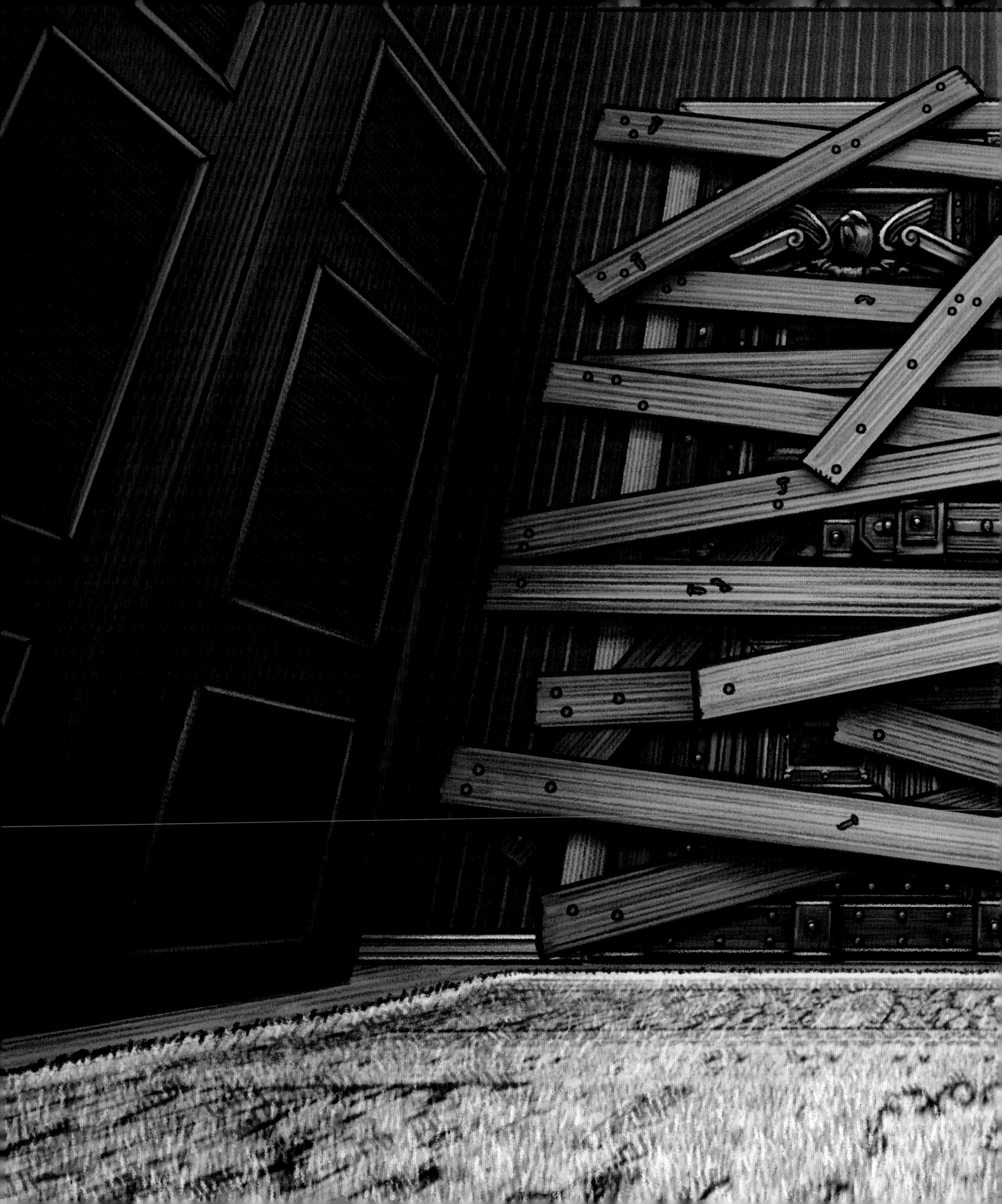

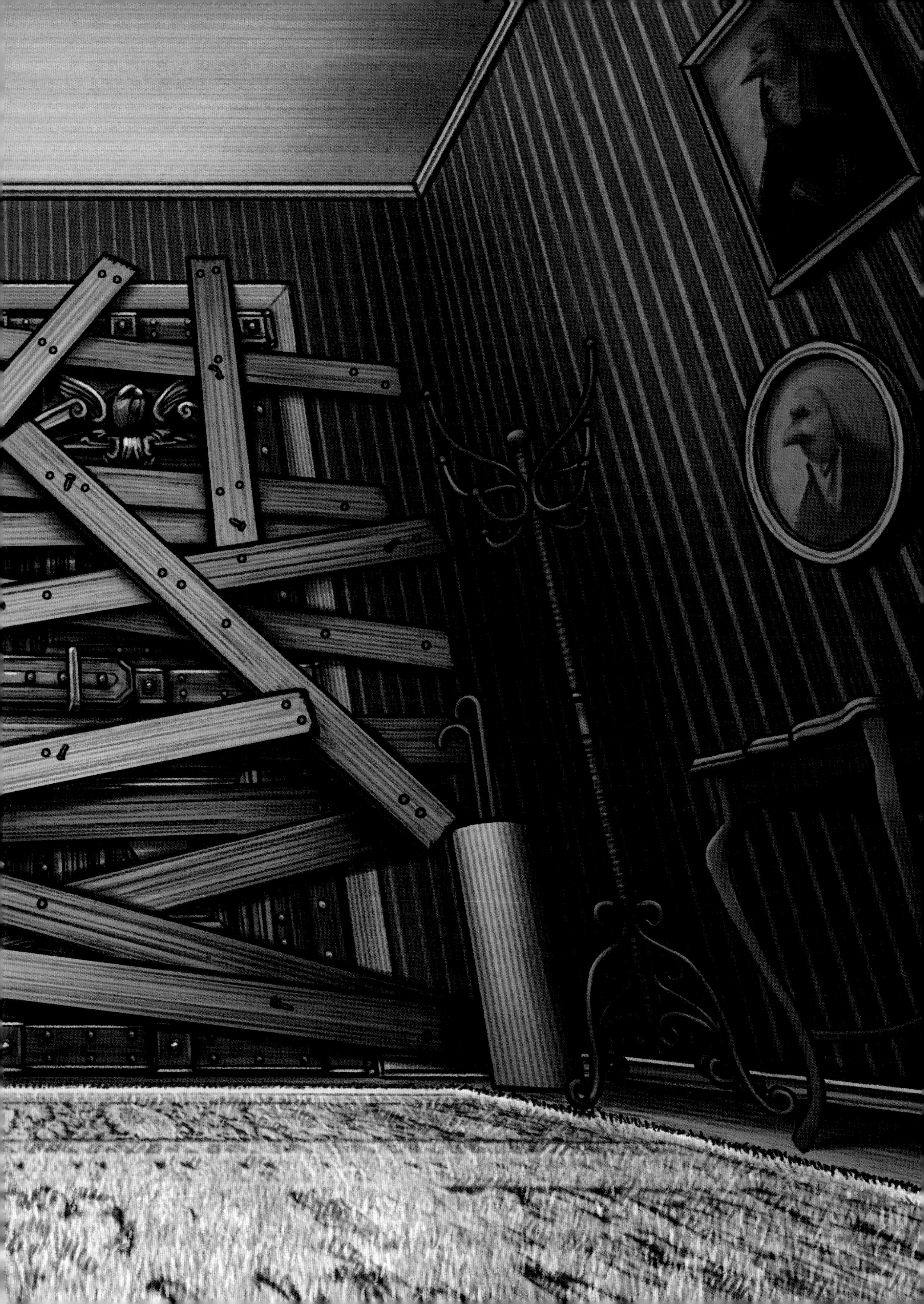

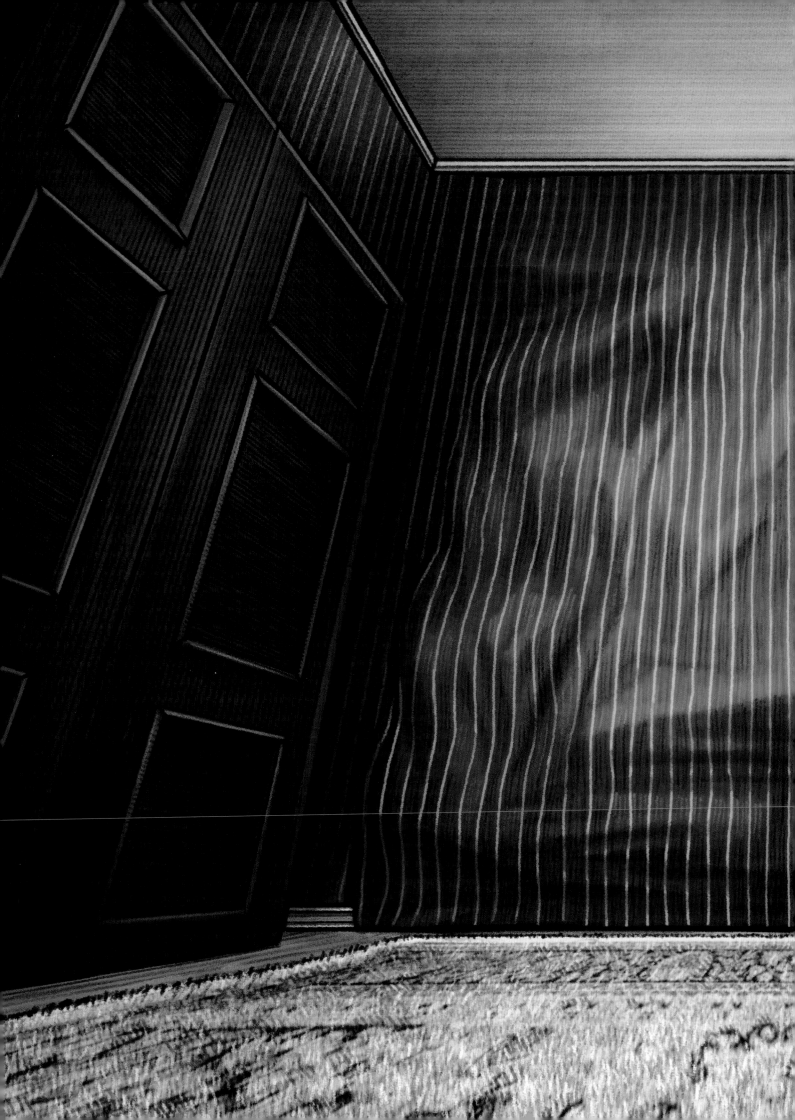

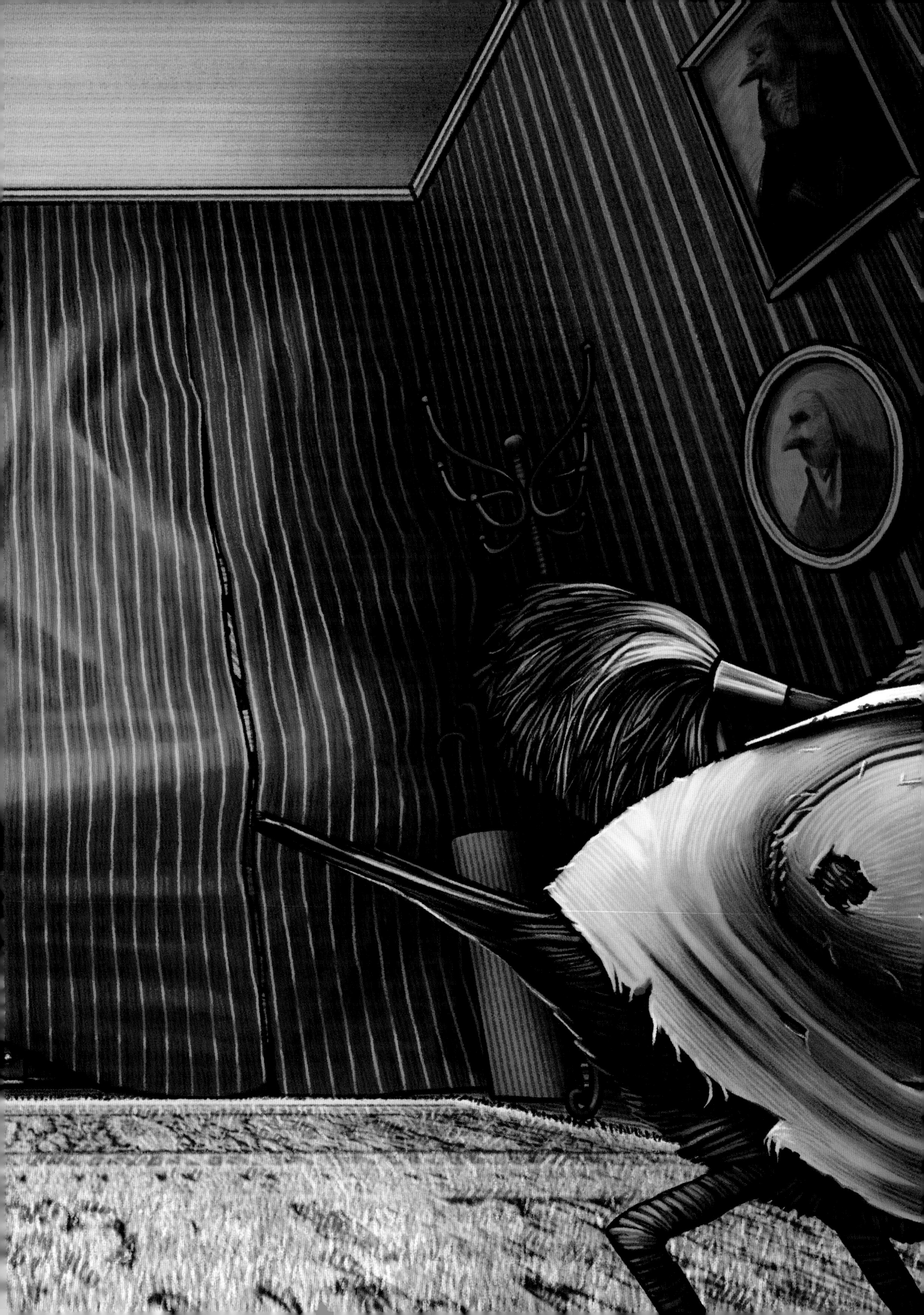

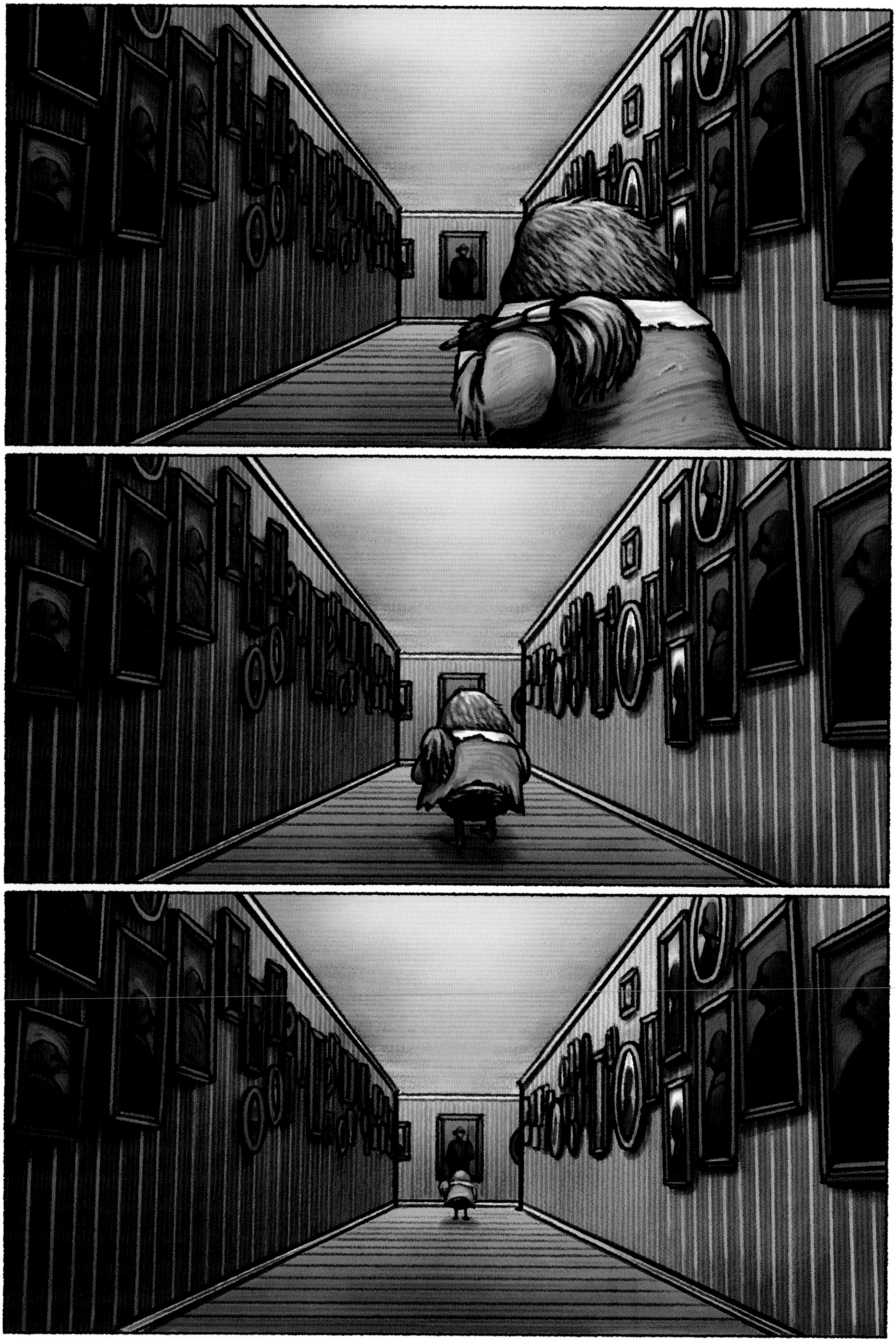

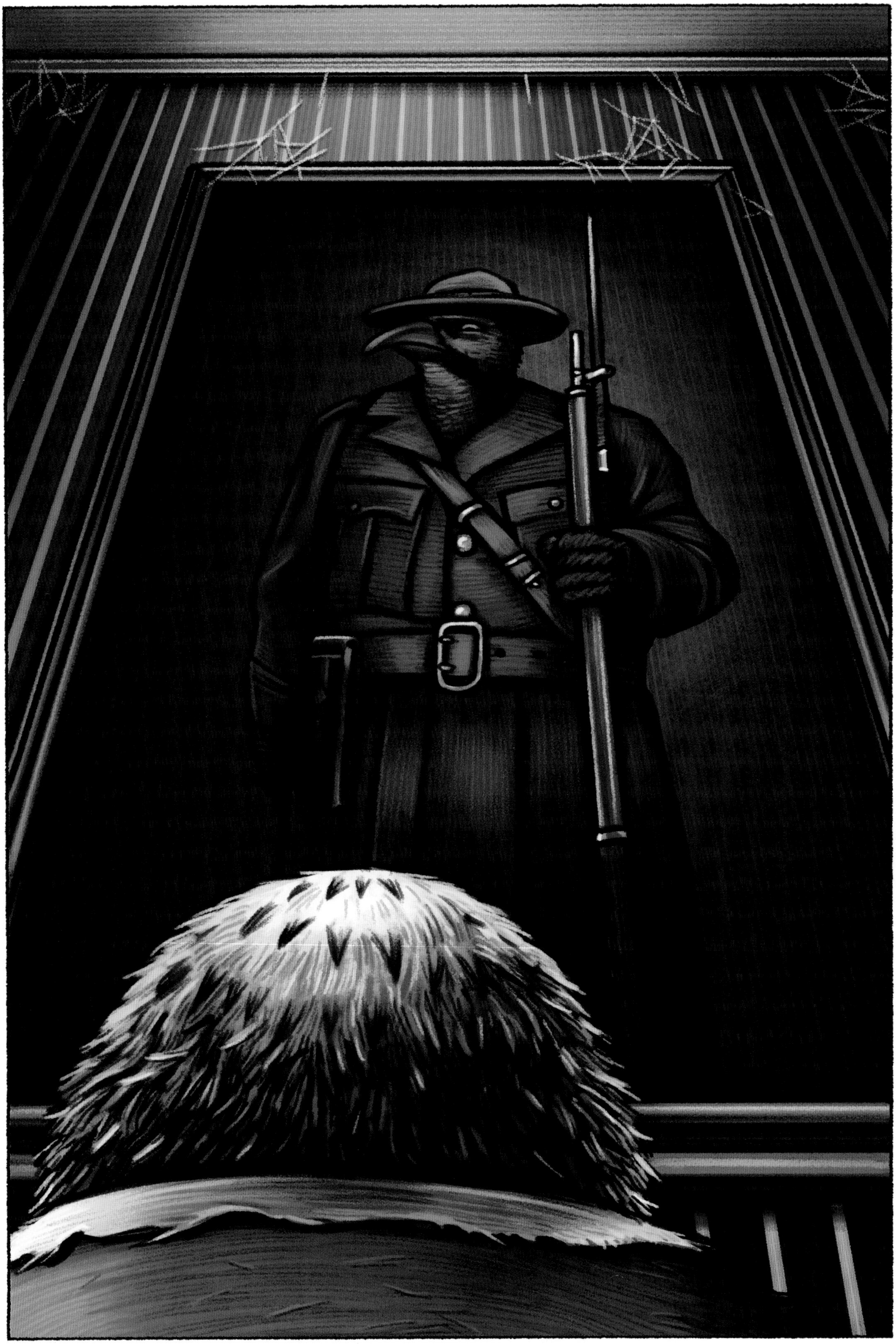

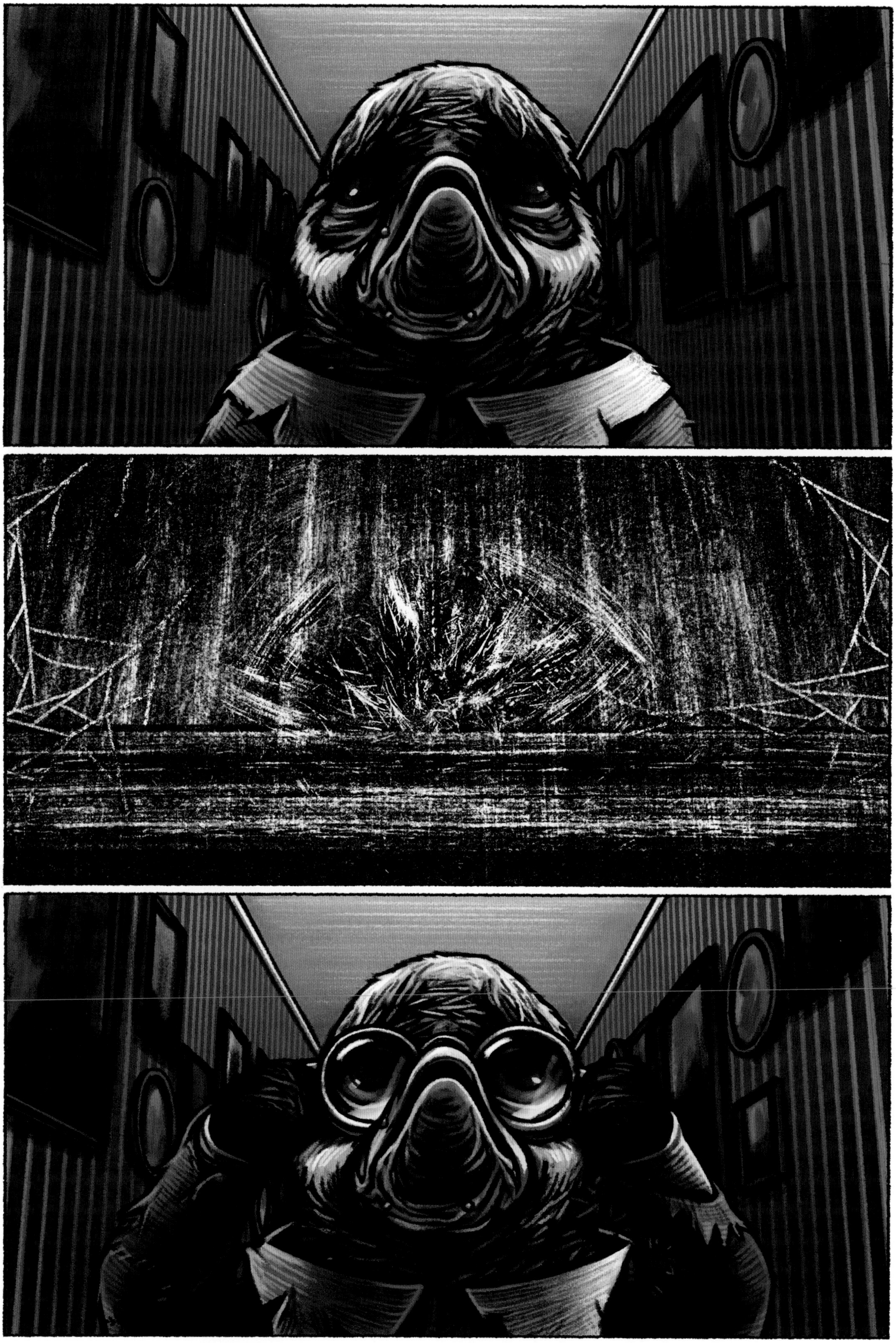

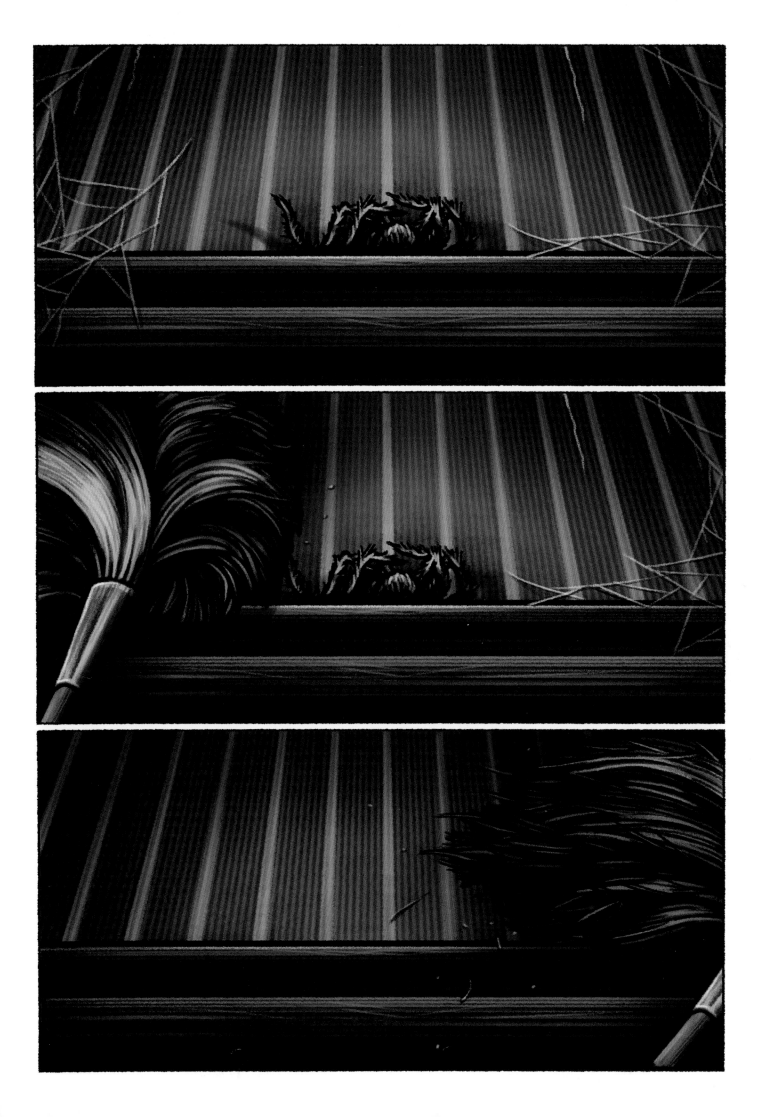

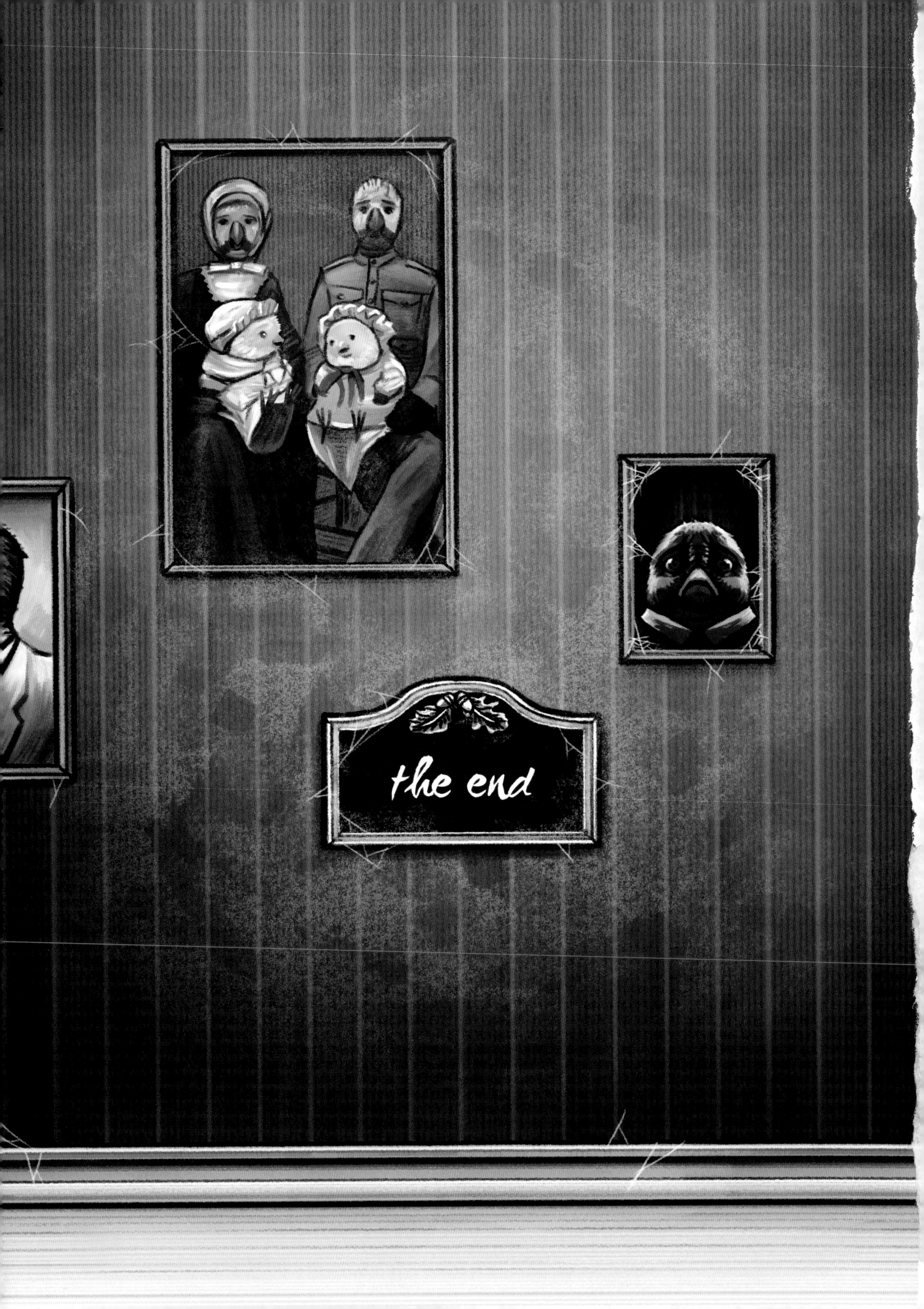
the end

Publisher . . . . Mike Richardson
Editor . . . . Jemiah Jefferson
Digital Production . . . . Nick James

Published by
Dark Horse Books
A division of
Dark Horse Comics, Inc.
10956 SE Main Street
Milwaukie, OR 97222

DarkHorse.com
International Licensing: (503) 905-2377

First edition: September 2014
ISBN 978-1-61655-469-9

1 2 3 4 5 6 7 8 9 10

Printed in China

Originally published in Finland as *Pikku Närhi*.
English translation by Lauri Ahonen.